HIGH CRIMES AND MISDEMEANORS
The Impeachment and Trial of Andrew Johnson

High Crimes
and Misdemeanors

THE IMPEACHMENT
and TRIAL
of ANDREW JOHNSON

by Gene Smith

WILLIAM MORROW AND COMPANY, INC.
NEW YORK   1977

Printed in the United States of America.

1 2 3 4 5 6 7 8 9 10

Library of Congress Cataloging in Publication Data

Smith, Gene
    High crimes and misdemeanors.

    Bibliography: p.
    Includes index.
    1. Johnson, Andrew, Pres. U. S., 1808-1875—
Impeachment. 2. Sumner, Charles, 1811-1874.
3. Stevens, Thaddeus, 1792-1868. 4. Reconstruction.
I. Title.
E666.S64   353.03′6   76-9838
ISBN 0-688-03072-6

HIGH CRIMES AND MISDEMEANORS
The Impeachment and Trial of Andrew Johnson

1

On the day in 1851 when the new Congress of that year assembled, old Henry Clay of Kentucky, tottering, months from death, left his seat in the United States Senate for the last time. In leaving, he passed a new Senator coming in to take his seat for the first time, Charles Sumner of Massachusetts. Compromise incarnate, Clay the creator of the Missouri Compromise and the Compromise of 1850, was giving way, so it was said, to conscience incarnate.

Charles Sumner in 1851 was forty years of age. The awkwardness of his youth which had made his schoolfellows address him as "Gawky" was gone, and he was one of the handsomest men of his time. He wore his free-flowing dark brown hair in a thick mane. It reached almost to the broad shoulders encased in jackets of dramatic plaid above lavender-colored or checked trousers tapering down to white spats. Lettered, eloquent, magnificent in his gestures and his deep rolling voice, he seemed born to be a Senator. He had never held a lower elective or appointive post.

He was from Boston, the son of a coldly formal lawyer-father and a distant mother. As a boy he did brilliantly at the

Public Latin School, memorizing vast sections of the classics, reveling in the discipline of verb declensions. He compiled thick notebooks listing historic events occurring on given days. Harvard followed, of course. A most serious freshman, he was absent for a grand total of three hours from the five hundred and eighty hours of classes, recitations and chapel exercises which formed the scholastic year. (His father wrote on his report card: "It is of little avail to have expensive and learned professorships established at college if a scholar does not devote his whole time to the duties prescribed.")

Aside from class assignments young Sumner's reading was enormous. Home on vacations he loaded his letters to friends with quotations from the classics and allusions to antiquity. He made Hasty Pudding. He went on to Harvard Law School and then, upon graduation, into practice. He was not a success. The merchants did not want as their attorney a young man given to quoting from Plato and Aristotle and the lesser prophets of the Bible. They in turn bored him with their money grubbing. He gathered what financial resources he had and in 1837 went to Europe. There he had his flowering.

His two-and-a-half-year sojourn abroad was miraculous. A young man of twenty-six with no important name or past came to the heart of civilization and without effort conquered it. Everyone who counted in the Old World took him up and passed him to friends—Wordsworth, Peel, Russell, Gladstone, Metternich, Louis Philippe, Cavour. He sat at the tables of Lords Fitzwilliam, Lansdowne, Wharncliffe, Leicester, Holland, Carlisle, Morpeth, the Duchess of Argyll and the German Crown Prince; they had him to shoots at their estates. In Paris he employed not one but two tutors that he might perfect his conversational French. In Rome and Florence he learned to speak Italian fluently. He mastered German. He attended classes, observed parliamentary debates, visited museums and cathedrals, dined out every night. It was his openness, his willingness to learn, that made friends of all he met, for he was unpretentious, kindly, a stranger to jealousy. Lovable, the Europeans said.

Still under thirty, Charles Sumner returned to the law in Boston. As before, he did not do well. To his few clients he talked far too much about everything. It was like being under Niagara, a friend said, the deep voice pouring out quotes and erudite allusions in a slow, rolling mass of words. (Mrs. Jefferson Davis remembered a sequence of his thoughts on the Indian Mutiny, lace, Demosthenes, jewels, Seneca's morals, intaglios, the Platonian theory and "quite an interesting résumé of the history of dancing.")

There was never any chitchat, no talk of sports, horses, dogs, and nothing about art and music that did not seem the forced result of an acquired, not a natural, taste. Nor did Sumner display any sense of humor, although, noted the young Henry Adams, he smiled grandly from time to time when someone made a joke. Nothing light or whimsical reached him, nothing ironical. "If one told Charles Sumner that the moon was made of green cheese," mused Oliver Wendell Holmes, "he would controvert the alleged fact in all sincerity, and give good reasons why it could not be so." Even Longfellow, his best friend, could not make clear to him that Lowell in his *Biglow Papers* was writing in New England dialect. "They are admirable, very good indeed," Sumner said. "But why does he spell so badly?"

There were those who found him heavy, portentous, Olympian. One wearied of the fact that "he was rarely without a pocketfull of letters from duchesses or noblemen in England," said Henry Adams; and Henry James would feel himself "rapidly stifling under the weight of that insensate and implacable egotism." But there were those who loved him. "It characterizes a man for me that he hates Charles Sumner," Emerson said, "for it shows that he cannot discriminate between a foible and a vice."

The eligible young ladies of Boston found him beyond reach. In a strangely adolescent fashion Sumner romanticized womanhood and spoke of what bliss must come to those who found love at first sight. He marveled at the courage of friends who entered into marriage—"Cupid's Tribunal" to him. Yet no girl could hold his interest even fleetingly. Several once arranged a contest, the prize to be a sum to which they all contributed. It would go to the girl who could hold Sumner in conversation for fifteen minutes. There was no winner. The prettiest charmer found he needed a larger audience than one.

Admittedly brilliant and the admired intimate of all who were best in the Boston of his time, Charles Sumner was yet a drifting man. "My mind, soul, heart, are not improved or invigorated by the practice of my profession; by overhauling papers, old letters, and sifting accounts in order to see if there be anything on which to plant an action," he said. "The sigh will come for a canto of Dante, a rhapsody of Homer, a play of Schiller." Despite his failure to achieve professional distinction he gained intellectual Boston's respect, and it was that Boston of Allston, Choate, Prescott, Bancroft which asked him to deliver the annual Fourth of July oration of 1845 in the Tremont Temple.

It was a great honor, conferred after much thought each year upon a praiseworthy younger man. Seated before the thirty-four-year-old Sumner, awaiting the traditional patriotic exhortation, was all of his Boston. Also in the audience were officers of the regular army and the state militia and the Washington Light Guard, and naval officers from the battleship *Ohio,* docked in the harbor. "What," Sumner asked, "is the true grandeur of nations?" Then, as one listener put it, "with quotations and illustrations from the history and literature of every nation and every time," Sumner damned officers "besmeared with gold" on their uniforms as the possessors of "barbarous" ways "typical of brute force."

"What use is the standing army of the United States?" he demanded. "What use is the navy of the United States?" He pointed out toward the battleship at anchor. Such as *that,* he boomed, cost as much as four Harvard Colleges. It was the first of that long list of speeches the content of which was to infuriate listeners. Yet in his strangely simple way he did not understand, never understood, why he made people so angry. Sumner was, said Richard Dana, like a "cat without smellers

. . . He has none of the delicate tests that, as he passes along, tell him what he touches." To his own satisfaction, he felt, he had told the truth. War was wasteful and murderous. Could there possibly be any other view?

The speech made Charles Sumner a name. He lectured and wrote in favor of peace, even as the United States in the next year went to war against Mexico. The young Illinois Congressman Abraham Lincoln also wrote and spoke against the involvement in Mexico, but no such attention attached to his remarks as to those of Sumner. There was no comparison between the two. Sumner was the foremost spokesman of peace in the nation. In demand now, he spoke of prison reform as well as of peace. But in the United States of the late 1840's there was a paramount cause which sought him out, a cause that men feared, and with reason, to follow to its logical conclusion. For that conclusion meant suffering, death, the Four Horsemen. No such hesitancies attended Sumner. He became, above all other men, the voice of Abolitionism. The young William Henry Seward of New York on a trip to the mid-South had seen little children tied one to the other being driven into a courtyard inn. He had watched as they were watered at a horse trough and then driven into sheds to cry themselves to sleep. They would never see their mothers again. They were being sent in chains to the Gulf States, to King Cotton. Seward would never forget. But Seward was suave, diplomatic, a politician. The young Lincoln had said he wished it were within his power to strike at slavery. But he did not say so in public. He smothered his feelings. That Charles Sumner could not do.

The great voice booming out, the long sentences thundering down, Sumner joined in the 1848 founding of the Free Soil party, which had but one platform: human slavery must never be extended. It must be eliminated throughout America. "But," a friend ventured, "you forget the other side." Sumner slammed his clenched fist on a table. "There *is* no other side!"

Despite the fact that the Abolitionists represented only a small fraction of thinking America, Sumner permitted no opportunity to pass without his ritual denunciation of slavery, whether in private conversations, wedding toasts, obituaries, lectures, letters. The South, he said, was simply a vast bordello, a "mighty house of ill-fame" where five hundred thousand women were flogged to prostitution. Slavery was the vampire, murderer, assassin, violator. It was sinful to speak of compromises, concessions, arrangements. "Nothing can be settled which is not right," he said. "Nothing can be settled which is against Freedom. Nothing can be settled which is against divine law."

Abolitionists in the eyes of the vast majority of Americans were slave thieves, disturbers of the peace, cranks. "The long-haired men and short-haired women peculiar to all reforms," said the journalist Donn Piatt. There was not the slightest proof that anything they said had any basis in fact, for only faith could make the Abolitionist believe that the Negro could in any way be the equal of the white man. But the belief that here was God's image in ebony was sufficient for Sumner. His denunciations of slavery grew more and more emotional. His face grew flushed and his voice choked in frenzy when he spoke of slavery, "the harlot . . . the harpy . . . the source of all our baseness."

Boston and the North intensely disliked human slavery, the fetters and chains, whips and auction blocks. But also to be considered were trade, America's coming greatness, Manifest Destiny. The permanency of the Union must be maintained. Slashing attacks upon the South must be moderated. But Sumner did not see it that way. "Convictions of the heart cannot be repressed," he said; "utterances of conscience must be heard. They break forth with irrepressible might. As well attempt to check the tides of ocean, the currents of the Mississippi or the rushing waters of Niagara."

He could not be ignored. Massachusetts and the North could not push aside the sound of that great voice crying, "It is not within the domain of expediency. To be wrong on this is to be wholly wrong." In 1851 the Massachusetts Legislature sent him to the Senate. He came to a Washington so southern-like as almost to resemble a raw Charleston or Savannah. The houses along the odoriferous river flats were ramshackle in appearance, and pigs and cattle freely wandered the dusty or muddy streets. The city had surface drainage with stepping stones across the gutters. Negroes lounged about. One did not bring one's better horses or carriages to this overgrown watering place, and most of the Senators and Representatives lived in southern-style boardinghouses placed along the north side of Pennsylvania Avenue from the Capitol to the Treasury. They ate in communal "messes." Society, the army and navy and the better old families were overwhelmingly southern.

The two houses of Congress contained men of a type Sumner had never seen before. At home they were great aristocrats, the owners of baronies consisting of thousands of acres and hundreds of slaves. They were colonels of militia regiments, adherents of the code duello, gallants with the ladies, students of Sir Walter Scott's novels of chivalry. In Washington they constantly spat into cuspidors, cursing the Yankee lowdowns who questioned the higher culture of the South. They saw themselves as the American versions of the elegant English gentleman, indeed, as the Cavaliers continuing the War of the Roses against the Puritan. Their section had more colleges, more money, more of the amenities of life than arid New England, but they openly carried pistols and Bowie knives. Alternately courtly and dangerously belligerent, they interpreted political opposition as a slight upon their honor. Abolitionism they looked upon as simple robbery.

Charles Sumner, the man of books and words, looked at these men prideful of their prowess with horse and whiskey jug, these mighty hunters and card players, and launched himself at them. His first speech in the Senate on the subject of slavery was an attack on the Fugitive Slave Law, which held that all citizens must assist a slaveholder attempting to repossess his property. It was, said Sumner's friend George F. Hoar, the speech of "the man who ever deemed himself sitting in a lofty pulpit with a mighty sounding board, with a whole widespread people for a congregation." It was delivered, as were all Sumner's Senate speeches, in the tones of a schoolmaster alternately harsh and then wondrously patient as he addressed scholars of no impressive achievement.

He was, he told the Senate, the slave only of principles: "I call no party master." He was after all, as he often said, "in morals, not politics." He would adhere to the law above magistrates. And so it was his duty to point out that the Fugitive Slave Law was unconstitutional, unchristian, wrong. There followed ritual denunciations from the southerners. His words, said Senator Jeremiah Clemens of Alabama, were the yapping of a puppy, annoying but of no moment.

One southern Senator was more tolerant. He was Andrew Pickens Butler of South Carolina, whose seat was directly in front of Sumner's. Butler was a red-faced, white-haired old man who had seen, he said, other men come to the Senate "reeking" of home prejudices. Eventually they lifted themselves above these transient influences. It would happen to Sumner. Often Butler asked Sumner to reach into his prodigious reading and flawless memory in order to verify classical allusions and quotations Butler was planning to use in speeches. Sumner obliged. The two became friends of a sort, Butler letting it be known that as he represented South Carolina, the most aristocratic state in the Union, he was conferring social standing upon the northerner. That boon did not protect Sumner from the obloquy of other southerners rising to condemn the series of speeches which confirmed him as slavery's greatest enemy. "Serpent . . . leper," he was called on the Senate floor, "sneaking, sinuous, snakelike poltroon."

The violence of the southerners' attacks alarmed Mrs. William Henry Seward, the wife of the Senator from New York. She told Sumner he should take precautions to assure his safety. "I am here to do my duty," he replied, "and shall continue to do it without regard to personal consequences." He went on his way, lecturing Senators friendly and unfriendly alike on their correct courses of action and the principles to which they should adhere, all the while littering his remarks with mention of his relationships with George Sand, George

14

Eliot, Disraeli and of what Macaulay had recently told him. Portentous and impressive even when the matter at hand did not appear of overwhelming importance—whatever he chose to discuss became, said George F. Hoar, "that upon which the foundations of heaven and earth rest"—he discussed the idea that one day he might fail of reelection by sighing, "Poor country—poor, poor country."

When newcomers arrived in Washington the first person they asked to have pointed out in the Senate Chamber was Charles Sumner. He did not disappoint them in their expectations of what a Senator should look like, for, he said, he never permitted himself, even in the privacy of his own chamber, to fall into a position he would not take in his chair on the Senate floor. (One Senator wondered aloud how Sumner must look in his nightshirt.)

Residing, so it was said, on Mount Sinai, the Senator from Massachusetts permitted himself always to speak in wild exaggerations. He could discuss a public-lands issue by saying it would make Council Bluffs a suburb of Washington and call the London reception of the would-be liberator of Hungary, Kossuth, a greater event than any of the victories of Julius Caesar or William the Conqueror. When it was remarked that his speeches contained few light remarks, his reply was, "You might as well look for a joke in the Book of Revelations."

Yet when Charles Sumner spoke on the issue of slavery it was said that here was the conscience of the nation speaking for a moral blockade of sin, Saint Michael with sword in hand battling Satan's demons. Women who refused to wear cotton because slavers produced it worshiped Senator Sumner.

Three years after his entrance into the Senate he broke with Butler of South Carolina. It was over yet another debate on the Fugitive Slave Law. The Senator from Massachusetts, Butler said, had taken an oath to support the Constitution and laws of the United States. Would he, asked Butler, live up to his oath? Would he obey the Fugitive Slave Law?

"Does the honorable Senator ask me if I would personally

join in sending a fellow-man into bondage?" Sumner asked, and then answered his question with a quote from the Bible: " 'Is thy servant a dog, that he should do this thing?' "

Butler replied that Sumner thus affirmed that he had perjured himself when he took his senatorial oath. Other southerners joined in to say that Sumner was rude, wanton, gross, vulgar, degraded, that he should be expelled from his post. He retorted that they might bear in mind that they were not back on their plantations "well-stocked with slaves, over which the lash of the overseer has full sway." In the end Butler told him they could have no further relations.

Two years passed. In the spring of 1856 the question of whether Kansas should be admitted to the Union as a slave or free state was debated. Something akin to civil war raged in a territory now called "Bloody Kansas." Butler spoke in favor of the settlers who wished slavery Sumner rose to answer. In his hand he held the already-printed proofs of the speech he would deliver. It was his invariable custom to prepare his speeches at home. (There, so his enemies said, he would practice his dramatic gestures before a full-length mirror, his figure illuminated by a Negro boy holding candles. The other roomers would be driven into the street to seek relief from the booming voice.*) He delivered almost no extemporaneous speeches. So there could be no doubt that he had taken time to reflect upon what he would say concerning Kansas and Butler's hopes that slavery would take root there. In fact he had told his friend Theodore Parker, "I shall pronounce the most thoroughgoing philippic ever uttered in a legislative body."

He began to speak on May 19, 1856. From the very first there was a distinct sexual overtone to his remarks. To make Kansas a slave state would be to perform "the rape of a virgin territory, compelling it to the hateful embrace of slavery." Here was the proslavery conspiracy made clear, "without a single rag, or fig-leaf, to cover its vileness."

---

* Sumner said there was no mirror and no Negro boy, that before delivery he recited his speeches in a low voice.

16

Three times he was interrupted by the president of the Senate, who called the southerners to order. Ostentatiously affecting not to listen, their noisy laughter and talk made it difficult to hear some of Sumner's words. But Senator Stephen A. Douglas of Illinois knew that indeed they were listening. "That damn fool will get himself killed by some other damn fool," Douglas muttered.

Sumner turned to the remarks of Senator Butler, who was not present. Whom did Butler represent? South Carolina, a state suffering from a "shameful imbecility" brought on by slavery. South Carolina's performance in the Revolution had been "pitiful" and indeed if everything of that cancer-stricken fief from its very beginnings down to the election of Senator Butler were blotted out from the pages of history, little would be lost. Yet Senator Butler, discharging "loose expectoration"— a reference to Butler's slight speech impediment—was found among those swearing his allegiance to slavery. "The Senator from South Carolina has read many books of chivalry, and believes himself a chivalrous knight, with sentiments of honor and courage.

"Of course he has chosen a mistress to whom he has made his vows and who, though ugly to others, is always lovely to him; though polluted in the sight of the world is chaste in his sight. I mean the harlot Slavery. . . . The frenzy of Don Quixote in behalf of his wench Dulcinea del Toboso is all surpassed."

It was getting late and Sumner had been speaking for three hours. He halted, indicating he would conclude the next day. When he had finished Representative John A. Bingham of Ohio told Senator Henry Wilson of Massachusetts that Sumner was in danger. He had gone too far. He should be given protection. Wilson recruited Representatives Anson Burlingame and Schuyler Colfax and went to Sumner. "I am going home with you today—several of us are going home with you."

"None of that, Wilson," Sumner said. He walked away alone and after a moment fell into step with William Henry Seward. Together they went toward the place where the horse

17

omnibus for central Washington City stopped. Seward asked Sumner if he intended to board the omnibus and Sumner answered that he was going to walk over to the Printing Office and check on the final proofs of the speech. That night Representative Preston Brooks of South Carolina found it difficult to sleep for thinking of the speech, which he had not heard but discussions concerning which he had listened to in the lobbies of several hotels. Brooks was in his midthirties, a six-footer with a four-in-hand dangling on his bosom and with his clothes worn a size large so that they hung loose upon him after the fashion of southerners of the day. He had fought in the Mexican War before coming to Congress, where he was not known as one of the violent southern fire-eaters. Perhaps in a spirit of whimsy, he had once introduced a resolution requiring all Congressmen to check their pistols in a special room before coming onto the floor of the House.

Brooks' father was a cousin of Senator Butler, the object of Sumner's scorn. As such Brooks was "kin." And of course he was a South Carolinian filled with South Carolina fire and dash. He considered what to do about Sumner's speech and was still thinking of what his course should be when the next day Sumner, going on for two more hours, finished. That was Tuesday, May 20, 1856. When Sumner sat down there was an offering of comments from other Senators. Mason of Virginia declared that Sumner's presence was dishonor itself. Douglas of Illinois, who wanted to be President and did not wish to offend southerners, said of Sumner, "Is it his wish to provoke some of us to kick him as we would a dog in the street?"

That night Brooks made up his mind. There was no consideration of sending Sumner a challenge to a duel. It was most unlikely that Sumner would accept. Northerners always declined. Furthermore, the act would establish Sumner as Brooks' social equal. In Brooks' view Sumner was no more than an insulting inferior. On such a man one used a horsewhip or cowhide. But it was difficult to get a really good grip on a whip handle, and Sumner was a tall, bulky man who could conceivably wrest the whip from Brooks' hand. If that happened and

Sumner were suddenly armed with Brooks' whip, Brooks would have no choice but to shoot him. He did not wish to do that.

So he selected for his chastising weapon a gutta-percha cane with a gold handle, the gift some months earlier of a friend. It weighed eleven and a half ounces and had a thickness of one inch at the top to almost five-eighths of an inch at the base. Its quality, the specific gravity, could be compared to hickory or whalebone.

On Wednesday, May 21, Brooks went to the Capitol grounds with his cane. He waited there for an hour and a half, pacing up and down from a bench to the Capitol steps and then back again. Representative Henry Edmundson of Virginia, who had heard it said that Brooks was going to take exception to Sumner's remarks, came upon him as he was walking from the steps back to the bench. "You are going the wrong way for the discharge of your duties," Edmundson remarked. Brooks asked him to come for a walk. Brooks would not be representing his state properly, he told Edmundson, if he permitted Sumner to say such things as he had said about South Carolina. And the Abolitionist fanatic had also offered deliberate insults to Senator Butler, an old man and a relative. Brooks was almost in the position of a husband whose honor had been outraged.

Sumner did not appear. Brooks discussed the matter with Representative Lawrence Keitt of South Carolina, a fire-eater. Really, he had no choice, Brooks said. It was his clear duty. The next morning, May 22, 1856, after an almost sleepless night, Brooks went again to the Capitol grounds and waited for Sumner to appear. He stationed himself in a gatehouse from which he could see all the likely approaches to the Capitol. If Sumner came on foot, he could be intercepted at the steps. If he came by carriage, there would be time for Brooks to run up the Capitol steps and get him at the carriage entrance on the other side of the building.

Edmundson of Virginia came up. "You are looking out," Edmundson remarked. Brooks told him his plan. But running up the steps was a bad idea, Edmundson pointed out. One was dealing here with a physically strong man, six feet two. It

19

wouldn't do to arrive winded and panting. Better to rethink the plan. They sat together in the gatehouse. Sumner did not appear. They must have missed him. They went up into the Capitol, where they parted.

Edmundson went into the Hall of Representatives, took his seat and sat through a eulogy to a recently deceased colleague. Then the session was adjourned. Edmundson got up and strolled into the Senate Chamber. The Senate was also in adjournment, with only a few people scattered about, but Edmundson saw his companion from the gatehouse sitting in a Senator's chair. "You are now a Senator?" Edmundson asked.

Another man had earlier taken note of the occupant of the chair. "How is Colonel Brooks today?" inquired Sergeant-at-Arms Joseph Nicholson.

"Well, I thank you. Come here, Nicholson."

Nicholson went and stood over him. "Do you see that lady in the lobby?" Brooks asked.

Nicholson turned and looked. She was seated on a lounge at the rear of the Senate Chamber. "Yes."

"She has been there for some time," Brooks said. "What does she want? Can't you manage to get her out?"

A joke, of course, Nicholson thought to himself. "No," he replied, "that would be ungallant. Besides, she is very pretty."

Brooks turned in his seat, looked again and said, "Yes, she is pretty, but I wish she would go."

He got up and walked out to the vestibule, Edmundson following. He could stand this thing no longer, he told Edmundson. He had scarcely slept last night, thinking of the vile insults. But there was a lady in the Senate Chamber, and one could hardly do what had to be done in her presence. So he would send in a messenger and ask his man to come into the vestibule. There he could be dealt with.

That wouldn't work, Edmundson said. The messenger would surely come back with a request for Brooks to come into the Chamber. Then Brooks would be back where he started.

They stood looking at Sumner as he sat at his Senate

desk with his head bent over envelopes he was franking. Several people stopped by his seat and attempted to speak with him, but he dismissed them, saying the mail would soon be going out and he wanted these copies of his speech sent on their way.

Keitt of South Carolina came in. Brooks made up his mind. The insults had been offered in there, in the Chamber, on the floor of the Senate. The floor of the Senate was the place to avenge them. The presence of a lady was unfortunate, but more important things were involved.

Brooks took his thick gold-headed cane and walked from the vestibule down the aisle to where his man was sitting. "Mr. Sumner," Brooks said.

Sumner looked up. Too vain to wear glasses, he saw only a blur. Had his eyesight been perfect he still would not likely have recognized the man who stood directly above him looking down, for he had never exchanged a word in his life with Preston Brooks.

"I have read your speech twice over carefully," Brooks said. "It is a libel on South Carolina and on Mr. Butler, who is a relative of mine—"

Sumner made a motion to stand up, and, breaking off his sentence, Brooks swung the cane in an arc and slammed it down on his head. Perhaps it was the result of that first stroke which made the doctor who later treated Sumner reflect that the ragged slash was very like one made by a flung brick. For it opened the scalp to the bone and sent a flow of blood pouring down Sumner's face.

Blinded, Sumner tried to get up. But as he did not shove back his chair, the tops of his thighs pushed up against his desk. Brooks, like a man cutting firewood with an ax, gripped the cane with both hands and slammed it down again on Sumner's head. Perhaps he landed five more blows before Sumner convulsively forced himself up, his legs ripping the desk from the iron plates which held it bolted to the floor. Brooks swung again.

With his arms stretched out in front of him, Sumner

staggered forward, trying to grab the flailing cane. He maneuvered by instinct, not really knowing or seeing, and never to remember what was happening. Brooks struck at him with the cane. In the almost empty Senate Chamber men broke off conversations and gaped. An assistant sergeant-at-arms, coming to his senses and taking in the scene, began to run across the Senate floor, shouting at Brooks to stop. The aged Crittenden of Kentucky had been talking with Pearce of Maryland when he realized what was happening and ran toward the men shouting, "Don't kill him!" Brooks' friend Keitt leaped in front of Crittenden, one hand waving a cane, the other reaching for a pistol in his pocket. "Leave them alone, God damn you!" Keitt shouted.

Sumner lurched into his desk. It overturned and crashed to the floor. That opened up the field of fire for Brooks, who slammed the cane onto Sumner's head a dozen more times. Sumner staggered to his right, Brooks staying out of reach of the waving arms as he swung the cane down. The cane snapped. Looking on from a distance, Toombs of Georgia thought to himself that it had been a remarkably silent affair, but that now the broken cane made a much louder sound than it had when it was whole.

The two men circled and reversed positions. Brooks backed up to have room to swing. Sumner lurched backward, Brooks moving forward with the stump of the cane raised over his head. Sumner reeled into a desk and appeared about to go down when Brooks seized his lapel, held him up and swung the broken cane. Splinters from it flew into the air as it came down on Sumner's head.

Sumner broke away, fell onto a desk, hung there for a moment and then slid into the Senate aisle.

There followed almost complete invalidism. Charles Sumner could not stand up without assistance, and even a few minutes of reading or writing tired him. He felt like a man of ninety, not forty-five, he told his friends. A physical weight seemed to be spreading over his brain. With it came the terrible

22

fear that his mind would be affected. Feverish insomnia plagued him.

Pale and thin, tottering when he tried to walk, he went off to the estate of Francis P. Blair at Silver Spring outside Washington and lay there in bed listening to the sounds of the springtime birds. Then after a few days he tried to go back to the Senate. After a few minutes he had to be helped away.

He went to a health resort in the mountains, then to a European spa. Agony followed him. He took cures, consulted eminent doctors. Nothing worked. Meanwhile his Senate seat remained empty. "A perpetual speech," it was called.

He wandered Europe, came back, went again. He could hardly walk: The Martyr Senator in the eyes of the North; the shammer in the South. His spine pained him. His mental state was frightful and his nervous agitation painful to his friends. Three years passed. The agony in his back was unbearable. He consulted a French physician who said that it was possible that the application of tremendous heat to the spine might ease the ghastly pain. Sumner asked that the treatments begin that very day.

The doctor asked if he wanted chloroform and then in answer to Sumner's question said that it was possible the use of a painkiller would weaken the treatment. That afternoon Sumner lay face down while the doctor applied white-hot material to his spine. No chloroform was used. The patient's hands clutched the table. He writhed.

The treatments went on for weeks, the doctor thinking to himself that never before had he seen such fortitude under pain and deciding, also, that never again would he subject a human being to such torture. But the fires worked. Sumner began to improve. Perhaps it was all psychological, and this was the purification of the flames. No one ever knew. Four years after Brooks' cane came smashing down, on June 4, 1860, Senator Sumner rose in the Senate to speak again.

"The Barbarism of Slavery" was the title he gave his speech. ("The Crime Against Kansas" was the title of the one four years earlier.) He spoke of what it meant to breed human beings for profit, the resulting damage to the parents and to the children. Chestnut of South Carolina answered: "After ranging through Europe, crawling through the back door to whine at the feet of British aristocracy, craving pity and reaping a rich harvest of contempt, the slanderer of states and men reappears in the Senate." Sumner remarked that he would add Chestnut's speech to the printed versions of his own. The words would be new evidence of the barbarism of slavery.

By then, 1860, Preston Brooks was dead, the victim of an unknown ailment which brought on strangulation. Four years earlier he had been arrested on a charge of assault as he left the Senate Chamber bearing the gold head of his shattered cane. A judge had fined him three hundred dollars. A motion was also made to expel him from the House of Representatives. It failed, but Brooks resigned. Then he went back to South Carolina to run again for the seat he had given up. He won it back with exactly six votes in the district cast against him. Women in the South sent him canes. He had restored the dignity and respectability of a Senate menaced by Abolition fanaticism.

In the North his name was Brooks the Bully, Bully Brooks. One day in Boston a little boy's father held the child up on the Statehouse terrace wall so that he could look over a sea of heads at an open carriage. In the carriage was Bully Brooks' victim. Shakily, he got to his feet. Many years later the little boy, who then held Charles Sumner's seat in the Senate, remembered the sound which rose from the throats of the assembled citizens of the Commonwealth of Massachusetts. "At the sight of him," wrote Henry Cabot Lodge, "a shout arose from that crowd the likes of which I have never heard since, and I have heard, in the course of my life, many crowds."

It would have been well for the South, the mature Senator Lodge reflected then, fifty years after Appomattox, if the South had heard the sound of that shout.

2

In February, 1861, young Charles Francis Adams of Boston paid a visit to Washington. The place appalled him. The House of Representatives was in his eyes some sort of national bear garden where frontiersmen and slave overseers roamed. They spat on the floors, drank bad whiskey and carried Bowie knives.

There was no style to the capital, Adams decided. The houses were modest and widely spaced, with sandy deserts in between. Only one street in the entire city was paved—Pennsylvania Avenue. The few grandiose government buildings, the Capitol, the Treasury, seemed incongruously placed in this provincial village.

Withal, a throbbing dread of the future hung over Washington. It was as if the city was mined and ready to explode. For the southerners were leaving, their carriages rumbling through the streets as they made for the depot and the trains. "Thank God! Oh, thank God!" Representative Lawrence Keitt's shouts had interrupted a wedding party two months earlier. "South Carolina has seceded! Here's the telegram—I feel like a boy let out from school." Once he had shouted,

"Leave them alone, God damn you!" as Crittenden of Maryland tried to get between Preston Brooks and Charles Sumner.

Other states followed South Carolina. By early February, 1861, Jefferson Davis of Mississippi, late Senator of the United States—he had cried as he took his departure—was preparing for his swearing-in as President of the Confederate States of America. Would there be a war? In the White House the outgoing President, James Buchanan, paced the porch, alternately weeping and praying. "Not in my time, not in my time," he kept repeating.

Young Charles Francis Adams was the grandson of President John Quincy Adams and the great-grandson of President John Adams. As a child he had known Senator Charles Sumner as a kindly, earnest friend. Along with others from Massachusetts he had interpreted the Brooks assault as an attack not only upon Sumner but upon Boston and the patriot tradition with which his own Adams family was so involved. It was the most natural thing for the young man to send in his card to Sumner when he visited the Senate and just as natural for Sumner to come out at once to say hello and take him in.

But Sumner was extremely agitated. "He talked like a crazy man," Adams remembered, "orating, gesticulating, rolling out" what he had to say "in theatrical, whispered tones." He seemed "super-heated, his nervous system overloaded." One question faced the nation in the crisis which was developing, Sumner told his young visitor. There was one point which must be decided, "the one true question of real statesmanship, the only question of true statesmanship, which has not even been touched." Yet he did not explain the one true question. His eyes gleamed with something "distinctive of insanity." All the Senators were in an uproar, Adams quickly learned, but Sumner was the worst.

After a while Sumner led his visitor toward the Senate cloakroom. As they walked along they met a rather tall, well-built man with black hair, deep black eyes and a swarthy complexion. In Adams' mind, he appeared to be a strong man physically and intellectually. Sumner introduced his visitor to

Senator Andrew Johnson, Democrat of Tennessee. Senator Johnson, speaking in what Adams thought was a rather formal fashion, remarked that he had sat next to John Quincy Adams when he and the ex-President had served in the House of Representatives. He had seen the ex-President stand up to say, "Mr. Speaker! Mr. Speaker!" and then drop his arm and sink down, to murmur a moment later, "This is the end of earth."

When the three had finished their brief talk Sumner and Adams walked on, but Senator Johnson had indicated the young man might call upon him during his Washington stay. Shortly thereafter Adams went to Johnson's room in one of Washington's hotels, every one of which was in Adams' eyes an "unkempt barracks." Johnson's room, containing a bed and some scanty furniture, was a miserable little place littered with folded speeches and copies of public documents. But by then Adams had had his fill of Sumner and his cry that the southern slaveholding class was an unholy combination of ruffianism and bluster. Johnson's calmness was appealing. That was the most outstanding thing about him, the young visitor felt, his nerve, his coolness. He spoke slowly and with no show of emotion about the problems the country faced as the states of the South fell away one by one.

While Johnson said he agreed with Adams' assessment of Sumner—"morbid and diseased" of late, "in fact, actually crazy"—the Senator's words were hardly less violent than those of his Massachusetts colleague. He denounced Senator David Yulee, who, typical of the departing southerners, had written the Florida Legislature to explain why he was leaving the northerners and westerners and coming home: "I am willing to be their master, but not their brother."

"Miserable little cuss," Johnson said of Yulee in his slow, even way. "Contemptible little Jew * . . . despicable little beggar . . . a damned blackguard, never owned the hair of a nigger." His solution for the crisis was, Adams learned, that a lot of people ought to be hanged.

One month later Senator Johnson rose to speak in the

* Yulee had changed his name from Levy.

Senate. It was the second day of March, 1861. In two days the new President, Abraham Lincoln, would be sworn in. Several days earlier Lincoln had slipped through pro-secession Baltimore. He had traveled at night to come to Washington and register at the Willard, where he received men frightened for their country and for themselves. (Sumner was among the callers. Six foot four himself, Lincoln looked at the towering Sumner and, as was his fashion with big men, suggested they stand back to back to see who was taller. That was not Sumner's way. Dignity affronted, he said it was a time to stand front to front, not back to back. "My idea of a bishop," Lincoln remarked when the Senator left.)

Johnson's speech two days before Inauguration Day, 1861, was to a Senate in which the seats belonging to six states were empty. Other seats soon would be. The families and hangers-on of the departed were gone. For the first time in years the galleries which so often echoed the sound of southern voices shouting down the representatives of the North possessed a Yankee twang. Yet compromise solutions were bruited about. "Let the erring sisters go in peace," said Horace Greeley's New York *Tribune*. "Would you forcibly hold the South?" asked Senator Lane of Oregon.

Within weeks Johnson would be the sole representative from a Confederate state who would refuse to follow that state out of the Union. Soon young Charles Francis Adams would be wearing the blue-trimmed-with-yellow of a Union army cavalry officer. Soon Washington would be filled with troops, wagon trains, mules, commission brokers seeking positions for clients, sutlers, liquor dealers, whores, gamblers, keepers of concert saloons with waiter girls, circus and bear shows, and Sanitary Commission and Christian Commission representatives carrying Bibles. Above all the other noises—the booming of artillery practice, drums beating, bugles playing—would be the zigzag sound of ambulances wending their way through the rutted streets as they sought smooth going to avoid jolting their mutilated and bloody occupants. And there would be other wagons with U.S. HEARSE on the sides.

28

No one could know of all those things when Johnson got up to speak. What was clear was that the Union of eighty-five years was collapsing. Yet there were men who did not wish to face it. Johnson addressed himself to such men.

"Have we reached a point at which we cannot talk about treason?" he asked.

"Show me who has fired upon our flag, has given instructions to take our forts and our customhouses, our arsenals and our dock yards, and I will show you a traitor!"

He had said what others were afraid to say: he had thrown down the gage of battle at his own South; and at the word *traitor* the galleries erupted into cheers. Clingman of North Carolina, who soon would be heading home, got up and shouted at the crowd, "Why, the Senate Chamber is becoming but a theater!" People yelled insults at him, drowning out the voice of the presiding officer who was calling for the sergeant-at-arms to make arrests. A moment later Johnson said, "I have done." But before he sat down a man in the galleries jumped up on a bench, waved his hat and shouted, "Three cheers for the Union and for Andy Johnson!" A great roar filled the room, completely submerging the voice of the presiding officer. When the cheers were finished the voice from the Chair could be heard ordering that the galleries be cleared immediately and that the persons guilty of causing the tumult be arrested. "Arrest and be damned," a man called down. "We are ready to go now!" And they went, pushing and shoving, hissing and clapping and shouting for the Old Flag and the Union and for the southerner who had the courage to fling defiance back into the face of his own southerners because he felt they were wrong.

Two days later, the day of the inauguration of Abraham Lincoln as President of the United States, *The New York Times* spoke of Andrew Johnson, of Greeneville, Tennessee, for most of his life, but now an exile from a home with which he would soon be at war. "The greatest man of the age," *The Times* said.

Fifty-three years earlier, on December 29, 1808, Andrew

Johnson had come into the world in a hovel. The shack belonged to a couple who worked for a hotel in Raleigh, North Carolina. Jacob Johnson carried the travelers' bags, took care of the horses, brought wood for the fire. Mary McDonough Johnson—everyone called her Polly—did washing and mended clothes.

Poor whites, crackers, the Johnsons had no prospects, no future. Jacob's duties at the hotel allowed him time to work as a porter at a bank and ringer of the town bell for weddings, funerals, fires, public announcements. In addition to her other tasks at the hotel, Polly Johnson served as maid to the wife of the hotel's owner when not caring for little Andy and his older brother, Bill. The couple saved no money, made no plans. Completely illiterate, they had signed their wedding license with X's.

Far above the Johnsons stood the planter aristocracy with its slaves and mansions and fine ways, its polished floors and old silver, the fox hunting and bookishness of a leisured class. Below were the Negro slaves. Jacob and Polly Johnson existed in a world in between, from which there was no escape. For North Carolina had no yeomanry, no middle class. Looking at their type, the Irish-born traveler E. L. Godkin reflected that here was the "most wretched, most cadaverous, most thinly clad, most lean, most haggard, most woebegone, forlorn, hopeless, God-forsaken-looking portion of the human race, the poor niggerless whites of the slave states. . . . I think I have never seen men in whom hope, energy, and courage, to all outward appearance, seemed so utterly extinguished as in these." Here was the English peasantry gone to bad seed. There was not even the opportunity to rise by mastery of an artisan's tools, for that was the province of the slave. To compete with him was deggradation.

The word the gentry used to describe the Johnson class of poor white was *mudsill*—the sill half-embedded in the dirt upon which the superstructure rests. "In all social systems," explained Senator Hammond of South Carolina, "there must be a class to do the mean duties, to perform the drudgery of life.

That is a class requiring but a low order of intellect and but little skill. Its requisites are vigor, docility, fidelity. Such a class you must have, or you would not have that other class which leads progress, refinement, and civilization."

Accepting, never questioning, the Johnsons lived on what the gentry permitted them. In December, 1811, when Andy was three, his father went along on a gentlemen's fishing trip. He was there to care for the horses, serve the food and drinks, clean the day's catch. The party was at Hunter's Mill on Walnut Creek, a few miles from Raleigh. The gentlemen grew boisterous. Someone launched a canoe. Three men piled in. The canoe drifted into ten-foot-deep water. One of the gentlemen, for a lark, rocked the craft. It went over. Colonel Tom Henderson, editor of the Raleigh *Star,* found himself dragged to the bottom by a reveler who could not swim. He fought his way up, dragging the other man with him. They went under again. December's icy waters closed over them. Jacob Johnson came running from shore, plunged in, paddled to the two men and dragged them to safety.

A month later, fatally weak from the results of the exposure, Johnson collapsed while pulling the rope of the town bell. Colonel Henderson wrote in his *Star* for January 12, 1812, that Johnson had "for many years occupied an humble but useful station in society. . . . In his last illness he was visited by the principal inhabitants of the city by all of whom he was esteemed for his honesty, sobriety, industry. . . . None laments him more (except perhaps his relatives) than the publisher of this paper; for he owes his life upon a particular occasion to the boldness and humanity of Johnson."

Jacob Johnson's relatives buried him in the town's potter's field. There was no money to erect a stone. For the next decade Polly Johnson and her sons Bill and Andy existed on her earnings as a washerwoman and sometimes weaver and spinner of cloth. It was a brutally impoverished poor-white-trash life made no better by Polly's marriage to a shiftless tramp, Turner Dougherty. There were no amenities, no refinements, not even the necessities of life in the Raleigh of the

1820's. "I have grappled with the gaunt and haggard monster called hunger," Polly Johnson's younger son said, later. He did not go to school for so much as one day. Schooling cost money.

Eleven years after his father's death, at the age of fourteen, Andy was stocky and dark, a street Arab. Apprenticed to a tailor, James Selby, he was legally bound—his mother had signed her X—to stay with Selby until he turned twenty-one. Bill had preceded him. The two brothers sat cross-legged on a bench, crouching over shears, needle, measuring tapes.

There was no fresh air. The tailor's wife gave the boys coarse and heavy homespun for their clothing. The hours were from early morning until evening, stitching, patching, binding, raveling. Outside the shop, North Carolina's gentry traveled the few blocks to the state capitol in heavy carriages driven by slave coachmen and attended by slave footmen in livery.

The pedigreed of Raleigh who came to the shop occasionally left a tip for the bound boy holding the horses. Beyond Andy's respectful manner there must have been something else, for one or two of the men gave a little time to instructing him. A patron gave him a book, a collection of speeches and essays, and one of the foremen read to him from it. Andy learned to read the book by relating what had been read aloud to the sight of the words. He did not recognize individual letters as such, only the words.

When Andy was sixteen he and his brother and two other bound boys threw some rocks at the house of a widow who lived outside of town. (She had two daughters Andy remembered as "right smart.") The widow did not take the prank well and threatened to go to the law. The boys panicked. On the night of June 15, 1824, Andy and Bill and the two other youths fled Raleigh. They made their way to Carthage, seventy-five miles away. There they opened their own tailor shop in a rented shack. Selby advertised a ten-dollar reward for their return, "Or I will give the above Reward for Andrew Johnson alone." If the boys were returned to Raleigh they could be in substantial difficulties, for the law was severe on runaway apprentices. They moved on to Laurens, South Carolina, and took over an abandoned cabin.

In late 1824 Andy took note of a young lady of Laurens and expressed his affections. She reciprocated them. But he was poor, functionally illiterate, a runaway bound boy. Her parents demurred. He understood and left Laurens and went back to Raleigh to make it up with Selby. But by then the tailor wanted no part of him, so he hung around the inn in whose courtyard shack he had been born. People were afraid to employ a boy still legally bound. Andy wandered away into Tennessee, came back. The older brother, Bill, was gone by then, headed west, eventually to Texas.

His mother and stepfather were as they had always been. They had nothing to lose by leaving town. And off to the west was the frontier where Andy could start all over. So in August of 1826 in a two-wheeled open cart drawn by a half-blind pony the family set out to cross the Eno, the Haw, the Yadkin, the Catawba, the Swannanoa, the French Broad, the Pigeon, the Nolichucky, to scale the Blue Ridge Mountains, to sleep in the open and be frightened by a bear and finally to come, after a month, to a valley between the Blue Ridge and the Cumberland Mountains, there to camp for the night at the flow of water later called the Gum Stream in Greeneville, Tennessee. He unharnessed the pony.

His mother got busy with dinner. He went to seek some corn fodder for the pony and met a little boy who led him to his father's farm. The father gave him what he wanted. The next day he met the little boy's older brother in Greeneville's post office-general store and told him he was a tailor. The brother said the only tailor in town was too old to work much anymore. Greeneville would offer opportunities for Johnson. The older brother ordered a suit on the spot and young Johnson, obtaining the material at the general store, immediately went about making it for him. But Andy had not yet decided to stay in Greeneville. The family moved on to Rutledge, then returned to Greeneville a few months later when word came that the elderly tailor there had given up his business. In Greeneville, Andy rented a cabin and put up a sign: A. JOHNSON, TAILOR.

Beyond the opportunity to have his own business, there was another reason for his return to Greeneville. On the morning after his arrival the young Andy Johnson, eighteen, passed the girls of the Rhea Academy standing on the sidewalk. "There goes my beau," Eliza McCardle whispered to a friend. Seventeen, brown-haired, hazel-eyed, she was the daughter of a deceased shoemaker. Andy Johnson stopped to ask Eliza McCardle directions to the post office-general store. After he left, the girls teased her about her new sweetheart. She said, "He's all right. I might marry him someday."

Andy had returned from Rutledge to Greeneville in March, 1827. He and Eliza were married two months later. Their home was a two-room cabin, each room about twelve feet by twelve, the front room being his shop and the rear their kitchen, dining room, bedroom and parlor. Eliza's dowry consisted of her schoolbooks. From them she taught her husband to read and write and cipher. Eliza was the only teacher Andrew Johnson ever had. Later, running for office, he often spoke of how he as much as anyone on the green globe had reason to admire and love the opposite sex, for one of their number had taken him in and taught him. That teacher was his wife.

Legs curled under him, he worked at his trade. *June 17th 1829. P. H. Nelson. To making vest $1.50. To BomBazett $1.50. To Cotton Lineing $1.50. August 13th 1830. To Makeing one coat for Wm Whinney $4.00. oCtob 3 1832. Dr. Hill To Cuting pants $.25. March 1840. To makeing one pare of pants for M. Payne $1.00.*

He read as he worked, a word at a time as he pulled a needle through the cloth. Prospering, he hired apprentices and a man to read aloud to him and his young employees. Eliza gave him a daughter, Martha, in 1828, and a son, Charles, in 1830. Both were born in the single room in which the family lived. In 1831, at age twenty-three, Andrew Johnson bought a house and lot at auction, paying about one thousand dollars. Three more children were born there.

He sent his daughter, Martha, to school and studied her books with her, an earnest, solemn man trying to make up for lost time. He wanted to know why things were the way they were, relationships between groups, what power was. For music, art, poetry, he had no feeling or interest. The entire town of Greeneville possessed fewer than one hundred standard works of literature and its cultural life could be defined by the fact that only once a waxwork show representing Napoleon and other important figures came to town, never to return. He did not care. The theater, games, sports held no attraction for him. Sometimes he played checkers, badly.

There was a tiny college four miles outside of town and every Friday night the students held debates. Andy Johnson got permission to participate. So every Friday night for years he trudged four miles to the debates to match wits and then four miles back home. As a speaker he was slow and heavy, but effective, capable of projecting a certain power. His voice was good, booming when he warmed up.

The students Johnson met made his tailor shop their headquarters during visits to town. Other artisans and mechanics dropped by, bricklayers, shoemakers, carpenters. East Tennessee was one of the very few districts of the South where such a middle class existed, for the mountain land was unsuitable for large-scale slave plantations. Yet the little town had its aristocracy. One member was Dr. Alex Williams, the owner of sixty-four foxhounds. By most of Greeneville, Dr. Williams was considered a giant of the time and referred to as "Alexander the Great." In turn, Dr. Williams and his set viewed Andy Johnson as a mechanic, a poor white, a mudsill one step removed.

The tailor shop became a gathering place for men like Andy. Those who met at the shop saw its owner as generous, kindly, thoughtful, anxious to understand things. Notably taciturn and reserved, he displayed no small talk, no gaiety, grace, informality. In his life there were only one or two close friends. The others about him were accepted impersonally as men who felt as he did. Yet he was something of a leader in the isolated little world of the tiny town set in the mountain country. It was his manner, the level stare, that commanded respect.

For years Greeneville had been governed by a wealthy clique, but in 1829 the tailor shop decided to run a slate of candidates for the town council. The tailor shop backed three of the twenty-seven men contesting the seven aldermanic posts. Johnson was one of the three. He was elected, receiving eighteen votes. During the two succeeding years he ran for alderman again, winning election each time. After that he stood for mayor and won. It was something of a blow to the well-bred of Greeneville to have as their mayor a man who still worked full-time as a tailor. A concerted effort was made to defeat him when he ran for reelection. The effort failed. He served his second term, ran again and was again elected.

The gentry did not accept Andrew Johnson even then. Once Dr. Williams gave a banquet to which all the local notables were invited, with the sole exception of Greeneville's three-time mayor. Shortly afterward Johnson spoke of his feelings to a young lawyer, Oliver Temple: "Someday I will show the stuckup aristocrats who is running the country. A cheap purse-proud set they are, not half as good as the man who earns his bread by the sweat of his brow."

The words were unusual for Johnson, for even in a private and casual conversation he almost always spoke in a formal manner. He was different when he made speeches. East Tennessee demanded of its political speakers that they supply entertainment and exhortation and spirit, and something of religion's uplift, but it was not only the needs of his listeners that made Johnson come alive on the stump. In front of the people he could bring forth fire and thunder. Perhaps it was something akin to that passion which takes possession of the performer and transforms him when a crowd is assembled. Then Johnson was at ease, open to a communicated excitement which enlivened that dark and somber face and made fiery that restrained tongue.

In 1835, Johnson ran for the lower house of the Tennessee Legislature. The slight by Dr. Alex Williams ("Alexander the Great") was widely known among the mountaineers of Greene and Washington counties, and they saw Johnson as their champion against the rich and pedigreed. He went to camp meetings and muddy crossroads where his voice, beginning low, would rise in volume as he invariably denounced the monsters out to destroy the liberty of the people. In Washington, President Andrew Jackson had in rough guests who put their muddy boots up on the chairs and spat on the carpets, acts that would be unthinkable at a European court but which were accounted as a triumph for American democracy. From the stump or a rude goods-box fashioned into a rostrum, Andrew Johnson proudly declared himself no colonel or lawyer but just a plain man working with his hands; and the similarity of names between the two Tennesseans made the people of Greene and Washington counties liken the young legislative aspirant to the Hero of New Orleans.

On Election Day, Johnson went to the border of the two counties where the votes would be counted and was there to hear his victory announced. Word got back to Greeneville, and a procession of men went up the rutted and unpaved highway past primitive farmhouses and shabby crossroads trading posts to welcome and then escort the winner home. The lawyer Oliver Temple was struck by how calm and unmoved Johnson was. That cold manner, Temple thought to himself, seemed to mean that Johnson was saying, "This is only what I deserve and shall expect in the future."

In the state legislature he impressed the more sophisticated of his fellows as a raw and callow primitive. He regularly denounced bills for internal improvements such as roads or canals, seeing them as big-money and big-city schemes to mulct honest people of their money. "A railroad!" he exclaimed. "Why, it would frighten horses." He was defeated in his run for a second term. He ran again and was elected.

He spoke against the letting of convict labor to compete with free mechanics by saying the practice degraded the working-man, who was the salt of the earth. And, as he often did, he offered his list of eminent artisans: "Adam, the father of the race, was a tailor by trade, sewing fig leaves together for aprons; Tubal-cain was an artificer in brass and iron; Joseph, the husband of Mary, was a carpenter, and our Saviour probably followed the same trade; the Apostle Paul was a tent-maker." He jeered at a bill which called for hiring a geologist to study Tennessee's mineral and agricultural resources, saying the money was spent for a man who went around peering at snails, shells, snakes, rocks and fossils. The project was a plot to rob the people of their liberty, another scheme of the few who would steal power from the many.

From the lower house of the legislature he went to the Tennessee Senate. In 1842 Andrew Johnson announced for the United States Congress. The laborers and mechanics backed him; what was called the better element opposed a rustic tailor with the twanging accent of the up-country hillbilly. He won, the first tradesman or artisan ever sent to Congress from a slave state, and traveled north to a Washington of forty thousand inhabitants, the biggest city he had ever seen. As Congressman he did not socialize, making only a few friends. He continually spoke out in favor of his projected Homesteading Bill, which would open up the vast western government lands to anyone willing to farm them. Thus would hardy farmers be given a stake in their country and their society. He rhapsodically described how from land ownership would grow a great independent class of men resolutely opposed to the outmoded Europeanized planter aristocracy, its manners and its thinking. The bill was routinely voted down. Its author was marked as a demagogue.

Much of Johnson's time was spent in the Library of Congress, doggedly studying and reading. He dressed, as he always had and would continue to do for many years, in clothing he made himself: a black broadcloth frock coat and waistcoat, black doeskin trousers and a silk hat. When he spoke he looked intently into the listener's eyes; listening, he hung his head and attentively heard any speaker out. A grim man. At home the tailor shop prospered even during its owner's absence, for he had chosen an excellent manager to oversee an operation which now employed half a dozen skilled craftsmen. By the standards of Greeneville he was well off, and eventually would own eight slaves, but by the standards of the South's congressional delegations he was the poor-white mudsill he had always been. (Landowners and cavaliers born to command would as a matter of course hold a man who was serious, economical and thrifty to be a contemptible Yankee-like plodder.) Johnson had strength of mind and character, said Jefferson Davis of Mississippi, but he would never permit himself to rise above his humble origins. Johnson was forever seeing slights where none were intended, Davis said, and then retreating, like the mythical character who gained strength by touching Mother Earth, to the methods of thinking and expression and the way of life which had given him birth.

What plain Andy Johnson of the stocky and peasant-like form and the heavy face thought of the great men of his South surfaced violently during a debate in 1846. Representative Davis rose on the slim, high-arched feet that people noted as belonging to a natural-born aristocrat and spoke in favor of a resolution expressing thanks to General Zachary Taylor for his victories in Mexico. Davis coupled praise of Taylor with praise for his own alma mater, the United States Military Academy. West Point to Johnson was gold braid and an officer class. He spoke out against the Taylor resolution and West Point. Davis countered by pointedly asking, "Could a blacksmith or a tailor construct the bastioned field-works opposite Matamoros?"

Davis had struck home. The rough brawler's stump manner of the harsh rises of mountainous East Tennessee showed itself. "I am a mechanic," Johnson snarled, "and when a blow is struck on that class I will resent it." He had not been raised to formal politeness in debate and now all veneer of it fell away. "I know," he went on, "we have an illegitimate, swaggering, bastard, scrub aristocracy who assumes to know a great deal, but who, when the flowing vein of pretension is torn off from it, is seen to possess neither talents nor information on which one can rear a useful superstructure. Sir, I vindicate the mechanical profession. I mean the man who earns his living by the work of his hands, and not by fatiguing his brain."

An impossible person, Davis and the other southerners decided. He would remain forever obsessed with his humble origins. But the exchange did not hurt Johnson in East Tennessee, where they said that Andy was not the kind of fellow to go back on his raising.

As United States Representative he declared the government should pay no more than one thousand dollars for the original copy of Washington's Farewell Address. Otherwise "by-bidders and sweeteners" would run up the price. He denounced the creation of the Smithsonian Institution, saying it would be better to set up a school for mechanics. He opposed increasing the pay of government clerks unless the government's pick-and-shovel men got a raise also, adding there were too many clerks in any event, for all they did was go "around the country blowing the horn of their bosses." At the end of each of his five terms as Congressman he campaigned in his aggressive style, answering opposition charges that he was a boor and demagogue by saying that those who opposed him, whether of his own Democratic party or not, were enemies of the people.

"These vandals and hyenas would dig up the grave of Jacob Johnson, my father, and charge my mother with bastardy," he would shout, and then inevitably recount his impoverished origins and say he was now the champion of the poor, that he was a tailor who always gave a good fit at the right price. Let the people honor him by permitting him to be their representative and together they would stand, "hand to hand, shoulder to shoulder, foot to foot, and make a long pull, a strong pull and a pull altogether." Sometimes he offered a song which he said the boys of Greeneville used to sing, and bawled out:

If you want a brand-new coat
I'll tell you what to do;
Go down to Andrew Johnson's shop
And get a long-tail blue.

If you want the girls to love you,
To love you good and true,
Go down to Andy's tailor shop
And get a long-tail blue.

He campaigned on the Democratic ticket against the Know-Nothings and their anti-foreign and anti-Catholic secret order with its passwords and midnight gatherings. "Show me a Know-Nothing and I will show you a loathsome reptile on whose neck every honest man should put his feet," he shouted at a meeting. "It's a lie—it's a lie," men yelled back. He could hear the sound of pistols being cocked. In his cool way he looked at the people and, after a tense pause, went on. The next day he was told that the Know-Nothings were organizing to stop a forthcoming speech. He went to the place set for his appearance.

"Fellow citizens," he said, "it is proper when free men assemble for the discussion of important public matters that everything should be done decently and in order. I have been informed that part of the business to be transacted on the present occasion is the assassination of the individual who now has the honor of addressing you. I suppose therefore that this is the first business in order. If any man has come here today for this purpose this is the proper time to proceed." As he spoke he pushed back his coat so that everybody could see that his right hand was resting on a gun butt. He let his words hang in the air, then said, "It appears that I have been misinformed. I will now proceed to address you on the subject that has called us together."

His enemies said he was a "mobocrat," "full of treason and hate against the rich." He was "leading a rabble against the better elements of society." "Robespierre was as bad, but

41

he used chaste language." "If Johnson were a snake," said an old Tennessee rival, Isham G. Harris, "he would lie in the grass to bite the heels of rich men's children."

"Whose hands built your Capitol?" Johnson replied. "Whose toil built your railroads and your ships? I have no quarrel with an aristocracy founded on merit and on honest toil, but for a rabble, upstart, mock aristocracy, I have supreme contempt."

In 1853, forty-five years old, he ran for Governor and won. At his inauguration he refused to ride in a carriage, but walked, like the common people who had sent him to Nashville.

"The Mechanic Governor," as he was called by the out-of-state papers, urged higher taxes for education, backed the establishment of agricultural and mechanical fairs, set up a state public library. In 1857 a rumor spread in Nashville that, aping the year's Sepoy Mutiny in India, the city's Negroes were going to rise in rebellion. Mrs. Lazinka Campbell Brown, a noted lady of the city, whose father had served in the James Monroe Cabinet and as Minister to Russia, was told that the slaughter would take place on Christmas morning. Nashville, it was said, would be awash in blood that day unless Johnson ordered cannon fired to intimidate the blacks. Half-amused and half-believing, Mrs. Brown and her daughter went to the Governor. The daughter remembered long afterward how Johnson listened to the tidings the ladies brought. Where, he finally inquired, was the evidence of any disturbance? "Upon whom am I to fire?" There was a quiet strength there, the daughter decided.

But with that strength went no humor, the Brown ladies saw. Once in their home the Governor met a woman with whose husband he had served in the legislature years earlier. He asked after the husband and learned from the woman that he had been dead for six years. "I thought I hadn't seen him in the street," Johnson said. Mrs. Brown later told Johnson she could hardly restrain herself from breaking out in laughter. He did not see that anything funny had happened. He was a man of most narrow views, a mutual friend said of Johnson. Mrs. Brown agreed and offered some remedial reading. One day when the Governor came calling she recommended Thomas Carlyle to him and took a volume down. He thanked her and went away, to return saying, "I can't make head or tail of that book." She looked down and saw she had given him *Sartor Resartus* (The Tailor Repatched). He had given no hint that it was applicable in any way to himself.

Johnson's constant insistence that mechanics and artisans were superior to all other men baffled Mrs. Brown. Why had he let his son Charles become a physician and his son Robert a lawyer if only men who worked with their hands were virtuous? "Because they had not sense enough to be mechanics," the Governor replied. As for himself, now freed forever from his tailor shop—although he still made his own clothing—"I thought better when I was on my tailor's bench." Success in the world's eyes would never change him, either. He said he had seen men who were in a position to have their own carriages refuse to speak any longer to poor people. He simply hated the rich, the Browns decided.

Devoid of any kind of outside interests beyond his involvement with his family, Johnson saw everything in political terms. When his arm was broken in a railroad accident, he took immediate note of the political sympathies of the doctor called to attend him. The doctor ruled that the arm must be rebroken and bent it around a fluted bedpost to do the job. The pain would have been frightful in any case, but the sharp edges of the post added an additional agony. Governor Johnson told people that the doctor could as well have used a round post, but had naturally not done so because he was a Whig treating a Democratic patient.

The Governor served two terms and then, in 1857, went to the United States Senate. The long and terrible schism between North and South was reaching the climax which would bring the hurricane, but Senator Johnson of Tennessee did not display notable foresight or concern. He did not wholeheartedly identify himself with his geographical section as did each of the other twenty-one southern Senators. His concerns lay elsewhere. In the Senate he repeated over and over the themes of his life and career: "I want no rabble here on one hand, and I want no aristocracy on the other." He pushed his Homestead Bill, voted against increasing the size of the army, against building a railroad to the Pacific. Once the other Senator from Tennessee, John Bell, indicated that he considered Johnson beneath him. It was the sort of bait to which Johnson always rose. "A gentleman and a well-bred man will respect me; all others I will make do it," he said menacingly. He would defend his rights "at all hazards and to the last extremity." The matter was smoothed over, but it was noted he had practically offered an invitation to a duel. "Now that I have them down, do you think I won't trample on them?" he had asked Mrs. Brown on his election to the Senate. "I tell you I will."

He did not foresee the holocaust that was coming. His remedy for the conflicts which divided the sections was adherence to the Constitution. Conversely, to break up the Union was to violate the Constitution. So there must be no war. The South simply had no choice but to remain in the Union.

Alone in that view among the southerners in the Senate, Andrew Johnson stood with them on the issue of human slavery. "If you liberate the Negro," he asked, "what will be the next step? What will we do with two million * Negroes in our midst? Blood, rape and rapine will be our portion. You can't get rid of the Negro except by holding him in slavery."

And, of course, southern-born and southern-bred, with the South in his voice and ways, he could never be wholly at ease with the men of the North. Once he heard the Massachusetts politician Benjamin Butler tell a Washington audience that the North would never be forced into war by Abolitionist fanatics like Charles Sumner. If war came, Butler added, the fanatics would have to climb over the bodies of men like himself. "Damn a Yankee who professes to be more of a southern man than I am myself," Johnson said.

* The slave population has been estimated at four million.

By 1860 hardly anything was discussed in the Senate but slavery, the possibility of southern secession, the establishment of an independent southern republic, the chances of war. Johnson doggedly kept pushing his Homestead Bill. Free land for free laborers. A chance for the common man. But the Homestead Bill was caught in the whirlwind. Were the territories whose populations would be suddenly expanded to enter the Union as free states? The South could not permit that. Would they be slave states? The North said no. The regional responses exasperated a Johnson who believed only that poor men must be given a chance. "Why lug slavery into the matter?" he asked. If the Ten Commandments were to be voted on "somebody would find a Negro in them somewhere."

Yet in those last days of peace Johnson repeated over and over that the Constitution was the life preserver to which they all must cling. One could understand why he felt that way, for if the South went out and he went with it, he would be a citizen of a republic whose leaders had passed laws in many states which said that no one who owned fewer than ten slaves could hold office. Yet plain Andy Johnson of Greeneville loved Tennessee, loved the South.

Tennessee, essentially a border state, decided to hold a plebiscite which would determine if the state went with the Confederacy or stayed with the Union. In the spring of 1861 Senator Johnson returned home to speak in every county of East Tennessee, to hark back to the Hero of New Orleans, Andrew Jackson, who had said in answer to Calhoun of South Carolina, "The Union, it must be preserved." The railroad home led through what was now enemy country. At one Virginia stop an armed mob came into the car. "Are you Andy Johnson?" a man asked.

"I am."

"Then I am going to pull your nose!" The man lunged forward. Johnson drew a revolver as the mob closed around him. The conductor came in, shouting, "No shooting, gentlemen, please! There are ladies in the car!"

With the weapon leveled Johnson forced the mob out.

As the train pulled away his shout reached down to them: "I am a Union man!"

In Lynchburg, Virginia, another crowd waited. "Hang him!" men were yelling as the train pulled in. "Here's the rope!" Johnson stood on the train steps challenging them to come ahead. At Bristol so large a mob gathered that word was telegraphed to President Jefferson Davis. The last thing President Davis wanted was a slaughtered martyr to the Union cause. The atrocity might incline undecided border states to cast their lot with the North. Davis telegraphed back that the train should rush through Bristol without stopping.

And so Johnson came to Greeneville. All he owned, all of his being, was there. He set out to keep Greeneville and East Tennessee as his native land, going from meeting to meeting to say that if war came the poor man of the South would have to fight for the King Cotton aristocrats and their hell-born and hell-bound rebellion. "I am for my country," he shouted in his booming stump-speaker's voice. His revolver was always on his hip. Other men, terrorized by the threats and violence, capitulated and declared they would stay with Tennessee if that state joined the Confederacy; in constant danger but cooler, less bitter, eloquent beyond what he had been in the past, he asked that Tennessee stay loyal. The election went the wrong way for him. By a vote of 101,000 to 57,000 the voters declared their state part of the Confederacy.

But he would not slip away like a coward. In a light carriage, accompanied by three friends, Johnson made for the Cumberland Gap and Kentucky. At Bean Station, Tennessee, a man called for a mob to arrest the fugitive. No one responded. It was typical of Andrew Johnson, Oliver Temple thought, that he would openly pass through mountain passes and narrow valleys perfect for ambush. Perhaps it was that courage and that deliberate way which brought him to safety. Behind him, in Greeneville, a banner waved in the main street: ANDREW JOHNSON, TRAITOR. Eight years would pass before he would see Greeneville again.

* * *

He came back to sit in a Senate hysterical with hatred of the South which had given him birth, to be a slaveholder among Abolitionists, a Democrat among Republicans, the sole representative of the slave states who still sat with Free Soilers. Alone, for his family was still in a Greeneville ruled by officers in Confederate gray, Senator Johnson voted for the call-up of the troops who would fight First Bull Run. He was appointed to the Committee on the Conduct of the War, and with its other members harangued the Union commander, George B. McClellan, for his desultory ways.

In Tennessee he was declared an "alien enemy" whose property was liable to confiscation. His two sons-in-law were members of the state's Union resistance, living in mountain caves from which they sallied forth to burn bridges and intercept Confederate troop trains. Johnson's wife and daughters and youngest son were virtual prisoners in their home. For months at a time he had no word of their welfare save for an occasional brief message smuggled through the lines to say they were at least alive. He kept to his tasks in Washington, and his fellow Senators viewed him now in a new light, for of all their number he had sacrificed the most for the Union: family, fortune, wife, children, home. There was something awesome about the one southerner who had stayed when all the others had left.

After the disastrous Union rout at Bull Run, Andrew Johnson rose in the Senate to say that the war should be fought, not for oppression or conquest, but to maintain the Constitution and the Union. He would suffer death gladly rather than see his Tennessee a part of an oligarchic empire. Only let the old Union be as it was and he would have all armies disbanded.

Within view of the Capitol one could plainly see the Confederate campfires across the Potomac in Virginia. There were those who said Lee would soon take Washington City. "Some of us," Johnson said, "would not feel so very comfortable if the rebels were to get this city. I do not think I could sleep right sound if they were in possession of it. I do not believe there would be much quarter for me." But, he added, the rebels, his people among whom he had lived all his life, would not take Washington City. "Yes, we must triumph. Though sometimes I cannot see my way clear in matters of this kind, as in matters of religion, when my facts give out, when my reason fails me, I draw upon my faith. My faith is strong, based upon the eternal principles of right, that a thing so monstrously wrong as this rebellion cannot triumph.

"God being willing and whether traitors be few or many I intend to fight them to the end."

Throughout the winter of 1861–62 General George B. McClellan drilled the troops of the eastern army of the Union. He was a student, a tactician and a perfectionist. But the Union general's lack of actual progress did not worry Charles Sumner. Sumner openly expressed the hope that the Union would not gain too quick a victory. For an easy triumph meant everything would remain unchanged, with the blacks still in a condition of slavery. "The longer our triumph is postponed, the more impossible this becomes," he wrote his British friends. Union defeats were Providence's way of forcing emancipation, and imposed "for our crimes toward a long-suffering race." In fact none of the military aspects of the war overly interested the Senator from Massachusetts. "It seemed," said George F. Hoar, as if he thought the rebellion would be "put down by speeches in the Senate, and that the war was an unfortunate and most annoying, though trifling disturbance, as if a fire-engine had passed by."

In contrast, Johnson and the other members of the Committee on the Conduct of the War constantly called for more aggressive war-making. No officer was vibrant enough for them, least of all McClellan. To lose a battle or even a skirmish made any soldier suspect in their eyes. Perhaps he was a traitor, a secret rebel sympathizer. Caution they interpreted as cowardice, retreat of any kind as treason. All save Johnson were Republicans, but they were not the same kind of Republican as Abraham Lincoln, who was a conservative. They were *Radical* Republicans. Only one general satisfied them, the militarily unlettered Ulysses S. Grant, a fighter. Out in the west Grant laid siege to Fort Donelson on the Cumberland River and took it after offering the Confederate commander the terms which made the name Grant suddenly world-famous: "Unconditional surrender."

The fall of Fort Donelson meant that the Tennessee capital of Nashville was open to the Union forces. The Confederate Governor and legislature departed for Memphis in the south. Soon Nashville was filled with running soldiers in gray who had escaped the Union dragnet around Donelson.

Under a February rain the rebel army roared through, looting as it fled. With the army went the students of the Nashville Female Academy and anyone else who could get away. The suspension bridge over the Cumberland fell into the waters after it had been set on fire. By February 20, 1862, the railroad bridge, the ordnance works and the trapped Confederate gunboats were burning. Under the smoky haze Nashville waited for the Yankees to come.

The Union troops marched into the capital bringing with them the newly appointed and army-commissioned Military Governor of Tennessee, Brigadier General Andrew Johnson. At Lincoln's request he had given up his seat in the Senate and position on the Committee on the Conduct of the War, knowing he actually would rule little more than the city of Nashville. His authority existed only through the intercession of Union bayonets. The hold was tenuous. Beyond the city limits stood the vast Confederacy. *"Go it Andy this is your day,"* read an anonymous letter addressed to the new Military Governor. *"The day is not far advanse when you will have your just day and that day cannot come until you are tared and fethered and burnt."*

Knowing that the rebels would soon return, the Military Governor ordered the destruction of almost two hundred homes to make way for fortifications. The work was done largely by slaves whose infuriated rebel owners were forced to supply their services and equip them with food and tools. Anyone who protested was instantly escorted to the outskirts of the city and told to move south. Some Nashville ministers spoke against the draconian rule of the new Military Governor and were promptly arrested and brought before him. General Johnson showed them a loyalty oath to the Union. When they refused to sign, he threw them into jail with orders that no visitors be admitted. "These assumed ministers of Christ," he said, "have done more to poison and corrupt the female mind of this community than all others, in fact changing their entire character from that of women and ladies to fanatics and fiends. Traitors and hypocrites, wearing the livery of heaven to serve the devil." He had the ministers brought to the city limits, where they were told to keep walking.

Outside the town, guerrilla bands burned houses, tore up railroad tracks, ripped telegraph wires and hanged men suspected of being sympathetic to the Military Governor and the Union. Food was a problem, with Union foraging parties in constant danger of ambush. In the summer Nathan Bedford Forrest, the Confederate cavalryman, came to menace the town. He cut the railroad and telegraph service so that Nashville became an island in a Confederate sea. With no cavalry fit to oppose Forrest's troops, there was nothing for the Union forces to do but cut trees and barricade the streets with them. The Confederates brought up artillery and bombarded Nashville. Dead mules, victims of the shelling, lay unburied in the broken streets and a plague of rats swept up from the river. Rumors said a vast force of rebels was on the way and would invest the city momentarily.

Johnson closed the saloons, fined Confederate sympathizers, impressed additional slaves into Union service, suspended newspapers and two pro-rebel publishing houses, took all horses for the army. He banished anyone he suspected of being a rebel spy and made up his own loyalty oath, far stronger than the one Washington dictated: it forced the oath-taker to swear he prayed for a Union victory and rejoiced in the triumphs of Union arms. "He keeps the screws tight down on their thumbs," wrote a New York *Tribune* reporter from Nashville. The Military Governor "daily thundered incoherent invectives against the 'hell-hounds of the hell-born and hell-bound Confederacy,' " noted Colonel Henry Stone of the Union army, whenever he "could find so much as an audience of one to listen."

Stone was not the only officer to find him a tartar. Johnson fought with all the Union commanders sent to Nashville. Running the city was largely a soldiers' operation and he might well have slipped into the background, but he did not. Each officer who arrived at the depot was served with a copy of the Military Governor's commission and instructions from President Lincoln. Johnson was the soul of Nashville's defense. As Forrest moved closer to the city and the Union lines contracted, the Capitol building became known as Fort Andrew Johnson. The situation was growing desperate. "I am no military man," Johnson told the officers around him, "but anyone who talks of surrendering I will shoot."

The Military Governor decreed that any time an insult was offered to a Union man five suspected rebel sympathizers must be imprisoned. He threatened hangings, confiscation, firing squads. All the while he cursed the high-born gentry he said had made the war. Someone remarked to him that central to the conflict was the question of human slavery; he snarled, "Damn the Negroes, I am fighting those traitorous aristocrats, their masters."

In September of 1862 the Confederate forces completely isolated Nashville. Surrounded by a populace largely hoping to greet a conquering rebel army, the Military Governor savagely questioned the bravery and motives of anyone who showed less fighting spirit than he. When a rumor spread that General Don Carlos Buell was going to flee with the Union troops, the Military Governor roared, "We are sold out! Buell is a traitor! He is going to evacuate the city and in forty-eight hours we shall be in the hands of the rebels." He turned to Colonel Granville Moody, a chaplain. "Moody, can you pray?"

"That is my business, sir, as a minister of the gospel."

Both went to their knees on opposite sides of the Governor's room. Reverend Moody launched into a fervent prayer that the city be delivered from its dangers. Responding with loud "hallelujahs" and "amens," Johnson made his way on his knees to the chanting clergyman, finally to put his arms around him as they beseeched the Almighty in unison. When the minister finished Johnson let out a last roaring "Amen!" and got up and took a deep breath. "I feel better," he said. Then, "Oh, Moody, I don't want you to think I have become a religious man because I asked you to pray. I am sorry to say it, but I am not, and have never pretended to be, religious. No one knows this better than you. But, Moody—there is one thing about it—I do believe in Almighty God! And I believe in the Bible, and I say I'll be *damned* if Nashville shall be surrendered!"

Grimly he fought on against the besiegers, self-sufficient, domineering, an impatient, rough and belligerent man in the eyes of all who knew him. He often said that before he would let the city go under he would burn it to the ground. He himself had nothing to lose, for he knew that if the rebels captured him he would be tarred, feathered and then hanged. Nashville was isolated from September to November of 1862 before Union forces broke through. By then the Military Governor was reunited with his wife, ending their year-long forced separation. Left behind in the comparative safety of Greeneville, Mrs. Johnson had been ordered out of their home directly after his appointment as Military Governor. Given thirty-six hours to get out of Confederate territory, she made her way to Murfreesboro with her two daughters, her youngest son and the grandchildren. There she was told she could not go through the lines. With night coming on she wandered from one home to another seeking shelter. Finally a woman took in the refugees on condition that they be gone by morning.

The next day Eliza Johnson led her party south to Tullahoma and then back to Murfreesboro. They spent the night in a deserted restaurant. There was no food, fire, bed or place to sit down besides the floor. She had candles and matches, some stale food from her lunch which she had saved for the children.

That Mrs. Johnson was the wife of the Military Governor brought her insults and threats in the areas south of his tiny dominion, but never by a look or word did she indicate her feelings. Finally she came to Nashville and, showing her order of expulsion from home, passed through the Confederate outposts and into the Union lines. Her husband wept when he saw her.

For two years he fought the war in Nashville and the surrounding countryside. Minnesota and Michigan regiments escorted him as he went to tell the people of Tennessee that they should support the Union. "The representatives of this corrupt, and if you will permit me almost to swear a little, this damnable aristocracy, taunt us with our desire to see justice done, and charge us with favoring Negro equality. Of all living men, they should be the last to mouth that phrase.

"Why, pass any day along the sidewalks of High Street where those aristocrats more particularly dwell—these aristocrats whose sons are now in the bands of guerrillas and cutthroats who prowl and rob and murder around our city—pass by their dwellings, I say, and you will see as many mulatto as Negro children, the former bearing an unmistakable resemblance to their aristocrat owners. . . .

"What do the Secessionists propose to do? They are ready for a return to a monarchy and the establishment of an aristocracy that should control the masses. Are you willing to quail before treason and traitors and surrender the best government the world ever saw? If the Union goes down we go with it. There is no other fate for us. Our salvation is the Union and nothing but the Union. The only inquiry must be, Are you for the Union and willing to swear that the last drop of your blood should be poured out in its defense?"

War swirled about, raids, charges, burnings, ambushes in which Military Governor Johnson and his escort came under enemy fire. Confederate officers, so said the rebel Knoxville *Daily Register,* argued with each other about who would get "Andy's scalp when the army reaches Nashville." Had he given in, the Confederate troops and provisions for Lee to the north would have moved in a straight line instead of by a forced circuitous bypass.

Officers who came to Nashville thought of Johnson as the grimmest sort of person. Carl Schurz, a German refugee from the Revolution of 1848 now a Union officer, found the Military Governor polite and kind, but distinctly plebeian. There was no "sunlight" in him, Schurz reflected, but "rather something sullen, something betokening a strong will inspired by bitter feelings. I could well imagine him leading with vindictive energy an uprising of a lower order of society against an aristocracy from whose lordly self-assertion he had suffered, and whose pride he was bent on humbling." The Military Governor had no culture, Schurz decided, and his mind moved in a narrow circle of ideas as well as words. In appearance he was somber and dignified, and his manner was calm, but Schurz could not rid himself of the impression that beneath this "staid and sober exterior there were still some wild fires burning."

To Schurz and others Johnson talked of nothing but political subjects, of how the rebels were no longer citizens, but public enemies. "The constant burden of his speech," Schurz wrote, "was that the rebellion against the government of the Union was treason, and that treason was a crime which must be made odious by visiting condign punishment upon the traitors. To hear him expatiate upon this, his favorite theme, one would have thought that if this man ever came into power, the face of the country would soon bristle with gibbets, and foreign lands swarm with fugitives from the avenging sword."

Schurz decided that a man must be a fanatic who talked of nothing else but punishment of traitors. He tried to suggest that there were other matters in the world fully as important as revenge, but the Military Governor greeted the idea with polite indulgence and then went on to speak of how the criminals would be branded with their crime for all time to come. "Indeed," Schurz wrote, "this seemed to constitute the principal part of his political program for the future." Schurz went away wondering if Johnson ever talked about other matters. Perhaps with his family and friends and neighbors, he decided.

Major Benjamin C. Truman was the officer assigned to the Military Governor as his personal secretary. He found his chief almost as single-minded as Schurz thought him. He took part in no games save for his occasional displays of bad checker playing. He never went to the theater * because, he told Truman, he had never visited a playhouse when young, and since then preferred to spend his time in work, study or sleep. Gambling he regarded as a wrong. "Never knew one card or one domino from another, and was never at a horse race." The Military Governor told his secretary that now and then in the past he had gone to a few circuses and minstrel shows and liked them, but, after all, he had "never had much time for frivolity." He did not do much drinking, not caring for champagne or mixed drinks, and he had never been in a barroom. When he drank he took Robertson County whiskey, some days two or three glasses at the most, but for other days and weeks none at all.

Occasionally, Truman found, Johnson could relax his harshness against the hellish rebels. That was when the rebels were feminine. One day the daughter of the owner of the Saint Cloud Hotel was arrested for spitting upon Union officers from the hotel porch. Laura Carter was a pretty girl of about twenty. The arresting officer told Johnson he was sorry he had to take her into custody. He first had tried to reason with the young lady, explaining she should behave herself since Johnson himself was staying at the hotel. Laura Carter had then replied that she would yet dance on Johnson's grave. "Oh, you mustn't mind these little rebels," Johnson said. "There is no harm in Laura. Dance on my grave, will she? She will plant flowers instead. I'll take care of her. Let her go."

Perhaps Johnson's Old South respect for women made him so understanding of Laura Carter. He treated all women with exaggerated deference, Major Truman noted. Only once

* When the tragedian John Wilkes Booth played Nashville in *Richard III* on February 1, 1864, the Military Governor did not attend.

in all the Nashville years did he permit himself to be disrespectful to a lady. A giantess, one of the largest human beings Truman had ever seen, called on Johnson. Her husband, a prominent Nashville rebel, had been sent to a northern prison at the Military Governor's order. She wanted to visit him and asked permission to go through the Union pickets surrounding the city. Johnson told Truman to make out the pass.

"And return," said the giantess.

"We don't want you to return," Johnson replied.

"Andrew Johnson," she roared, "do you know what I ought to do? I ought to take you across my knee and give you the biggest spanking you ever had in your life!"

"Madam, it would take the whole Union army to spank you," he said. But he gave her the pass that would allow her back. In a rare moment of levity Johnson said to Truman, "If her husband had any sense of gratitude, he'd send me a letter of thanks for sending him to a northern prison."

In the North, Andrew Johnson's name became a byword for courage and steadfastness. It was impossible not to admire a man who had given and risked so much, and then had become the hated foreign proconsul among his own people. In early 1864 Major Truman ran into an old friend who was a correspondent for the New York *Herald*. The friend was visiting Nashville with General Daniel Sickles. "The President has sent him here on an important mission—can't you guess it?" the friend asked. Truman said he could not.

"He has come down here to look after Johnson," the friend said.

"To look after Johnson?"

"Yes, to look after Johnson. To see what he is doing. To look into his habits. The President wants Johnson on the ticket with him if his habits will permit. And the General has been sent here to investigate."

Sickles completed his research and went back to report to the President. In June the Republican party, renamed the National Union party for this election, nominated Andrew Johnson, the leading war Democrat of the country, to run for

Vice President on the ticket headed by Abraham Lincoln. The man Johnson would replace, Hannibal Hamlin, was from Maine. His inclusion on the ticket in 1860 led to charges that the Republicans were strictly a northern, sectional party. With Andrew Johnson, Democrat of Tennessee, on the ticket, Lincoln could hope to garner votes in the border states and from Democrats in the northern states who resented the claim that theirs was the party of treason. Here was a Vice Presidential candidate, shouted Horace Maynard in his nomination speech, who had "stood in the furnace of treason." The delegates exploded in applause. (So violent was Johnson's well-known hatred of the Confederacy that Charles Sumner was heard to say that he wished the ticket were turned around, with Lincoln running in the secondary place.)

Johnson campaigned in the border states and the Midwest, calling for the destruction of the Confederacy and denouncing Lincoln's Presidential opponent, the former Union army leader General George B. McClellan. That officer, so hesitant in battle, had decided that the bloody stalemate of the war must be resolved by vigorous northern peace overtures. No viewpoint could be more opposed to that of either Lincoln or Johnson. But as Election Day approached, McClellan's position appeared to be gaining strength in a North weary of death, and Lincoln told his intimates that his Administration would lose the election. (Her husband's opinion terrified Mrs. Lincoln; she said to her maid that he *must* be reelected if only so that she would be in a position to pay the extravagant clothing bills she had compiled.)

As a Vice Presidential candidate Johnson happily asked people what they thought of a ticket consisting of a former rail-splitter and a former tailor. (Lincoln, far less wedded to his origins, never made any conspicuous references to these former stations in life. The rise from them did not hold any of the romance for him that it did for his running mate.) On the stump Johnson threw aside restraint, as he always had. Addressing a group largely made up of Negroes, he cursed the "damnable aristocracy" which had made playthings of black women for so long. He promised that future laws would protect people of color. So would the people "break down an odious and dangerous aristocracy."

But once those laws were in effect, he asked, would the blacks in their turn shun "the path of lewdness, crime and vice"? Men and women shouted back, "We will! We will!" and Johnson shouted that if they did then as in days of old, a Moses would arise to lead a downtrodden people to the Promised Land. "You are our Moses," voices cried out. Carried away, Johnson forgot that he routinely employed the word *nigger* and had even once said of the distinguished leader Frederick Douglass, "He's just like any nigger, and he would sooner cut a white man's throat than not." In response to enthusiastic cries of approval, the candidate called out, "Humble and unworthy as I am, if no better be found, I will indeed be your Moses, and lead you through the Red Sea of war and bondage!"

The statement was given wide publicity. It underlined Johnson's implacable hostility to the Confederacy. At the same time it may have angered some border-state Democrats whose adherence his nomination was supposed to assure. Abraham Lincoln knew he was in deep trouble when he told a war-weary North that his reelection would mean more fighting. The President wrote out a memorandum which he had his Cabinet members sign. It was an offer of cooperation with his presumed successor, McClellan, intended for delivery when the voters named McClellan to Lincoln's office.

Only timely Union victories in the field saved Lincoln and Johnson. The Administration was returned to power by the electorate. Johnson was Vice President-elect. A strong man, Lincoln had said of him. And his inclusion upon the ticket showed Europe that not all southerners were rebels. That fact might convince England to continue its nonrecognition of the Confederacy, the primary aim of Secretary of State William H. Seward's foreign policy. Would the President have picked Andy Johnson as his running mate in other circumstances? It is more than doubtful. Lincoln appeared to wonder, at the moment of Johnson's nomination, if he had done the right thing in supporting him for the Vice Presidency, saying that he hoped that Johnson was the right man for the job. Then he let his voice trail off in a manner that indicated that he was not certain Johnson was a good choice.

One month after the 1864 election the Confederates stormed Nashville again. The Vice President-elect's family had returned to Greeneville, which was once more in Union hands. He sent them a letter there that spoke of his rundown condition. "My mind is tortured and my body exhausted," he wrote. "Sometimes I feel like giving all up in despair, but this will not do. We must hold out to the end; this rebellion is wrong and must be put down." By then it was obvious that the South's strength was ebbing away very quickly.

The new year of 1865 came in. Inauguration Day was to be March 4. Tired and ill, the Vice President-elect wrote to the secretary of the Senate's Chief Clerk. He asked if he could take the oath of office in Nashville and so spare himself the long trip north to Washington. Six other Vice Presidents had not been in Washington for the ceremonies, the Clerk replied. But President Lincoln learned of Johnson's letter and, wishing him present, telegraphed to ask that he come to the capital. Still suffering from what was diagnosed as possible typhoid, the Military Governor did not commit himself to attending the inauguration. On January 24 Lincoln wired that the Cabinet had discussed Johnson's possible nonattendance and had unanimously decided that it was best that he be present for the ceremonies on March 4. "Be sure to reach here by that time," the President telegraphed.

On February 25 Johnson left Nashville, thin and worn. There were alarms in Kentucky—bushwhackers were planning to ambush him, it was reported—but on March first the Vice President-elect reached Washington. He took rooms, a suite of bedroom and parlor, on the second floor of the Kirkwood House at Twelfth and Pennsylvania. For the next two days he remained indoors as heavy spring rains soaked the capital.

On March 3 he resigned as Military Governor and Brigadier General. Accepting the resignation, Secretary of War

Edwin M. Stanton said Johnson had served "in a position of personal toil and danger perhaps more hazardous than was encountered by any other citizen or military officer of the United States." Even in his personal life he had given as much as any man. His eldest son, Charles, had died in Union uniform after a fall from a brother officer's horse. His daughter Mary Johnson Stover's husband had died fighting against the rebels. His son Robert had entered an army in whose camps every kind of vice was to be found and had emerged as a hopeless wastrel and drunkard. Mrs. Johnson and their youngest son, Andrew, had both contracted consumption in the lean days when they were virtual Confederate prisoners at Greeneville.

The night before Inauguration Day the Vice President-elect went to a party given by John W. Forney, the Secretary of the Senate. Johnson did not want to go, but Forney told him that the party was intended to be a victory celebration. Johnson owed it to the war Democrats to put in an appearance. The epithet *Copperhead* was widely used to describe those Democrats who had been at best lukewarm in their support of the Union cause, and Johnson, the antithesis of the Copperhead, should not only be present at the victory celebration but should become a prominent member of the Administration. Then Democrats would not forever be condemned for failing to back the war. The Vice President-elect attended the affair with his Nashville aide, Major Truman.

It was a good time to throw a party. The rebs were on the run and the war would soon be over. The North was rich and prosperous. On the following day the Administration would begin another four years. When Secretary of the Navy Gideon Welles drove home at midnight with Secretary of State Seward the party was still going strong.

The next morning the Vice President-elect awoke with an aching head and queasy stomach. At ten-thirty Senator James Doolittle of Wisconsin arrived at the Kirkwood House to pick up Johnson. Hannibal Hamlin, the outgoing Vice President, joined them. The three drove to the Capitol through a drizzle which, added to the rains of the previous few days, had turned Pennsylvania Avenue into a sea of mud.

They arrived and went up to the Vice President's Room, where General Charles Hamlin, the outgoing Vice President's son, was waiting for them. Outside, the Senate Chamber became filled, the ladies resplendent in gig-top bonnets and hoops. A South American diplomat got his feet tangled in a crinoline, tripped, rolled down the aisle. Wearing dress uniform with gold lace and epaulettes, "Fighting Joe" Hooker took a seat. The Radicals' favorite, Hooker was the handsomest soldier of his time. He had once been feared as the potential leader of a Radical coup d'etat. Foreign ministers arrived in court dress, and the judges of the Supreme Court in their black silk gowns, with Chief Justice Salmon P. Chase at their head.

A few minutes before noon Johnson said, "Mr. Hamlin, I am not well and need a stimulant." He was acutely nauseous. Perhaps it was stage fright, perhaps the results of the previous night's indulgence, perhaps an effect of his lingering illness. "Have you got any whiskey?"

"No," Hamlin said. "When I became Vice President I gave an order prohibiting the sale of liquor in the Senate restaurant. But if you desire, I will send across the street for some whiskey." A messenger was told to go get a bottle. When he returned Johnson took a water glass and filled it—to the brim, Hamlin noted—and drank it down. The oath-taking speech he would soon make was going to be the effort of his life, Johnson said. He filled another glass. "I am not fit to be here, as I was slow in recovering from an attack of typhoid fever. I will take some more of the whiskey, as I need all the strength for the occasion I can have."

It seemed like quite a large quantity of liquor to Hamlin, a teetotaler; but, he thought to himself, Johnson was probably a hard drinker who could easily consume a considerable amount of whiskey. Certainly there was no indication that the alcohol was causing any ill effects.

It was time to go. Hamlin and Johnson got up and arm

in arm they left the room with the departing Vice President's son, General Hamlin, following. They were hardly out of the room when Johnson excused himself, hurriedly turned back and, almost bumping into General Hamlin, quickly returned to the room. Looking in, General Hamlin saw he was filling up a third glass with whiskey. Johnson came back, rejoined the outgoing Vice President and went into the Senate Chamber.

The spectators had arrived wearing rain gear, but many were soaked nevertheless. A humid warmth rose from the packed rows of seats. Hamlin went to the rostrum and Johnson sat down directly below him at the Chief Clerk's desk. Hamlin began his farewell speech, to hold up as the Cabinet came in. He continued, then paused as Mrs. Lincoln, in black velvet trimmed with ermine, took her seat. The President was in the President's Room signing last-minute bills of the outgoing Congress.

Hamlin finished his speech and said, "Is the Vice President-elect now ready to take and subscribe the oath of office?"

"I am," Johnson replied. He was to make a brief speech —the schedule called for five minutes or a little more—and then take his oath of office from Hamlin. He would then join the others who would watch Lincoln take the oath and deliver his Second Inaugural Address outside on the East Portico.

Johnson went to the rostrum. The first words that came out were a stammering series of disconnected sentences. Understandable, Hamlin thought to himself, the emotion of the moment, the return to the Senate Chamber where Johnson had served with such distinction. But it kept up. "Your President is a plebeian—I am a plebeian—glory in it," Johnson called out. His face was beet-red.

He was here, he went on, at the call of the American people, and "not presumptuously to thrust myself into a position so exalted." There was a strange belligerency about the words. No one had accused him of thrusting himself forward. "Tennessee has never gone out of the Union," he shouted. "I am going to take two minutes and a half on that point—I want you to hear me. We derive our power from the people—

You, Mr. Chief Justice Chase, are but a creature of the people. I want you to hear me two minutes on that point."

He began to list the members of the Cabinet, telling each he was a "creature" of the people. "You, Mr. Stanton, Secretary of War, and you, Mr. Speed, Attorney General, and you—you—" he stopped. "Who is the Secretary of the Navy?" he mumbled. "Welles," stage-whispered John Forney, his previous night's host. "You, Mr. Welles, Secretary of the Navy."

It began to dawn upon the listeners that something was wrong. Johnson waved his arms, and his voice rose and he lapsed into the chanting and twanging southernisms of the Tennessee hill country: "I'm a-goin' for to tell you, here, today. Yes, I'm a-goin' for to tell you all, that I'm a plebeian! I glory in it. I am a plebeian! The people, yes, the people of the United States have made me what I am. And I am a-goin' for to tell you here today, yes, today, in this place, that the people are everything!"

Attorney General Speed turned to Secretary Welles. "All this is in wretched bad taste. The man is certainly crazy." Welles looked at Secretary Stanton, who sat at his right. Stanton seemed petrified. "Johnson is either drunk or crazy," Welles said to Stanton. Postmaster General Dennison squeezed his eyes shut and sat immobile. Supreme Court Justice Nelson's mouth hung open with amazement. Senators were whispering, "Is the man crazy?" As the raving went on, people twisted in their seats or covered their eyes. Several Senators turned sideways, seeming to cower in an about-face position.

"Humble as I am, plebeian as I may be deemed," Johnson kept shouting. He waved his fists. President Lincoln came in, seated himself, listened a moment and then let his head droop slowly.

"I, a plebeian, elected by the people the Vice President of these United States, am here to enter upon the discharge of my duties!" Johnson yelled. He waved his arms at the assembled Diplomatic Corps swathed in court dress of gold lace, swords, knee breeches, cocked hats, plumes. "Gee-gaws!" he shouted. "I, though a plebeian boy, am authorized by the principles of the government under which I live to feel proudly conscious that I am a man!"

He had long exceeded the time allotted for his speech. Forney stepped up and put a note on the rostrum telling him to stop. Johnson ignored it. Cries of "Tell him to stop!" could be heard, and finally Hamlin, sitting behind him, leaned forward as unobtrusively as possible and hissed, "Johnson, stop!" The hoarse voice kept ranting on about its owner's rise from humble beginnings and the greatness of the occasion. Hamlin desperately leaned forward and grabbed the tail of Johnson's coat and yanked it.

Finally, after fifteen ghastly minutes, he finished. Hamlin jumped up to administer the oath and Johnson, stumbling over the words as he repeated them while adding his own comments on how he could agree with the oath in all respects, was sworn in as Vice President. Then he seized the Bible and turned to the audience, yelling, "I kiss this Book in the face of my nation of the United States." He appeared to want to go on, but was halted. Scheduled to swear in the new Senators for the new Congress, he was far too befuddled to administer the oaths. Forney did it hurriedly and the ceremonies in the Senate Chamber were concluded. All stood to go to the East Portico where the President would speak. Senator John Henderson of Missouri, the chairman of the committee to escort the President, offered Lincoln his arm. Lincoln took it while turning to a marshal and saying, "Don't let Johnson speak outside."

They all moved to the East Portico. Senator Preston King of New York, who had been active in getting Johnson his nomination, shepherded the new Vice President along. His face red, Johnson waved both arms and beamed as cheers for Lincoln came up from the waiting crowd.

The President waited for the applause to die down. He put a copy of his speech on the podium before him, and at that instant the sun came out from behind the clouds. ("It made my heart jump," Lincoln said later.)

The President read out his seven-paragraph speech and left, to stand on a reception line that night and greet the hundreds who came to congratulate him. One young Union army nurse thought that something almost akin to a halo's light beautified that plain, sad face when the President left the line to take the hand of a young lieutenant who had left a leg in the trenches before Petersburg. "God bless you, my boy!" Abraham Lincoln said in the thin yet gripping voice with which he had delivered his Second Inaugural Address earlier that day:

> *Fondly do we hope—fervently do we pray—that this mighty scourge of war may speedily pass away. Yet, if God wills that it continue until all the wealth piled by the bondsman's two hundred and fifty years of unrequited toil be sunk, and until every drop of blood drawn with the lash shall be paid by another drawn with the sword, as was said three thousand years ago, so still it must be said, "The judgments of the Lord are true and righteous altogether."*
>
> *With malice toward none; with charity for all; with firmness in the right, as God gives us to see the right, let us strive on to finish the work we are in; to bind up the nation's wounds; to care for him who shall have borne the battle and for his widow, and his orphan—to do all which may achieve and cherish a just and lasting peace among ourselves, and with all nations.*

In the crowd that listened was the holder of a ticket obtained from ex-Senator John Hale of New Hampshire's love-struck daughter. Wearing a tall silk hat, John Wilkes Booth stood on a stairway just above and behind the President.

Preston King took the Vice President to the estate of the Francis Blair family in Silver Spring, Maryland, where Sumner had gone when Brooks finished with him. There Johnson spent the next two weeks. He issued no statements, made no comments on what the newspapers were calling "the most incoherent public effort on record," the "spewings of a drunken boor," an "exhibition of drunken impertinence." To think, said the New York *World,* "that one frail life stands between this insolent, clownish creature and the Presidency!" Senator Sumner convened a caucus of Republican Senators and unsuccessfully urged them to move that Johnson resign. The speech, Sumner said, was the "most unfortunate thing that had ever occurred in our history."

It had taken only a few minutes for Johnson to destroy the country's picture of him as the determined man who had given so much to the Union cause. Secretary of the Treasury Hugh McCulloch remarked to the President that the nation had an immense stake in his life, considering the character of the man who would succeed him in case of his death. Lincoln hesitated a moment and then said with what McCulloch considered unusual seriousness, "I have known Andy Johnson for many years. He made a bad slip the other day, but you need not be scared, Andy ain't a drunkard."

Less than a month later the Confederate capital of Richmond fell to the Union army. Four years of crying "On to Richmond" were at an end. Washington exploded with joy. All the public buildings were illuminated, artillery salutes were fired, strangers embraced in the streets, bunting and flags were everywhere. From the steps of the War Department the Vice President addressed a great throng. He said he would repeat for them what he had recommended as the proper treatment for the South's leaders when the war first broke out in 1861: "I would arrest them, I would try them, I would convict them, and I would *hang* them." The newspaperwoman Jane Grey Swisshelm wrote that she was unable to convey the man's earnestness. "There was no rant, no bluster; it was deep, calm, conscientious conviction, and made me shiver."

Johnson had returned to himself. None of the ravings of his awful inauguration speech, but all of his long-held beliefs came forth. When he mentioned Jefferson Davis the crowd roared "Hang him!" Yes, Johnson shouted back, hang him twenty times, hang him as high as Haman. "Leniency for the masses—*halters* for the leaders!" He was so bloodthirsty, so filled with hatred, Mrs. Swisshelm thought. Rather let him be like the Negro who refused to swat the fly, for there was room for both of them in the world. "Let there be no hanging," she said to him when he finished his speech. "Disenfranchise them."

"Mrs. Swisshelm," he replied, "a very good way to disenfranchise them is to break their necks!"

The next day President Lincoln left General Grant's headquarters at City Point in Virginia and steamed up the James River to Richmond's wharves. A cloud of smoke hung over the beaten city whose streets were filled with shattered bricks from shelled buildings. The fleeing Confederates had burnt the bridges, blown up the storehouses, fired the gunboats. Lincoln came ashore holding the hand of his son Tad. Surrounding them were the twelve sailors who had manned the oars of the longboat. Almost unnoticed, the President began to take a little walk.

A Yankee newspaperman who had entered the city with the Union troops saw him and went up to a group of Negroes who had been told by a Union officer to start cleaning up some of the debris.

"Do you know that man?" the newspaperman asked the Negroes.

"Who *is* that man, master?"

"Call no man master. That man set you free. That is Abraham Lincoln. Now is your time to shout. Can't you sing 'God bless you, Father Abraham'?"

At once they broke into a stumbling rush to the landing party. "Saviour! My Jesus! There is the great Messiah!"

One old man fell on his knees in the dust and took the President's hand and covered it with kisses; and Abraham Lincoln took off his hat.

He went from there to the Confederate White House, to sit in Jefferson Davis' chair and to ask if he might have a glass of water. He went, also, to the home of someone he had known long ago, before civil war put his friend into the field at Gettysburg as leader of that charge remembered afterward as the high-water mark of the Confederacy.

"Is General Pickett's wife here?" he asked when a woman came to the door.

"I am General Pickett's wife."

"Madam, I am George's old friend Abraham Lincoln."

"The President of the United States!"

67

"No, only Abraham Lincoln, George's old friend. And this is George's baby?" George Pickett, Jr., stretched out his hands. Lincoln fondled him. "Tell your father that I will grant him a special amnesty—if he wants it—for the sake of your mother's bright eyes and your good manners."

Two days later, on April 6, the Vice President also came to Richmond. He met the Assistant Secretary of War, Charles A. Dana, who had been sent down to gather official Confederate records. Johnson launched into an impassioned speech on the monstrous sins of the Confederacy and the need for rigorous methods of punishment. The lecture went on, Dana estimated, for twenty ringing minutes. Finally Johnson paused, and Dana managed to say that without doubt the Vice President's remarks were very impressive and worthy of consideration. But why, Dana asked, were they being addressed to a relative nobody? Let him rather go to the President and Congress. This observation did not cool Johnson's passion. "Mr. Dana," he said, "I feel it to be my duty to say these things to every man I meet."

On that day, April 6, Mrs. Lincoln also came to Virginia. Escorting her, as he had to the Inaugural Ball, was Senator Charles Sumner. He was one of the few people in Washington who did not dislike Mary Lincoln. In her youth she had been a southern belle in Kentucky—all her relatives felt that she had married far below her station—and as a product of a southern finishing school she spoke French. She and Sumner wrote each other notes in French and exchanged copies of the latest books from Paris. They liked to talk of poetry. She sent him flowers from the White House conservatories. For Sumner's kindnesses to a worn and unhappy woman, President Lincoln esteemed the Massachusetts Senator. (And of course the Senator was also important to Lincoln's guardianship of the government. "Don't I manage Sumner well?" he once asked. "He thinks he leads me in all things." Sometimes after their conferences Lincoln would send a messenger racing after the departing Senator to beg that he come back for a moment. The President had just thought of another matter on which he must have Sumner's guidance. "The only man living who ever managed Charles Sumner or could use him for his purpose," said Senator Shelby Cullom of Illinois.)

Sumner had brought along his friend the charming nobleman Adolphe, Marquis de Chambrun, for the expedition south. After seeing Richmond—where Sumner took the gavel of the Confederate Congress for a souvenir—the party joined the President. Together they toured hospitals and attended parades. Despite the poisonous Washington gossip that Mary Lincoln was a traitor who had sent secret messages to her relatives in the Confederate army, she was heart and soul for the Union. Twice, de Chambrun noted, she spoke to her husband of what should be done with Jefferson Davis: "Do not allow him to escape the law—he must be hanged!"

Both times the President replied, "Judge not, that ye be not judged." In his own mind he had long since decided to give the South the gentlest kind of peace. The rebels were now erring brothers returned to the fold. "Let 'em up easy," he said to the Union officer commanding at Richmond. "Let 'em up easy." Later at a Cabinet meeting he would toss his hands in the air as a man does when he shoos sheep and declare that he hoped the Confederate leaders would go to Europe, Mexico, South America, anywhere, just so long as they vanished.

As the party steamed north along the Potomac to Washington, President Lincoln read aloud from Shakespeare. He came to some lines from *Macbeth,* read them, paused, and read them again. Sumner never forgot.

> *Duncan is in his grave;*
> *After life's fitful fever he sleeps well;*
> *Treason has done his worst; nor steel, nor poison,*
> *Malice domestic, foreign levy, nothing*
> *Can touch him further.*

When they reached Washington, April 9, 1865, Mrs. Lincoln said, "That city is full of our enemies." With an impatient gesture the President replied, "Enemies, never again must we repeat that word."

By then Lee and Grant were in correspondence across their lines. On the day Lincoln came home Lee put on a magnificent dress uniform with red sash, a presentation sword and clean spurs. Turning to General William Pendleton, his chief of artillery, he said, "I have probably to be General Grant's prisoner and thought I must make my best appearance." As it turned out there were no prisoners. Later Lee rode among his men to tell them they were all paroled. They must now go home, he said, and put in a spring crop.

When Grant's telegram reported that the Army of Northern Virginia had stacked arms at Appomattox Courthouse, Washington was flung into a frenzy similar to the wild celebration that followed the fall of Richmond six days earlier. An illuminated sign dominated the long view up Pennsylvania Avenue to the Capitol: "This is the Lord's doing; it is marvelous in our eyes." Again there were artillery salutes, bands, parades. The war was all but over, even though in North Carolina the fighting continued. A last weak force of Confederates there under General Joseph Johnston maneuvered back from the onrushing forces of William T. Sherman.

On April 11 the President spoke to a crowd gathered in the White House grounds. Mrs. Lincoln had asked both Sumner and the Marquis de Chambrun to attend. But only de Chambrun came, to watch and listen and then speak with the President later as Lincoln lay resting on a sofa. He would hold out for clemency for the beaten South come what might, the President said. That had been the theme of the speech.

Reading it the next day, Sumner would be appalled. There was no talk of hanging or of widespread confiscation, still less wholesale enfranchisement of the Negroes. "Alas! Alas!" Sumner wrote a friend. Upon hearing of Lee's surrender, the White House had sent special word to Sumner to apprise him of the fact. Attached to the message were flowers. But that was hardly enough. So many hundreds of thousands had died, so many hundreds of millions of dollars were spent. Had this enormous sacrifice been made only for the South to be magnanimously forgiven? With the black man still effectively in chains? In the view of Sumner and the other Radicals the South must be crushed. Never again could a swaggering plantation aristocracy hope to sit in the councils of the nation as equals to the men of the North, who had made the war and now must make the peace. It would be the concern of Congress, not the Executive, as to when and under what conditions the South would be permitted back. So said the Senators and Representatives in speeches, in manifesto, in private conversation and to the face of Abraham Lincoln.

Yet there the President stood on a balcony reading his clemency speech by the light of a candle. Tad Lincoln sat at his father's feet, catching the pages the President dropped as he finished with them. "Another, another," Tad kept saying. Across the Potomac at Arlington one could see the former residence of Mrs. Robert E. Lee. Brilliantly illuminated, the great house was surrounded by colored lights that blazed on the lawn. As ex-slaves by the thousands gathered to sing "The Year of Jubilee," rockets shot off into the night.

Let 10 percent of the qualified voters of a southern state take an oath of allegiance to the federal government, Lincoln said. Let them organize a state government. Then let them come back into the Union with all former privileges. Do not, he said, tell the erring brethren that they were irremediably evil. Consider the new state governments as the egg is to the fowl. Soon the little egg would be a complete bird.

But there were those Republicans in Congress, Radical or not, who wanted far more. They demanded that the southern states muster a majority of all voters to swear allegiance, repudiate all Confederate debts, admit complete responsibility for the war—and enfranchise all Negroes. That Negroes were barred from voting in almost every northern state was beside the point. The North had not enslaved Negroes. Nor had the North lost the war. The President turned to the subject of the vote and the freedmen. "I myself would prefer that it were now conferred upon the very intelligent, and on those who served our cause as soldiers," he said. That was not nearly enough for men like Sumner. In the Senator's view, Lincoln's proposed policy would enfranchise any ex-Confederate who signed a piece of paper, while strenuously restricting the number of black voters.

But below Lincoln in the darkness, John Wilkes Booth heard what the President said about letting certain blacks vote. He turned to his brutish companion, Lewis Paine, grabbing his arm. "That means nigger citizenship!" Booth hissed. "Now, by Christ, I'll put him through." He began to speak of shooting Lincoln as he stood there on the balcony. Years earlier Booth had been present when John Brown was hanged for inciting Negro rebellion. Now Lincoln was doing John Brown's work. One had been a criminal. What was the other?

Booth's voice was attracting attention and Paine urged that they leave. "That is the last speech he will ever make," Booth muttered as they departed. Previously he had only talked of kidnaping the President. The ransom he would demand was the freedom of the legions of Confederates held in northern prisons. That great host of men would go back to the South, rejoin their units and then sweep the Yankees away. But something new had grown in Booth's mind in these last few days of apparent northern triumph. Was not Brutus a hero, he asked himself.

On April 13, two days after the speech, Senator Sumner visited the White House for an illumination display. Sherman in North Carolina was on everybody's mind. For it seemed impossible that the Confederacy's last army under Joseph Johnston could long withstand Sherman in the wake of Lee's surrender of the Army of Northern Virginia earlier in the week. The next day at a Cabinet meeting the President said that after the illuminations he had dreamed the same dream which preceded nearly all the great events of the war. In the dream he found himself moving toward an indefinite shore in a singular, indescribable vessel. The reappearance of the dream must signal another important piece of news, he said. "I think it must be from Sherman."

That news would be the final end of the war. The President began speaking to his Cabinet of the peace that was coming and mentioned his last night's visitor, Sumner. A notable humanitarian, Lincoln said. But it was fortunate that the war would end when Congress was not in session. Without men like Sumner around, the executive branch could decide the future and present it as a *fait accompli* when the Senators and Representatives convened again. Luckily that would not be for months.

The Cabinet meeting ended. General Grant had sat in. He and Mrs. Grant had been invited to go to the theater that night with the Lincolns. But the General was not anxious to attend. He did not care much for theater-going. In addition, Mrs. Grant did not care for Mrs. Lincoln, who had insulted her during the Virginia expedition by intimating that Mrs. Grant had the position of First Lady in mind for herself. The Grants decided to go to New Jersey to see their children, who were in school. At the War Department the President asked if Secretary Stanton's aide Major Thomas Eckert might join the theater party. Stanton curtly replied he had work for Eckert that night. He was not the kind of Cabinet officer who considered a Presidential request a command.

Imperious, domineering, violent, Stanton could tear up a written message from the President and throw it into the wastepaper basket in front of the messenger's eyes. Earlier in the war he had remarked that explorers were foolish to go to Africa seeking gorillas when a flawless specimen had been found in Springfield, Illinois. (He also called the President "that giraffe.") His idea of humor was to threaten to throw people in jail. On numerous occasions he would jump off the high stool upon which he perched behind his desk and rush up to a petitioner, whom he would whirl about and then shove through the door. Radical-leaning, he had learned to hate and distrust McClellan so much that the General actually came to believe that Stanton wanted to wipe out the Union army to vent his spite.

The Secretary of War saw spies and plots everywhere, and filled the Old Capitol prison with his victims. But for all the brutality—which became the most dangerous when he

73

lowered his voice—Stanton had learned to esteem Lincoln. He recognized him as the leader of leaders. While the rest of Washington reasoned that the assassination scares were over once the President could safely walk through the streets of Richmond, Stanton said that the President should not expose himself so freely in public places.

That morning Booth went to Ford's Theatre to pick up mail sent to him there and learned the President would attend the performance that night. The opportunity had come. Theaters had figured in his previous kidnaping plans. Now he could strike an even stronger blow in a theater. He wrote a long letter to the *National Intelligencer* explaining what he was going to do. In the street he met a friend and gave him the sealed letter, asking that it be delivered to the newspaper after eleven o'clock that evening. The friend agreed to do as Booth asked. As they talked, a long line of Confederate officers trudged up Pennsylvania Avenue, prisoners. "Great God!" Booth cried. "I no longer have a country!"

He rode away to the Kirkwood House. One of Booth's little band of conspirators was staying there, his rent paid by Booth himself. For George Atzerodt had no money. A drunkard, clownish, the German-born Atzerodt made a living of sorts by running a scow across the Potomac at Port Tobacco in southern Maryland. The name of the town served as his nickname. Mrs. Mary Surratt, the mother of one of Booth's other men, John H. Surratt, intensely disliked Port Tobacco. Mrs. Surratt ran a Washington boardinghouse which Atzerodt occasionally visited. After he left, there were always empty liquor bottles to be picked up and thrown out. Vacillating, irresolute, Atzerodt stuck to Booth for the money in it. His Kirkwood House room contained a bankbook and some coiled rope originally intended for tying up the kidnaped Lincoln. In addition, two carbines were hidden between the mattress and the bedsprings. All had been left there by Booth.

John Wilkes Booth, however, had not come to the Kirkwood House to seek Atzerodt. He would see him later and tell him there was not going to be a kidnaping as originally planned. He would outline Atzerodt's role in the new plan. Listening, Atzerodt would stammer and whimper, saying he had engaged for an abduction but not a murder. Booth would tell Port Tobacco they were in it too far to back out now, and the roles must be played out.

That would be later. But in the early afternoon of April 14, Good Friday of 1865, Booth took out a card and on it wrote: *Don't wish to disturb you. Are you at home?* The clerk took the card to Suite 68, on the second floor. He returned a moment later saying there had been no answer to his knock. At Booth's request the clerk then put the card in the box for Suite 68, whose occupant was the Vice President of the United States.

That night Johnson ate in the Kirkwood House dining room. Afterward he chatted with former Governor Leonard Farwell of Wisconsin, who was also staying at the hotel. Farwell was going to the theater that evening. Would the Vice President like to join him? Johnson declined. He read in his room, then turned off the gas light. He was sleeping when around ten o'clock George Atzerodt, a Bowie knife in a sheath at his side, came into the hotel barroom. Atzerodt idled there for a while before drifting away, unable to bring himself to do what Booth had ordered: go up to Suite 68, knock on the door and, when it opened, plunge the knife into Johnson's heart.

Booth did better with his choice to kill Secretary of State Seward. At about the same moment that a bullet crashed into Lincoln's brain a knife ripped down at Seward where he lay in bed recuperating from a carriage accident. Only good luck saved the Secretary's life from Lewis Paine's ferocity.

Many of the people in Ford's Theatre thought the explosion of John Wilkes Booth's one-shot Derringer was part of the play. Then an athletic and handsome man—one of the handsomest actors of his time—leaped from the Presidential box to the stage. The footlights illuminating him, he waved a dagger, ran backstage and through a rear door to the street. Later people remembered that he had shouted, "Virginia is avenged. *Sic semper tyrannis!*" *

But he limped as he ran. His foot was broken. He flung himself on a waiting mare, put spurs to her and rode. He galloped to one of the bridges leading south, crossed and joined Davy Herold, a druggist's clerk. Herold had accompanied Lewis Paine to Seward's and had waited outside while Paine ran amok, fracturing the skull of Seward's son, knifing a military nurse and then finally assaulting the Secretary of State. The sound of the carnage inside frightened Herold and he fled to a previously designated rendezvous place. There he and Booth waited for the others of the assassination plot to appear. None of them did. Booth and Davy Herold rode south.

Behind them, stumbling and awkward, six men carried Abraham Lincoln out of Ford's Theatre to a boardinghouse across the way. There he was put into a little room. Behind him was blood on the floor and on the rocking chair in which he had sat, a screaming woman—his wife—and soldiers with drawn sabers pointlessly yelling at the playgoers, "Clear out, you sons of bitches!" In front of the theater was a widening circle of people shouting, then whispering, that the President had been shot, and that the army surgeon who first reached him had said, "His wound is mortal. It is impossible for him to recover."

Seated in the orchestra, ex-Governor Farwell heard the shot and saw a man plummet onto the stage and then run for the rear exit. He heard Mrs. Lincoln shrieking that her husband was shot. The Vice President came into his mind. He rushed out of the theater and at top speed ran for the Kirkwood House. Perhaps as he raced along he passed the terrified George Atzerodt looking for a good place to fling away his unused Bowie knife. In the end, hopelessly wandering and fearful of what would come next, Port Tobacco threw knife and sheath into the gutter.

* Thus always to tyrants.

Breathless, Farwell arrived at the hotel. Word of what had happened in the theater had not preceded him. Shouting at the desk clerk to guard the stairs, Farwell ran up to Suite 68.

"Governor Johnson!"

Farwell beat on the door, forgetting for the moment that Johnson was no longer Military Governor, but Vice President. That was what had sent Farwell flying through the suddenly alarmed streets of Washington, under whose spring moon men were gathering to ask, "For Christ's sake, what has happened?" and to hear in response, "The President has been shot!"

"Governor Johnson!" he screamed, pounding on the door. "If you are in this room I must see you!"

Johnson got out of bed. He did not strike a light. "Farwell, is that you?"

"Yes! Let me in!"

He opened the door. Farwell burst through, slammed the door behind him and fastened the latch. A moment later, when Farwell had finished, Johnson swayed and then staggered into his arms. They held each other tight.

Charles Sumner was at home, sitting with two other Senators over a bottle of wine. A servant burst in on them. "Mr. Lincoln is assassinated in the theater. Mr. Seward is murdered in his bed. There's murder in the streets."

Sumner said, "Young man, be moderate in your statements. Tell us what has happened."

"I have told you what has happened."

They made for the White House. Everything seemed in order. Sumner asked the guard pacing his beat if the President had returned from the theater. No, the soldier replied. "They say the President has been assassinated," Sumner said. A porter sought out Captain Robert Todd Lincoln, the President's twenty-one-year-old son. The men took a hack to the theater.

They passed the guards and entered the house to which the six bearers had brought the President. Mary Lincoln rushed up to Sumner and asked if her husband was dead. He replied he had just come and knew nothing, but he had brought her son with him. Sumner went into the room where Abraham Lincoln lay. He sat down near the bed, took Lincoln's right hand and spoke to him. A doctor said, "It's no use, Mr. Sumner. He can't hear you."

"No," Sumner said. "He isn't dead. Look at his face. He is breathing."

"It will never be anything more than this."

All night, until past seven the next morning, Sumner sat and listened to that breathing. There was something musical about it, he remembered later. Almost like a melody.

Secretary of War Stanton had been visiting Secretary of State Seward, who was still recuperating from the injuries he had suffered when he attempted to halt his runaway carriage horses. When Stanton returned home he found a band and a crowd waiting for him, asking that he make them a little speech. He said a few words and then locked up the house. Mrs. Stanton was in the children's nursery. Someone knocked at the door. Mrs. Stanton answered and a moment later came up to say to the Secretary, "Mr. Seward is murdered."

"Humbug!" he snapped. "I left him only an hour ago." He went downstairs and said to the man at the door, "What's this story you're telling?" The man repeated what he had said to Mrs. Stanton, and as he spoke people came to say the President also had been attacked.

Outside the house men were yelling, "Kill the god damn rebels! Kill the traitors!" Stanton went to Seward's home, where he confirmed the attack on the Secretary of State. He then joined Secretary of the Navy Welles in sharing a hack to Ford's Theatre. Terrified, the driver was incapable of handling the reins. So Chief Justice David K. Cartter of the District of Columbia Supreme Court shoved him aside and jumped up on the box. The Chief Justice took the two Cabinet ministers through the surging crowds. They came to the house where

Lincoln was dying. Both Secretaries peered down into their chief's face.

It came into Secretary Welles' mind—Father Gideon, Lincoln used to call him—that the features were so calm and striking that never before had the President seemed more impressive. But as he stood looking on, the appearance began slowly to change, the President's right eye swelling as much of the face became discolored. At six in the morning, having stood all through the long hours, Welles would take a seat at the foot of the bed.

Stanton looked down and listened to the labored breathing rise and then almost die away before it rose again. Like an Aeolian harp, he thought to himself. Stanton had heard that breathing before. It was when he held his sick child in his arms. The child had died. He collected himself and became in that moment the functioning government of the United States. There was no one else.

The Secretary of War told David Cartter, the judge who had driven the hack to the theater, to go into an adjoining room and start taking evidence from people who had witnessed the assassination. Convinced he faced a gigantic rebel plot, Stanton sent messages alerting all troops in Washington. Soon one could hear the sound of bugles and the long roll of the drums. Beneath a moon flashing in and out from behind scudding clouds, cavalry patrols plunged through the streets. Rumors spread that the rebels were going to burn the city. People told each other they were afraid of being murdered in their beds.

In the room where Lincoln was dying, Stanton dictated telegrams to New York ordering that detectives be sent to the capital. He ordered General Grant to return from Philadelphia. He sent word to railroad authorities for special safety arrangements for Grant's train and ordered all approaches to Washington blocked with troops. He halted all rail traffic south and sent word to Chief Justice Salmon Chase that the President could not live and that Chase must hold himself in readiness to administer the oath of office to Lincoln's successor. Aside from his whispered orders and his dictation of bulletin after bulletin for the newspapers there was no other sound in the room, no conversation, as every Cabinet member save Seward came to look on.

Stanton ordered the entire cast of *Our American Cousin* put under arrest. He dictated an official notification of Lincoln's death, which could be handed to the Vice President as soon as the President's life ended. Midnight came and passed. Sumner sat holding the President's hand, his head dropping so that it was bowed almost to the bloodied pillow. Towels were put on the pillow. Soon they also were stained. When Mrs. Lincoln entered, fresh towels were put on the bed so that she would not see the terrible flow of blood. She looked at her husband and then broke the silence of the room crowded with the men who had served him. "Live! You must live!" she screamed. "Bring Tad—he will speak to Tad—he loves him so!"

In the Kirkwood House, Johnson waited with Farwell. A messenger arrived from Stanton saying the Vice President should come. Major James O'Beirne, commander of the Washington provost guard, said a detachment of troops must go along. But Johnson did not want an armed escort. He pulled his hat down over his face and, with only Farwell and O'Beirne, he walked the two and a half blocks to the boardinghouse and the President.

He looked down at Abraham Lincoln. The other men in the room had served together for years, had lived through the war together, Stanton, Welles, Attorney General Speed, Surgeon General Barnes. Johnson was almost a stranger to them. Some had seen him only a few times in their lives, and one memory dominated: Inauguration Day.

Minutes later someone came from the front parlor to say that Mrs. Lincoln would be coming up in a moment. Sumner indicated to Stanton that the First Lady detested Johnson. To Mary Lincoln, the high-born southerner, Johnson would always be a mudsill tailor. Stanton said to Johnson there was no need for him to remain. The Vice President returned to the Kirkwood House and was not in the room when Mrs. Lincoln, screaming, fell in a faint on the floor. "Take that woman out and do not let her in again," Stanton rasped, and his order was obeyed. That night no one thought of questioning his authority in any matter.

Dawn came, and with it an April rain. It had been an early spring and the lilacs were in bloom. (Ever after Walt Whitman was unable to scent lilac fragrance without being reminded of this day.) Chief Justice Chase got up from his sleep and went to Seward's house, where the wounded Secretary lay in a stupor. His next stop was the Kirkwood House, where he found the Vice President calm and grave, his passions spent after a night of pacing the floor and cursing the rebels.

At the little house in Tenth Street the death struggle began. The flow from the wound ceased, and the breathing became more labored. Robert Lincoln put his head on Sumner's shoulder and sobbed. At twenty-two minutes past seven in the morning Abraham Lincoln's heart ceased to beat.

Coins were put over the eyelids and a white sheet drawn over the face. Stanton said, "Now he belongs to the ages." Nine hours had passed since Booth pulled the trigger.

People began to leave. As she came down the steps Mrs. Lincoln muttered, "That terrible house." Sumner drove away with General Henry Halleck. Before dropping Sumner at his home, where guards sent by Stanton paced, Halleck had the carriage halt at the Kirkwood House. There he said to Johnson, "With a view to your personal safety I advise you never to go out except in a carriage and accompanied by a sufficient guard." By those words Johnson learned that Lincoln was gone.

At the house in Tenth Street the haggard Cabinet men gathered in the back parlor. They all signed a letter to Johnson saying that he was now the head of the government. Attorney General Speed had prepared the letter and Stanton suggested that Speed go with a second Cabinet member to give it to the new President. Secretary Welles thought that Stanton believed he should be the Cabinet officer to accompany the Attorney

General. But the spell of Stanton's power was broken. Perhaps it was because Lincoln no longer lived, or that no vast rebel plot had materialized. For the men did not name him to go with Speed. Postmaster General Dennison suggested Welles should go, but Father Gideon said that Secretary of the Treasury McCulloch should be the man. He was next in rank to the absent Secretary of State Seward.

At the Kirkwood House the two Cabinet members talked with Chief Justice Chase and decided that Johnson should take the oath at ten o'clock, two hours later. It was one month and ten days since the fifty-six-year-old Andrew Johnson had taken his Vice Presidential oath. Chase went to the office of the Attorney General, where he looked up the precedents involving the two previous Vice Presidents, Tyler and Fillmore, who had succeeded to the Presidency. Chase also read the pertinent clauses in the Constitution. Then he made his way back to the Kirkwood House. All his life Chase had pursued the highest office within the gift of the people. Lincoln had said Chase was almost insane in his desire to be President. Now he was to be instrumental in giving it to Andrew Johnson. As he arrived at the Kirkwood House the Chief Justice saw old Francis P. Blair and his son Montgomery, who had taken Johnson to their estate for two weeks to recover from his Vice Presidential inaugural. For years the Blairs had been Chase's political enemies. He decided that at this moment old resentments should be buried, and greeted them.

Together the three men entered the hotel parlor, where they found a dozen or fourteen men, among them McCulloch and Speed, and ex-Senator John Hale of New Hampshire, whose daughter had given the pass to Booth so that he could stand near Lincoln at the previous Presidential inauguration. Soon Bessie Hale would write a heartbroken letter to Edwin Booth saying that if necessary she would marry his brother at the foot of the scaffold.

Chase read the oath aloud, and Johnson repeated it after him. Chase said, "You are President. May God guide, support, and bless you in your arduous labors."

Johnson leaned forward to kiss the twenty-first verse of the eleventh chapter of Ezekiel: *But as for them whose heart walketh after the heart of their detestable things and their abominations, I will recompense their way upon their own heads.*

3

Late that day the Cabinet met at the office of Secretary of the Treasury McCulloch. To be at the White House across the way would have been out of the question. For Lincoln had been returned there, his body draped in a Union flag and borne by a patrol whose officer walked bareheaded. He was placed in an upper room to undergo an autopsy.

Lincoln's presence would have alone been inhibiting, but in addition the men did not wish to intrude upon the former First Lady. Raving, screaming, her shrieks penetrating the closed doors of her bedroom to unnerve the servants speaking in subdued tones in a building whose every light was darkened, Mary Lincoln sat with her children and her dressmaker, the former slave Elizabeth Keckley. She would allow no one else near her. Her terrible wails rose and fell, and with them came frightful words. Johnson had killed her husband, Johnson the demagogue, the drunken poor white, she screamed.

Secretary McCulloch had been busy before the new President and the Cabinet ministers came into his room. Word came from New York's Wall Street * that the price of U. S.

* Stock markets remained open on Saturdays.

84

Government bonds was sharply down. Working through an agent, McCulloch had the Treasury Department enter the market with substantial funds. The bonds steadied. The Secretary did not consult the new President when he made his move. Perhaps he would have felt ill at ease doing so. All the Cabinet men felt uncomfortable in the presence of their new chief. Deferentially, they talked with him about an inaugural address, all of them being against it. To their relief he agreed with them, indicating his acts would disclose his policies. He hoped they would stay on in their jobs and help him with his new work. The man had some poise and dignity, McCulloch noted thankfully, and Welles thought he conducted himself admirably. The meeting adjourned. The Cabinet agreed to meet with the President the next day, Easter Sunday.

At about the same hour that President Johnson spoke for the first time with his Cabinet another group of men gathered in Washington. They were all Radical Republicans. For years they had opposed Lincoln's policies of reconciliation toward the South. Lincoln had always regarded the eleven states of the Confederacy as the territory of the United States and the citizens of those states as his countrymen. The Radical Republicans viewed them as enemies to be crushed. They held that view for a variety of reasons. Some were ardent, idealistic Abolitionists or northerners ambitious for industrial expansion rather than agricultural development. Others were westerners who wanted money spent for railroads to their areas and beyond. Still others were self-made frontiersmen who hated aristocrats. Their feeling for the downtrodden slave merged with desire for revenge and money, glory and position. Above all, they wished the South kept in a subservient position. The day of the cavaliers must never come again. No more plumes and swaggering and magnolia dreams.

The most prominent member of the little group that met on April 15 was Senator Benjamin Franklin Wade of Ohio. (Sumner was not present. His role was to expound principles and expose error, not offer practical solutions.) Rough, profane, a fighter, "Bluff Ben" Wade had had an impoverished youth. He worked as a laborer helping to build the Erie Canal. Then he studied law and eventually went to the Senate. He hated flowery talk or cosmopolitanism, holding it to be intolerable pomposity. A musician was to Wade a "fiddling cuss." After seeing a performance of *Othello*, he wrote to Mrs. Wade: "I do not believe there is a house of ill fame in the city except the very lowest where such conversation would be tolerated. And then, after the obscenity, they must all be butchered before your eyes. I think Shakespeare was a coarse vulgar barbarian."

In debate Wade could be brutal. "Can you find a meaner specimen of a man on the face of the whole earth?" he asked the Senate while discussing President Franklin Pierce. "Why, my friends, you could not find a meaner specimen of a thing for President if you had imported a baboon and put him there. He has no will of his own. He is hardly a moral agent. He cringes before his masters like a caged bear."

On the day after Sumner was struck down by Preston Brooks, Wade put two loaded pistols on top of his Senate desk. No one doubted he would use them if necessary. Earlier he had let it be known that if any southerner cared to challenge him to a duel he would accept. The weapons would be squirrel rifles, to be used at a distance of twenty paces. Each contestant would wear a white patch pinned over his heart. In debate Wade's hair would stand up like bristles while he unbuttoned his vest, shoved up his coat sleeves, tore off his cravat and yanked at his collar. When the war finally came he took his squirrel rifle and followed the army to Bull Run in a carriage. When the troops poured back in retreat, Wade blocked a road with the carriage. He halted fleeing soldiers by threatening to kill them. From then on no General was aggressive enough for him. In Wade's view McClellan was a "stupid ass" and so were most West Pointers, the graduates of "a useless school for conceited aristocrats."

As chairman of the Committee on the Conduct of the War, he and his principal associates, Zachariah Chandler of Michigan and Andrew Johnson of Tennessee, pilloried a series of Union commanders. "I would burn those pontoon bridges in the faces of the soldiers," he told McClellan when that officer discussed lines of retreat, "and let them know they had got to whip the enemy or be lost. Let them come back in their coffins." (Johnson remarked that the chairman expressed himself rather roughly, perhaps, but was essentially right.)

Wade eventually came to think of McClellan as an outright traitor. He blamed Lincoln for not firing the General and said the President's delay in dislodging him had cost one hundred thousand casualties. "When I think of these things," he wrote Chandler, "I wish the d---l had Old Abe." Later on even Grant was not fighter enough for him. He went to Lincoln to demand Grant's removal, and Lincoln, in his way, said, "Senator, that reminds me of a story."

"Bother your stories, Mr. President," Wade replied. "That is the way it is with you, sir. It is all story—story. You are the father of every military blunder that has been made during the war. You are on the road to hell, sir, with this government, and you are not a mile off this minute." In private conversation he referred to Lincoln as a "fool" and "poor white trash" essentially southern in background although "spawned" in Illinois.

Were the President and Mrs. Lincoln "aware," he wrote on an invitation to a White House ball, "that there is a civil war? If they are not, Mr. and Mrs. Wade are, and decline to participate in feasting and dancing." The President was too sluggish, too much the tool of traitors—likely including his wife, Wade said. Traitors! It was a constant theme with him, as with Johnson and as with Stanton.

When Lee finally surrendered, Bluff Ben Wade's joy was tempered with apprehension as to Lincoln's future course. When, during the Virginia visit, Lincoln had said he would permit the dispersed Confederate legislature to convene in Richmond, Wade had exploded. (He and Chandler and a few other Radicals had also gone to Virginia, but carrying carbines and wearing navy Colt revolvers and bandoliers of ammunition.) Wade and the others objected so strongly that Lincoln was forced to cancel his plan for the meeting of the Confederate legislators. The Radicals were still fuming over Lincoln's plans when Booth's bullet changed everything.

"I would sacrifice all—sons, kindred, friends and everything," Wade had once said. What was one more life when so many had died? His associates agreed with him. "I believe the Almighty continued Mr. Lincoln in office as long as he was useful, and then substituted a better man to finish the work," Chandler wrote Mrs. Chandler. Booth's bullet was a "godsend."

That was the theme of Wade, Chandler and the other Radicals on the day Lincoln died. But their manner of expressing themselves disturbed Representative George Washington Julian of Indiana. Their profanity was "intolerably disgusting" as they talked of Lincoln's conciliatory policies. Yet, Julian reflected, despite the brutal phaseology, they were correct in their views. "Weakness" had been put to flight and "the righteous ends of the war" would be brought to fruition by the new President.

The Radicals adjourned their meeting after writing a letter to President Johnson. His "old associates" from the Committee on the Conduct of the War would like to meet with him. Would he see them the following day, Easter Sunday? He sent back word that he would with pleasure.

That night, Saturday, Senator Sumner called on the President at the Kirkwood House. Fastidious, cultured, everything Bluff Ben Wade was not, he nevertheless shared many of the latter's views. He lectured Johnson on the needs of the ex-slaves. Johnson listened.

In the morning the President and Cabinet met again at the Treasury. They talked about the expected surrender of General Joseph Johnston to Sherman, of how the states of the South would best be governed, of the funeral planned for Lincoln. Stanton came in an hour late, yet filled with ideas and vitality, as always.

As they met, parishioners went to church to hear sermons preached on Lincoln and Booth, now positively identified as the assassin. George Templeton Strong of the Sanitary

Commission was at Trinity in New York, thinking to himself that the great tragedy was for the greater good after all: "It is plain to everybody that there can be no terms with the woman-flogging aristocracy; Grant's generous dealing with Lee was a blunder. Let us henceforth deal with rebels as they deserve: the rose-water treatment does not meet their needs." When the minister asked prayers for all the bereaved and afflicted families of the land, especially for that of the late leader, Strong reflected that perhaps Lincoln had done his appointed work and that the time had come "for something besides kindliness, mercy and forbearance." Vengeance and judgment were needed now, Strong said to himself. Lincoln's "goodness might have been abused by the rebels," Strong wrote in his diary that night. "Perhaps God's voice in this tragedy is, 'Well done, good and faithful servant. Thou has done thy work of mercy. To others is given the duty of vengeance. Thy murder will help teach them that duty.'"

Trinity's minister, the Reverend Francis Vinton, spoke of Samuel, who, "knowing his stern mission from God, took Agag and hewed him into pieces for the Lord. . . . In this stern spirit should the leaders of the rebellion be dealt with."

A few blocks from Trinity, at the Custom House, people wept and cursed as they held a memorial meeting. A man got up and said, "Be still!" The death was providential. God had removed the man of mercy so that real justice and punishment could be meted out to the rebels. "Hang Lee!" roared the crowd. Sermons followed: let there be damnation for the rebels, the hangman's rope, exile, confiscation of property.

In Washington the journalist Jane Grey Swisshelm remembered how she had remonstrated with the then Vice President who had shouted on hearing of Richmond's surrender, "Jeff Davis ought to be hung twenty times as high as Haman!" The new President had been right, she wrote, for the rebels were of "irredeemable depravity." Would that God would strengthen Johnson's hand in ridding the world of reptiles who could only give up their fatal sting when they were slain. The new President was Joshua succeeding Moses, Mrs. Swisshelm decided. The Almighty had tested the rebels with Lincoln's mercy; they had spurned it and shot him in the back. Their punishment would be Andrew Johnson.

In Washington, Sumner's friend the Marquis de Chambrun noted how the clergymen, the newspapers and the public meetings talked of nothing else but vengeance. One hundred thousand telegrams, he heard, had poured into Washington containing the word "hang." Sherman's men, he was told, had fallen upon four hundred Confederate prisoners at the General's North Carolina headquarters and slaughtered them to the last man.* Lincoln's old friend Orville Browning listened as his law partner excitedly told him there was only one thing to do: depopulate the South and repeople it. Drag the rebels from their homes and dispose of them. If this was to be the prevailing doctrine, Browning said to himself, slaughter, fire, anarchy and then despotism were in store. He went to his Presbyterian church and heard from his minister that the President had been removed because he was too lenient. Now the minister trusted the country "had an avenger who would exercise wrath."

In Boston the Reverend J. M. Manning compared Lincoln to Moses. Each had been taken away after the long journey even as the Promised Land came into sight. " 'I have caused thee to see it with thine eyes, but thou shalt not go over thither.' . . . Perhaps it is better for us that we should be orphans today. . . . His paternal heart, had it still throbbed in life, might have proved too tender for the stern work we are yet to do." Reverend Manning was echoed by the Reverend James Reed, also of Boston: "It may be that he who was the best leader in time of war is not best fitted for the new exigencies which are arising. . . . Certain it is that our President would not have been taken away, if he had not finished his appointed work."

The Reverend W. S. Studley of Boston said, "In dealing with traitors, Andrew Johnson's little finger will be thicker than Abraham Lincoln's loins."

* Untrue.

Herman Melville wrote:

> He lieth in his blood—
>   The Father in his face;
> They have killed him, the forgiver—
>   The Avenger takes his place.
>
> There is a sobbing of the strong,
>   And a pall upon the land;
> But the People in their weeping
>   Bare the iron hand:
> Beware the People weeping
>   When they bare the iron hand.

Wade led in the Radical Republicans. "Johnson, we have faith in you," he cried. "By the gods, there will be no trouble in running the government now!"

The President smiled.

4

Across the face of the South a great army was marching. It wore no uniform but the color of its skin.

Save for the little group of Confederates under Joseph E. Johnston in North Carolina, the war was over. The President of what had been the Confederate States of America was a fugitive. Union troops patrolled Richmond. What had been the War became The Lost Cause.

And the blacks knew it. And so they left the plantations and fields and mills. Great masses of them came down the lonely roads past burned buildings the war had left behind. They simply appeared, stayed for a while, and left. Now they could go where they wanted without asking Master's permission. It was Freedom, Jubilee. Wanderers, the countless black men and women and children vaguely searched for a son or daughter sold long ago, or for a white man who had once been kind.

It was planting time, but slavery had seen hundreds of other planting times since the first slave ship docked. Now these last slaves were free. And General William Pendleton, who had watched as Lee dressed to go and see Grant, went into the fields himself, he who had been chief of artillery of the Army of Northern Virginia. He was not the only gently raised southerner who suddenly found himself a field hand. Thin and wasted horses pulled plows steered by white hands; or, typically, a man hitched himself into the traces and pulled while his wife steered and their daughters dropped seeds contributed by charitable organizations with roots in the North.

"O God, what can I do?" wrote one southern lady on the day Booth's bullet took Lincoln. She wore homemade shoes of cloth. "I who have never been taught any work that seems to be needed now! Who is there to pay me for the few things I know how to do? I envy our Negroes who have been trained to occupations that bring money; they can hire out to the Yankees, and I can't."

There were no glass panes left in the windows of the dilapidated trains swaying over the broken roadbeds, no needles or thread to mend the tattered uniforms worn by the ex-soldiers. There was not, people said, a comb with all its tines to be found in any southern state, nor a complete set of china. People fashioned cups from gourds. Everywhere were ruined bridges, broken mills and factories, houses without roofs, chimneys without houses. The railroad water tanks were gone, the trestles down, the yards and gardens overrun with weeds. The Chivalry of America was starving. What had been their property cavorted in the towns, subsisting on what the Union soldiers and the northern charities handed out.

Many southerners could not get it straight that the four million were free. "If I don't own them," one bewildered woman said of her slaves, "who does own them?" She did not understand, but other southerners did. For they saw their former slaves baptize themselves in the South's rivers, to come from the waters screaming, "Freed from slavery! Freed from sin! Bless God and General Grant!"

And in Washington the President's language was so violent in a second meeting with the Radical Republicans that even Wade thought him too enthusiastic in his determination to deal out punishment. Wade, who himself could say the blacks of the South would only be truly free by their killing half the whites.

As the great black masses marched, a very great fear spread over the South.

Abraham Lincoln lay at rest upon a catafalque lined with white satin and in a coffin covered with black, with lilies at the head and roses at the foot. The East Room's chandeliers drooped black alpaca; so too did the doors, the windows, mirrors, columns of the portico outside. The face, exposed, seemed somewhat darker than in life. Otherwise it was unchanged.

Standing alone at the foot of the coffin, motionless, his arms crossed upon his breast with his hands resting on his collarbones, Andrew Johnson listened to clergymen praying for the fallen leader. Mary Lincoln was upstairs, prostrate. At the end President Johnson stood for a long moment looking down at the face in the coffin. Then came the six gray horses with a black hearse and a riderless horse behind, and the slow parade to the music of regimental bands playing a dead march. Thousands looked on, filling the sidewalks and every roof and window. The Twenty-second United States Colored Infantry led the mourners, its band playing a dirge. A group of Treasury Department men carried a flag with a gash made by Booth's spur. Draped on the Presidenital box at Ford's Theatre, the flag had tripped him and then sent him tumbling to the floor with a broken foot bone. Until the funeral began, the flag stood by the entrance to the new President's temporary office in the Treasury Building: a reminder.

At Fifteenth Street and Pennsylvania Avenue one of the horses pulling the President's carriage reared. The situation was dangerous and so Johnson got out and with his companion Preston King took seats in another carriage. The procession halted at the Capitol, where Lincoln would lie in state. Afterward the Johnson carriage was blocked in traffic. Secretary Welles gave him a lift. Two days later Washington's officialdom again assembled to put Abraham Lincoln on the train for

Springfield and a sepulcher. The cavalry detachment which had attended him in life surrounded not his successor, but Secretary of War Stanton. Once again the guns boomed and the dirges played and Lincoln went home.

That night, April 21, at eight o'clock, the President convened a Cabinet meeting. He did so at Stanton's urgent request. A telegram had been received from General Sherman in North Carolina. Sherman had outlined the surrender terms he had offered Joseph Johnston, commander of the Confederacy's last army. Johnston need only surrender and disband his forces, Sherman had told him, and the rebel states could return to the Union, their legislatures intact, with arms held under their own control in their own armories, with all political rights guaranteed. Southern citizens could even sue the federal government for the value of the emancipated slaves. That would mean the war had changed nothing except for the fact that the North had proved that, this time, it could beat the South. Such was Stanton's viewpoint, expressed in frenzied fashion to the President and the Cabinet. Sherman's thought was that he was complying with Lincoln's "Let 'em up easy."

What was the man thinking of, Stanton asked? These were terms "no truly loyal man could have agreed to, and little short of treason." General Sherman must be insane or a traitor. Earlier in the war there had been rumors that Sherman was a certifiable lunatic. His later successes had put the stories to rest. So it must be that he was a traitor. Stanton was famous for divining what was in a petitioner's mind and deciding the reply even before the man finished speaking. Now, his brain working at lightning speed, the Secretary of War poured forth theories on the form Sherman's treason would take. Perhaps he would march on the capital, like the Legion commanders of the Roman Empire. Perhaps he had secretly captured the fleeing Jefferson Davis and been bribed by the money of the Confederate Treasury. At the outbreak of the war Sherman had been serving as the head of a Louisiana military academy. Perhaps he had been imbued then with traitorous sentiments which were only now coming to the fore. Was this new development related to the murder of Lincoln? Stanton was in his element, seeing conspiracy, plots, treason and more treason.

The men decided that orders must go out to Sherman to rescind his offer to Joseph Johnston. Then Grant must rush to North Carolina and take over from his subordinate. But what would happen, asked Attorney General Speed, if Sherman arrested Grant? There seemed no real answer, and only Stanton and Speed thought such an event possible. The men agreed to keep the whole thing secret. Grant took a train south.

Even though he had agreed that nothing should be said to anyone, Stanton could not keep silent. He told Charles Sumner that Sherman was attempting to throw away all that the war was fought for. He told the Washington newspapermen. Even before Grant arrived at Raleigh, Sherman learned that the Secretary of War had entirely forgotten who burned Atlanta and marched to the sea. Stanton was now calling the General who had scourged the South a blunderer, madman, traitor.

Always volcanic, a fevered talker (it was almost easier to describe what he neglected to say at a meeting than to itemize what he did discuss), Sherman exploded. Stamping around his headquarters, he poured invective into the ears of his staff. Cigar ash spewed in all directions as he raged. He had simply wanted to end the war, he shouted. To be hard on the South now was like slashing away at the crew of a sinking ship. Did Washington want perpetual guerrilla warfare? Did they want anarchy? In the end Johnston surrendered on the same terms given to Lee. No political overtones were attached to the simple demand that his men stack arms and go home.

The question remained: What came now? No one knew if those areas of the continent which went by the names of Virginia and Alabama and Mississippi were still states of the American Union, contingents of a defeated enemy country, or simply nonexistent. (Sumner said that as political entities they had committed suicide.)

Throughout the war the North had never recognized

the Confederacy as an independent nation although it had conceded to Richmond the usages of warfare.* The South had been looked on as an absolutely integral part of the United States which was temporarily in rebellion. But the concept of a rebellion meant that the question of treason did not pertain. It also implied that the South was an entity commanding the loyalties of its people. But how could the southern states be recognized as government units, now the war was over, when Lincoln had never seen them as such during the war? He had never even conceded that Jefferson Davis was President of anything.

Andrew Johnson's view had been somewhat similar. Tennessee, he held, had never been out of the Union. (He had shouted it several times during his Vice Presidential inauguration harangue.) For if Tennessee had been out of the Union, how could he have been its Military Governor; how could he have run for the Vice Presidency while a resident of that state; how could he now be President of the United States if he came from a place not part of the United States?

But if Tennessee and the other states had never left the Union, they were then functioning units under the Constitution. And the Constitution regarded all states as equal. Congress could not make southern states live under conditions from which northern states were exempt. States simply could not secede from the Union, was the concept. But if they were never out of the Union, why weren't they represented at Washington during the war?

They could not go out. But they had. That seemed to cover it. Rich when they left—Louisiana was second in the prewar Union in per capita wealth, South Carolina third, Mississippi fifth, Georgia eighth—they had also owned a proud and illustrious past. They had helped make the revolution in 1776. Washington, Jefferson and Madison were Virginians. That heritage could not be undone.

Yet the Radicals wanted to wipe out the old names and

* Not to have done so would have logically called for murder charges against every southern soldier.

97

border lines of the late Confederacy and substitute new entities. They would be called the Territory of Lincoln, the Territory of Grant, the Territory of Sherman, the Territory of Sheridan. Thus the states who had tried to break up the country would be prevented from returning as accepted equals of those who had paid so great a price to subdue them.

But the war had been fought to preserve the Union, not to set up new Territories while destroying old states. "Join the Army and Help Save the Union." That had been the recruiting appeal. It was not, after all, the Abolitionists who made the war.*

Suppose, the Radicals said, the southern Representatives and Senators were permitted to come back to Congress. They might combine to repudiate the national debt which the war had created. (They would hardly want to help pay for having been beaten.) Suppose they tried to get the United States to assume the war debt of the Confederacy, redeem its bonds and certify to the value of its currency with Jefferson Davis' picture on it? Could such things be tolerated?

And the ultimate irony was that freedom for the Negroes meant that the three-fifths clause in the Constitution was abrogated. That clause—an agreement with the devil, a covenant with hell in the view of Abolitionism—had in apportioning state congressional representations according to the size of the given district's population counted each slave as three-fifths of a man. Now he would be counted 100 percent. That meant larger southern congressional delegations. It would almost be comical to think about it—save for the bleached bones of three hundred thousand Union army men lying in graves strewn from the Potomac to the Rio Grande.

Supine and silent, the South waited for the North to decide. Its accumulated wealth was dissipated by the war. The

---

* Early on it was not uncommon for men to declare they would resign their officers' commissions if the war for the Union was perverted into an attack on slavery; and for the two years of the war prior to January 1, 1863, the fighting had gone on with no move to emancipate the Negroes.

value of the land was gone because there were no slaves to work it. Two hundred and eighty thousand Confederate soldiers were dead out of a population of less than three million white men, a decimation for which modern history had no parallel. The loss created vast gaps in the social structure. The flower of two generations was gone.

Timidity and a desperate desire to please now replaced the arrogance and headstrong attitudes of what was called "Before the War." Those who had gone into battle carrying champagne and patés and English hunting pieces were now living off the garbage of the Union garrisons. Fear of Union vengeance mixed with fear of the great roaming black crowds. Fear of the blacks was greater.

But the problem would take care of itself, the southerners told each other, for within a short while the blacks would all be gone. They would never work without the threat of the lash, and so eventually they would all starve, leaving no more trace behind them than did the eastern Indian tribes of Colonial days. Their value was the same. What good was the Comanche to the western frontiersman?

The few who lived, southerners said, would be a pauper class. They would steal but that could be endured. Petty theft was not considered a crime under slavery. "Taking Massa's chicken to put in Massa's nigger" had been an acceptable fact of life. Since the Negro was ineducable, it could be expected that he could never be weaned from taking what he liked.

But what if, like a domestic animal who has escaped and fled to the woods, the black man turned wild? That was what southerners were almost afraid to ask each other. During the war the Negroes had for the most part stayed at home and quietly and loyally done their work. But with peace and the great wandering masses there came stories of a new breed of blacks. One heard them singing in the woods. The sound had in it something of the mystery and menace of limitless far-off Africa, the Dark Continent, and license and orgy. Through the dirtied and broken windows of the decaying Great House one saw their dark forms dancing in religious frenzy. Their one-time masters asked themselves if Christianity had lost its hold upon them, to be replaced by the "trance meetings" and voo-doo paganism of their past. Rape by slaves had been all but unknown in the prewar South, but suddenly there were fear-some stories. White women who had spent the war years alone with their children on plantations entirely staffed by blacks no longer went out without carrying arms.

In the streets of Oxford, Mississippi, L. Q. C. Lamar, back from the war, saw how the white people walked in the roadway rather than on the sidewalk where they might meet with their former property. The northern journalist Whitelaw Reid saw a drunken Negro sergeant, one of the two hundred thousand blacks who had served with the Union forces, take a sword and one by one cut the buttons with CSA on them from the tunic of a former Confederate officer. The man stood quietly while the job was done. "Let traitors take a back seat," the new President of the United States had said again and again.

"The bottom rail is on the top," the Negroes of the South were saying, and the phrase flashed from mouth to mouth so that it dominated thinking in the South. *The bottom rail is on the top.*

"The Negro," said *The New York Times* of May 17, 1865, "misunderstands the motives which made the most la-borious, hard-working people on the face of the globe clamor for his emancipation. You are free, Sambo, but you must work."

Disregarding the blacks, there was for the moment no route back for the white South. One had to take the oath of allegiance to the Union to practice law, to marry, to set up in business, even if the business was chopping mortar from bricks of the artillery-smashed buildings. The oath demanded that each southerner swear he or she had never offered "aid and comfort" to the rebellion. Few southerners could legitimately swear such an oath. But Union army squads went around in-cessantly making people hold up their right hands. A cavalry officer remembered later how he administered this pledge of loyalty to the Old Flag: "You do solemnly swear (Look here! Take that cigar out of your mouth!) that you'll bear true faith and allegiance to the United States of America; that you'll serve them honestly and faithfully (Stop that damned talking in the ranks!) against all enemies and opposers whomsoever; (Johnny, bring me that demijohn) that you'll observe and obey the orders of the President of the United States (Take off your hat and keep your hand up!) and the orders of the officers appointed over you: so help you God. Now—git!"

The trappings for Abraham Lincoln's funeral still hung in place in the East Room. The sound of hammers striking nails when the crepe went up had seemed to the half-mad woman upstairs like guns firing. Afraid that the dismantling noise would similarly upset her, Mrs. Gideon Welles, the only outside visitor Mrs. Lincoln would see, urged that the trappings stay. So they hung in place through the remaining two weeks of April and then into May.

Robert T. Lincoln called upon President Johnson twice to say that his mother would remove herself from the White House as soon as possible. The President said he understood. (In the South word of the meetings of the two got transmuted into a rumor passed from man to man: the former President's son had slain his father's successor.)

Johnson temporarily stayed in the opulent home of Representative Samuel Hooper of Massachusetts, who had returned to Boston. Each day the President went to an office in the Treasury Department. He was always accompanied by Preston King and a squad of armed soldiers. At the Treasury the Secretary, Hugh McCulloch, waited anxiously to see whether Johnson's behavior on Inauguration Day was an aberration. McCulloch would remain in an adjoining room listening to the President's constant and bitter denunciations of traitors. The Secretary of the Treasury decided that if he had not known otherwise he would think the President was dead drunk all the time, for Johnson simply could not rid himself of the habit of making wild charges in the strongest language, a trait derived from his earlier days on the stump. Typically, the President told a delegation from Illinois that Lincoln's assassination was not the crime of one man, but a product of "that source which is the spring of all our woes. The American people must be taught—if they do not already feel—that treason is a crime and must be punished."

"This infernal rebellion" needed justice, the President constantly repeated. That justice must be merciless, for what might be mercy to the individual might be cruelty to the State. "I hold this: robbery is a crime; rape is a crime; murder is a crime; *treason* is a crime and *crime* must be punished. The law provides for it and the courts are open. Treason must be made infamous and traitors must be impoverished."

He was even more outspoken with old friends than he was with strangers. Senator Chandler remarked to the President that a few hangings would make everything well; Johnson replied that his friend could not know the full enormity of Jefferson Davis' crimes, that he was unaware of the suffering which the rebellion inflicted upon Union men in the South. "No punishment could be too severe." He would establish a precedent that would prove forever to be a "terror" to men who conspired to overthrow the government. The President was so heated that Chandler told Wade and former Vice President Hamlin that "Johnson has the nightmare."

But of any kind of intoxication there was no sign, Secretary McCulloch saw. Usually the President worked from nine to five, taking time out for a luncheon consisting of tea and a cracker. McCulloch often saw him at night. There was never a sign of drinking.

One theme Johnson always sounded to visitors was of the guilt of the fugitive Jefferson Davis. On May 2, assured by Stanton that there was definite proof, the President issued a proclamation flatly declaring Lincoln's assassination was planned by Davis and several other named "rebels and traitors." One hundred thousand dollars' reward was offered for the capture of Davis, with twenty-five thousand dollars each offered for the other men. One of them, Beverly Tucker, safe in Canada, responded through the Montreal newspapers. Why, asked Tucker, had Booth called upon Andrew Johnson the day he shot Lincoln? Booth was known to be a heavy drinker. Was it not likely he had met Johnson "in the lower circle they were both known to frequent, and thus to have formed an intimacy which a common vice begets?"

Johnson was ambitious, Tucker pointed out. And what was the future of this ambitious man after his Inauguration Day display? "The crimson blush of mingled indignation and shame mantled the cheeks of ambassadors, senators, justices, and lesser dignitaries that witnessed the disgusting scene. . . . The prayers of the whole people, friends and foes of President Lincoln, ascended to heaven, that his life might be preserved and thus spare them the humiliation of having such a man to rule over them. Are we to believe that all this passed unnoticed by Andrew Johnson?"

Booth by then was dead upon the lawn of a Virginia farmhouse, shot by his own hand or by a half-deranged Union sergeant, it has never been determined which. "Dead men tell no tales," Tucker said.

Charles Sumner had decided Davis was guilty of ordering Lincoln's death: "He is an assassin. A man who serves slavery must be an assassin." But the matter did not greatly interest him. He visited the President not to talk of individuals but of entire peoples. He told the President that his guide should be not so much the Constitution as the Declaration of Independence: "All men are created equal." The President smiled. There need be no problem between himself and those who shared Sumner's views, he said. "I mean to keep you all together."

Sumner felt the battle of his life was ended. The President was going to carry the good fight and win. By then the summer heat of Washington was on its way, and Sumner decided to go home to Boston. He called to say good-bye to Johnson and also to talk about suffrage for the Negroes, apologizing for always returning to the subject. "Have I not always listened to you?" Johnson asked pleasantly.

Sumner acknowledged that he had, and went on to recommend that the South be ruled by military governors who would firmly impress upon the people, with bayonets if necessary, the North's determination that the blacks were to be granted equal rights. Then, their educations advanced in this way, the ex-slave owners of the southern states could be handed over to Congress when it convened in December, seven months hence. Congress would determine the future of the ex-rebels. The President listened attentively, and his manner was friendly. Sumner went off to Boston to tell his friends no trouble was in the offing, the President understood everything.

That Sumner believed this to be so gave him an enormous sense of relief. Now that the war was over, northern interest in the freed Negroes was ebbing away. There was very limited support for the idea that they should be given the vote. Certainly, reasoned George Templeton Strong of the Sanitary Commission, the blacks ought to have as many rights as the southerners who had tried to destroy the country. On the other hand the average field hand had no more use for the vote than his mule did. One might as well let the cows and horses have ballots. The northern journalist Whitelaw Reid toured a South which seemed to him like a crushed and divided Poland living under foreign domination and wrote of his interview with a black man in Georgia:

"What do you think of Andy Johnson?"

"Who him?"

"He's President of the United States. Do you know what that is?"

"Who him?"

"Who?"

"Why, Pres'den'?"

Yet the Radicals wanted to give this man the vote, Reid wrote. But Charles Sumner said both privately and publicly that illiteracy and ignorance should be no bar to suffrage, that many very intelligent people could not read or write. Was it fair to punish Negroes because their former masters had kept them in bestial ignorance?

Whitelaw Reid looked at an aged Negro studying the first reader with a group of black children aged four to fourteen and it came into his mind that this was perhaps the most suggestive and touching sight he had yet seen in his tour of the beaten South. The old man wore glasses he tied around his bullet-shaped head with packing cord. He wanted, he said, to learn to read his Bible. One heard stories of other ex-slaves who cut switches for their volunteer teachers, that they might be scourged into learning. It was glorious and pathetic that they hungered so, northerners said; glorious that after centuries of being forced to live like animals they retained the desire for education and enlightenment; pathetic that they thought learning to read would immediately make them like the Old Miss of prewar days, who got to dress in lovely clothing and sit in the Great House "keeping parlor."

Northerners as well as southerners asked: Could blacks safely be handed the vote? Could they make the leap from near-barbarism into the American democratic tradition, whose development had taken centuries? Even freeing them so quickly had not come easily to Lincoln. He had long considered a scheme of gradual emancipation which would free the last slave by January 1, 1900. He had never completely made up his mind as to whether the black could ever approach equal status with the white man. Secretary of State Seward, although always hating slavery, thought blacks hopelessly incapable of competing with whites. "They are God's poor. They always have been and always will be so everywhere," he told a friend. "They are not of our race. They will find their place. They must take their level."

It was a tortuous problem. The German immigrant Carl Schurz confessed to himself it was natural, and terrible, that southern whites thought the Negroes belonged to them. Something of that acceptance of Negroes as chattels had permeated the North for generations past. Charles Sumner could say the Negro was so like the white man that really he did not deserve a special word to define him but that if one was needed he should be called a "Unionist." But for every Charles Sumner there were thousands of northerners who thought of the Negro as semihuman. (General Sherman said there was not a man of his army who wanted to serve with Negroes.) It was really a moot point as to whether the black man was educable at all, reflected Whitelaw Reid as he looked at the old man with the glasses tied on by a cord. It was an open question whether he could rise to independent thought. It was even, Reid thought, a matter for comment that he could learn to read. The concept of Negro ability to learn was so new, Reid wrote, that the attempt to teach him must be regarded as an experiment.

While the experiment went on, while the South waited, the former Confederacy sank into anarchy. Lawless bands of ex-soldiers and deserters from both sides roamed the land, with only the widely spaced Union garrisons and patrols offering the hope of a minimal keeping of the peace. On the night of May 10 one of the patrols flushed Jefferson Davis out of a Georgia hiding place. Alerted that Yankee cavalry was in the vicinity, Davis seized a cloak and prepared to run for it. But it would have been impossible for him to escape, and he surrendered. Only then did he realize that in the rush to get away he had put on his wife's cloak. (It got out that the defeated enemy leader had dressed himself in hoops, skirts, petticoats, ladies' shoes and a big bonnet. A huge roar of laughter swept over the North.) Surrounded by his captors, Davis was handed a copy of the President's proclamation charging him with direct complicity in Lincoln's murder. "The miserable scoundrel who issued that proclamation knew better than these men that it was false," he said.

Heavily guarded, the former President of the Confederacy was taken to Fortress Monroe in Virginia, where he was put into a casemate to await the North's decision as to his fate. The gunroom of the casemate's embrasure was closed with thick iron grating. The doors were fastened with crossbars and padlocked. Secretary of War Stanton, occupying the post Davis had once held, ordered the commandant of Fortress Monroe to enforce strictest security for the state prisoner. Guards kept him under surveillance twenty-four hours a day. Some of his jailers amused themselves by addressing Davis with the diminutive of his first name. The light in his room was never extinguished. His eyes, always weak, tortured him.

Davis' nerves began to give out. Then the commandant, authorized by Stanton to manacle the prisoner if he considered it necessary, decided to do so. An embarrassed Ohio captain told the former president of the Confederate States of America that he was to be put in irons. Davis said he could not permit such an insult to his person. The captain ordered an armorer to do his duty. Davis fought, and underwent the humiliation of being physically held down while heavy leg irons were put on. When the men left he lay rigid for a long time and then arose to find that he could do no more than shuffle around. He was now the perfect symbol of the proud South brought low.

On May 22, 1865, six weeks after the assassination, Mary Lincoln left the White House almost unnoticed. Still disconsolate, she manifested that irrational worry over financial matters which would eventually cause her son Robert to put her in a mental institution. She drove to the station and a train headed for Chicago. From there she sent Charles Sumner three indications of her esteem: her late husband's cane and the letters of consolation upon his death sent to her by the Queen of England and the Empress of the French.

On the day after she left, the armies of the North began their last great parade. To see what Washington called the Grand Review people jammed the capital, some paying to sleep in horsecars. The reviewing stand was in front of the White House. The platform was covered with gay bunting, pots of flowers and cacti in bloom, banners with the names of all the great victories of the Boys in Blue: Antietam, Shiloh, Vicksburg, Gettysburg, Atlanta, Richmond. The journalist Noah Brooks thought that above the twenty-mile-long marching columns there seemed another moving assemblage, those who had "made the South all billowy with graves." Two armies, he thought: the glittering, cheered and cheering one below, and, moving with silent tread above, another host, noiseless. And at their head, of course, Abraham Lincoln.

Andrew Johnson sat in the middle of the stand and for six hours gazed upon the Army of the Potomac, the cavalry twelve abreast, the infantry twenty-five to a marching line. As each corps commander or divisional General came by, all on the reviewing stand got to their feet and colors dipped and swords rose in salute. Then the officer dismounted, orderlies taking his horse into the White House grounds. He then joined the other dignitaries, to shake hands with each and become a part of the reviewers. Family members of important Generals were on the stand; when Grant sat down he took his son on his lap.

On May 24, the second day of the Grand Review, Sherman's Army of the West paraded by. Long-limbed midwestern farmboys for the most part, they were not considered in the same parade class as the easterners upon whom the departed McClellan had stamped his spit-and-polish ways. But as Sherman turned down Pennsylvania Avenue he looked back and saw the gleaming bayonets riding with the shot-riddled battle flags and thought to himself that here were troops equal to any in the world. A few minutes later he was walking to the platform where the President and the others were waiting to shake hands.

Smiling, hands gesticulating, talking quickly as he always did, Sherman went down the line greeting each man. He came to Secretary of War Stanton. Harsh words and violent threats were an integral part of Stanton's character. Perhaps he had already forgotten or dismissed the fact that he had questioned Sherman's patriotism when Sherman offered easy surrender terms to the Confederate Joseph Johnston. Stanton put out his hand. Sherman looked at the hand and its owner, gave a brutally cool little bow and moved on.

By that evening the last of the troops had gone by. The mighty Union army of the war was no more, its members melting into the people from whom they sprang and into history.

It was time to make the peace. Five days after the parade Andrew Johnson, seven weeks President of the United States, declared, without consulting anyone in the adjourned Congress, what Reconstruction would be.

5

He issued two proclamations. One concerned the state of North Carolina. He was appointing, he said, a Provisional Governor, William Holden of Raleigh. Holden was to call a constitutional convention and supervise the choice of delegates who would make arrangements for the election of permanent office-holders. The new legislature must ratify the Thirteenth Amendment ending slavery, repudiate all Confederate debts and declare secession from the Union to be illegal.

That was all.

Then the federal government would withdraw all its troops from the state. North Carolina could then return to what she had been before the war, free to do as she wished. Once a state, always a state.

The President's other proclamation gave complete amnesty and pardon to hundreds of thousands who had participated in the rebellion. There were several classes of exceptions, including officers above a certain civil and military rank and anyone who owned property valued at twenty thousand dollars or more. Persons denied amnesty were at liberty to sue for pardon personally. The proclamation indicated the President would be generous in granting forgiveness.

The terms of both proclamations were unbelievably, inexplicably, mild. Men's mouths gaped open when they read them. There was no mention anywhere of assuring civil rights of any type to the ex-slaves, still less an indication that the rebel states would be forced to grant them the vote. There was no mention of hanging traitors, no threat of confiscation. Where were the halters, gibbets, firing squads? Under the President's terms North Carolina would be in a position to elect Senators and Representatives for the new Congress which would convene in half a year. Men who had been in the field fighting the United States when the last Congress adjourned would be members when the next one met.

Charles Sumner was absolutely bewildered. The President had turned a "somersault." He must be suffering from "strange hallucinations," Sumner said. "How easy it was to be right!" the Senator wrote Bluff Ben Wade. "The President seems to have made an effort to be wrong." Where were the hangings Johnson had spoken of so often? What of the lesson to traitors he had promised a thousand times?

Uncomprehending, refusing to believe it was really happening, the Radical Representative George S. Boutwell of Massachusetts rushed to the President and presented a raft of objections and questions. Johnson soothed him, and Boutwell understood the President to say that North Carolina was an experiment and that there would be no more such proclamations until the success of the experiment was gauged.

Boutwell went away somewhat mollified but still uneasy. Two weeks later the same terms were given Mississippi and days later Georgia, Texas, Alabama, South Carolina, Florida. All rushed to hold conventions and ratify state constitutions which uniformly barred Negroes from voting. The President suggested to the Provisional Governor of Mississippi that blacks who could read and write and possessed property worth $250 be given the vote, but the suggestion was ignored. Johnson dropped the matter. He would stand on the Constitution. The Constitution expressly gave to the states the right to confer the franchise and to determine the conditions which voters must meet. All but six states of the North forbade Negroes to vote, and those six imposed qualifications not asked of whites. Under the Constitution, the federal government could not force northern states to enfranchise Negroes, so how could it do so in the South?

In New Orleans the journalist Whitelaw Reid saw an astonishing change in the people. Before the North Carolina proclamation, he wrote, they pleaded and made entreaties; after it they made threats. Men who had fought four years to destroy the country were now experts giving lectures on their rights under the Constitution. The newspapers dropped the obsequiousness of the first weeks after the surrender, dropped the word *rebel* in favor of *Confederate* and began hinting that any Yankee innovations were temporary. "Men quoted the North Carolina proclamation, and thanked God that there had suddenly been found some sort of breakwater against northern fanaticism."

Everything was changed. Soon the New Orleans *Picayune* was editorializing on the ladies of the city, "the noble women of New Orleans, who have had courage to believe that misfortune can exist without guilt, and, refusing to worship the rising sun, have turned aside from the prosperous and the powerful" to reach out to the returning Confederate soldiers. Reid heard men talk about "soon putting an end to the careers of nigger agitators in Louisiana." He went on to Vicksburg, Mississippi. "Wait till Johnson gets things a-going here," a man said to him there, "and we'll make a contract law that will make a nigger work."

Soon the new state legislatures were hard at work on what were called Black Codes. In the eyes of the South the codes were an attempt to define rights the Negro had never had before, to express in law the transition from slave to citizen, an adaptation of the existing law to apply to peculiar and particular cases. The southerners felt they expended rather than restricted. They would regulate family life, conduct, morals. The Black Codes would declare that henceforth it would be permissible for blacks to learn to read and write, that they might own their own homes and testify in court. Without such codes, said the southerners, the blacks would wander about and revert to barbarism. Disease would ravage them, and they would perish from starvation while dragging the whites down with them.

To the North the Black Codes were a southern denial of defeat in the war, slavery under another name. For the codes, varying from state to state, generally forbade Negroes the right to buy public property, enter a plantation without consent, preach the gospel without a license from a recognized church, own or carry firearms, enter into a railroad car or stagecoach. Blacks were forbidden to follow any trade or business but farming unless possessed of a special permit, and black employees on white-owned farms were forbidden to sell poultry or farm products. Children were to be apprenticed with or without parental consent. White persons associating with Negroes were to be declared vagrants. Any black who signed a labor contract and did not live up to it was to be sent to prison, or his services for the life of the contract could be sold to the highest bidder. In Mississippi the legislature ruled that any black without lawful employ could be declared a vagrant. If he was unable to pay the vagrancy fine he could be hired out to work without wages for anyone who could pay his fine.

A storm broke in the North when the Black Codes became known. Newspapers said the North would convert the South to a frogpond before permitting such laws to be enforced. Newspapers began running daily columns under the standing headline "SOUTHERN OUTRAGES."

The uproar amazed the southerners. That was the tragedy, thought Carl Schurz: the two sections simply could not understand each other. Schurz met a southerner who said that when he told Negroes to go to their quarters they refused. The man felt himself in mortal danger from such insolence. A Georgia planter told Schurz of a black laborer who objected to being whipped, thus furnishing conclusive evidence of his unfitness for freedom. Another plantation owner came to the federal General commanding a local garrison and complained that the blacks were dancing and singing. The officer pointed out that laboring men did such things in the North. So what? The planter went away saying the northerner did not understand. Meanwhile the gardens were covered with grass and weeds, and the woods came back to reclaim the fields. Under the Codes the whites offered contracts to the blacks which called for five- or six-month services until harvest time. Payment would be made after the harvest was sold. The Negroes refused to accept the contracts, for doing so would be like returning to slavery. Plows rusted, mill wheels did not turn.

It did not matter, the freedmen told each other. For soon there was going to be wholesale redistribution of land. Northern white men had come among them to say that at Christmas the ex-slaves would be given forty acres and a mule. The white men had little striped poles which they offered for sale. The ex-slave only had to pay what he could afford for the poles and then stick them in the ground. With the arrival of Christmas whatever area he had enclosed would be his.

The pathetic savings of a lifetime—a gold piece Master gave on a long-ago birthday; a silver dollar earned for special work—went to buy the little striped poles. One ex-slave showed the written guarantee he had received, unable to read the words: *Whereas Moses lifted up the serpent in the wilderness, so also have I lifted this damned old nigger out of four dollars and six bits.* When federal commanders found the sellers they were prosecuted, but all over the South from cabin to cabin word spread that the great day of Jubilee was coming on the birthday of the Lord Jesus, for on that day the land would be handed out.

During that summer of 1865 a steady stream of applicants for Presidential pardon came to Washington. By then the President was in residence in the White House, with his oldest daughter, Martha, the wife of Judge David Patterson, serving as official hostess in place of her mother. Martha had arrived from Greeneville in mid-June, bringing her young son and daughter and little brother, Andrew Johnson, Jr. Her mother—the First Lady now—remained in Greeneville with the

113

other children and grandchildren. Wan and emaciated from consumption, Eliza Johnson was a sick woman slipping into complete invalidism.

The White House Martha Johnson Patterson took over was in wretched shape, partly because of the war's chaos and partly because of the protracted seclusion of Mrs. Lincoln. During that time unsupervised strangers had wandered about taking swatches of the wallpaper for souvenirs. The sofas were verminous, the curtains in shreds. Martha Johnson Patterson was the most capable of the Johnson children. Born when her father and mother lived in a tiny log cabin, she had gone with them to Washington to attend the Academy of the Visitation in Georgetown while he served in Congress. She had been something of a favorite of their fellow Tennesseans President and Mrs. Polk and had often been at the White House during her adolescent years.

Now in a calico dress and apron she rose with the sun and applied herself to the intensive cleaning the Executive Mansion required. Dark-haired, with a broad brow and large eyes, she dressed in the evening in robes of soft rich tints with a shawl of lace around her throat. She wore a single white flower in her hair. People who expected her to be a nouveau loaded with garish ornaments found her instead quiet and simple. "We are plain people from the mountains of Tennessee, called here for a short time by a national calamity. I trust not too much will be expected of us," she told one caller.

The unending stream of men who came to the White House during that first summer of peace were all of a type. They were bronzed, tobacco-chewing, outdoor men carrying canes and talking politics. They were the gentry of the South.

One White House employee said he could tell from their faces just what clause of the exceptions in the amnesty proclamation a man came under—civil official, soldier, or owner of property exceeding twenty thousand dollars. By far the greatest number of petitioners were in the last category. They jammed the antechambers and stairwells of the White House, an entire civilization's elite coming to stand in line so that Andrew

Johnson of Greeneville, Tennessee, might pass upon their pleas.

For the President was taking the whole process into his own hands. From nine in the morning until three in the afternoon he sat conducting interviews. There was no board of appeals or even a preliminary screening. A petitioner handed his card to the White House doorkeeper and then waited. Sometimes a man came back day after day for a week to spend his time lounging about with other ex-Confederates. Each was waiting for admission to the President's office on the second floor. There the President sat with three army aides, one of whom, a young major, had a stack of precious pardons a foot high piled in front of him.

Whitelaw Reid looked in one day. Two or three rebel Generals were in a reception chamber, Reid noted, as many former members of the rebel Congress, and, in the only chair in the room, a former secretary of war of the Confederate States of America.

Shown into Johnson's presence, a petitioner was greeted with a cool bow. The President did not offer to shake hands. The man stated his case. His whole future could depend upon these few moments; without a pardon he could not receive or transfer titles to any kind of property or do any kind of business.

Many attempted to indicate that at heart they always opposed the rebellion. One Alabaman told the President he had been a Union man for all the four years of the war. "I am delighted to hear that," the President said. However, the man went on, he was somewhat implicated in the rebellion by virtue of his very profitable sales of cotton to the Confederate government, sales which had resulted in his emergence from the war with a worth in excess of twenty thousand dollars. Hence his need for a Presidential pardon. "Well, sir," Johnson said, "it seems you were a Union man who was willing to let the Union slide. Now I will let you slide." The man was shown out. Sometimes Johnson could be even more brutal, telling rich men they should give all their money away to the poor and thereby put themselves into a pardonable category.

But his decisions were haphazard. An Alabama man said he'd been an uncompromising rebel who had done all he could to further secession. He added that he had fought in the Confederate army and regretted that the war had ended as it had. "Upon what ground do you base your application for pardon?" asked the President. "I do not see anything in your statement to justify you in making such an application."

"Mr. President," the man said, "I read that where sin abounds, mercy and grace doth much more abound, and it is upon that principle that I ask for pardon." He left with the pardon in his hands.

Other men did not get firm answers. The President might indicate that the pardon was made out and waiting but that he was not prepared to deliver it quite yet. But, the petitioner would ask, was not the case decided? Oh, yes, the President would reply, the pardon would be given in good time. But not just now. The petitioner would leave. "Not quite humiliated enough yet," an official whispered to Whitelaw Reid.

Such cases were relatively rare. By far the greatest percentage of applicants were given pardons. Provisional Governors of the late rebellious states sent in names by batches, and pardons came back by telegraph. Soon southern papers carried advertisements for self-appointed "pardon brokers" who promised quick action. Without exception they had nothing to sell, but they congregated in Washington's saloons and hotel lobbies speaking of their influence with the President. (One White House doorkeeper made a good thing of telling the "brokers" that he would arrange for the clients' petitions to be put on top of the piles on the President's desk. Trapped with marked money by a government detective, he was discharged. The President issued a statement saying intimations that money could secure pardon were an intolerable insult to himself and every member of the government.)

But the "pardon broker" business flourished nevertheless. Soon women of doubtful reputation dominated the field. It was said that these members of the demimonde had an avenue to the President through his son, Robert Johnson, who had come to Washington ostensibly to aid his father in his work, but actually to sadden him by drinking heavily in the Washington saloons. An amiable young man, Robert had emerged from the army as a drunkard. He was put into sanitariums, shipped away on a navy cruise by Secretary Welles, lectured at, but nothing worked. The President sadly said that, of his three sons, one was dead and another just as good as dead.

All Washington rang with the beseechings and demands for pardons. Rumors had it that an ex-Confederate colonel was in charge of the whole matter. And as the summer went on the southern atmosphere of Washington, gone for four years, returned. The former rebels came back to congenial surroundings. Sumner was in Boston, where he was spending much time with the vacationing Stanton. Congressmen were at their homes. The last of the volunteers were being rapidly mustered out of uniform. So in Washington one heard little but southern voices uttering southern aspirations and southern prejudices. By early August it was apparent that almost anybody could get a pardon. Even General James Longstreet, Lee's second-in-command at Gettysburg and one of the South's half-dozen most illustrious soldiers, came to ask a pardon. But for him the President drew the line. "There are three persons of the South who can never receive any amnesty: Mr. Davis, General Lee and yourself," he said to Longstreet. "You have given the Union cause too much trouble."

Longstreet was not deterred. "You know, Mr. President, that those who are forgiven love the most," he said.

"You have very high authority for that, but you can't have amnesty," Johnson replied. (But in time Longstreet would have his pardon and rise to high federal position.)

That the likes of James Longstreet should even dream of seeking amnesty, that he should *dare* to come to the White House, was an outrage to many northerners. Even Wade Hampton, said the New York *Herald* of August 27, the Beau Sabreur of the South, Jeb Stuart's successor as commander of Confederate cavalry, who spoke of dying in the last ditch of the Confederacy, "now bellows lustily for pardon. Who next?"

That Washington was filled with southerners and that Andrew Johnson's days were spent with ex-rebels worried Republican Senator William Pitt Fessenden of Maine. He went to the President and said things were moving too quickly. President Buchanan had gone too far in his attempts to placate the South, Fessenden pointed out. Now Johnson was imitating him. The results in the first instance had been frightful, and it would be even worse now to let the ex-Confederates end up controlling the country after so much blood and money had been spent to conquer them. Fessenden also urged others like himself to talk to Johnson "so as to have somebody about besides Democrats and Secessionists."

Other men were also rising to arms. "Aren't you ashamed to give Lee the privilege of being president of a college?" * a southern Unionist wrote Johnson. "Satan wouldn't have him to open the door for fresh arrivals, and *you* have pardoned him." † The cartoonist Thomas Nast turned out drawings which represented the President flinging pardons right and left. He drew Secretaries Seward and Welles as washerwomen, busily cleaning the besmirching stains of endless pardons from Union battle flags. He showed Johnson as Iago telling a wounded and wondering Othello in Union army uniform that he was still his friend. *Love thy neighbor* is Andyjohnsonism gone berserk, Nast explained.

Another cartoon showed Columbia on her throne looking at a long line of former rebels, Lee and Wade Hampton among them. All were bowing, kneeling, creeping and crawling for their pardons. Looking on was a one-legged black soldier. "Franchise?" asked the caption. "And not this man?"

The veteran Abolitionist Wendell Phillips said, "Better, far better, would it have been for Grant to have surrendered to Lee, than for Johnson to have surrendered to North Carolina." Sumner wrote Bluff Ben Wade, "The course of the President is

* Now Washington and Lee University in Lexington, Virginia.
† No pardon was issued to Lee.

so absurd . . . it must fail." But "meanwhile the rebels are springing into their old life. This is the President's work. I do not understand the President."

Wade himself was baffled by the actions of the old associate to whom he had cried when Lincoln died, "Johnson, we have faith in you!" Was it possible, Wade wondered, that the Andy Johnson who once denounced traitors and every Union soldier who lost a battle, was turning into an apostate? The form of government of the United States was proven a failure if it permitted Johnson to present this olive branch to the South on a silver tray, Wade decided. Lincoln's high-handedness had been bad enough, he told Secretary Welles. To get more of the same from Lincoln's successor would be beyond toleration.

But Welles saw that Wade had not yet given up, that he was trying to make Johnson rethink what he was about. In fact Wade was making every effort to turn Johnson back to his old ways. For, he wrote to Sumner, "to admit the states on Mr. Johnson's plan is voluntarily, with our eyes open, to surrender our political rights into the hands and keeping of those traitors we have just conquered in the field. It is nothing less than political suicide."

Andrew Johnson had been a silent, self-contained man all his life, the stolid, gloomy face showing no response to what people said, the few sentences offered in reply giving little indication of his inner feelings. He had no friends to whom he spoke openly, no desire or need to confide in anyone. A very suspicious type of man, said his confidential secretary, Colonel William Moore. A badger who had to be smoked out of his hole, said President Zachary Taylor's son Richard, who had served as a Confederate General. Completely unwilling to show his feelings to his advisers, thought the Secretary of the Navy, Gideon Welles.

Held by his interior needs to the safe, narrow limits of his early inclinations and leanings, Johnson used few stars to steer a course. He disdained religion. His secretary Frank

Cowan took note of the monosyllabic "old Saxon terms" the President used when discussing what he considered religious frauds. Of history he had little knowledge.

People of consequence naturally offered Johnson their views. "For God's sake move cautiously and carefully," wrote the newspaper publisher Joseph Medill from Chicago. "Don't show so much eagerness to rush into the embrace of the $20,000 rebels. They will suck you like an orange and when done with you throw the peel away." But he did not listen. In years past, faced with a problem, he would sit in the workroom of his tailor shop alone, thinking. Now in the White House he retired at night to his study with a pot of coffee and his cat, and again sat alone. His wife's advice had once meant a great deal to him, but consumption had made Eliza Johnson thin and emaciated, a hopeless invalid. She would soon be coming from Greeneville to be with him, but her strength was limited. Coughing spells wracked her. She could only walk a few steps without aid. He could not look to her for emotional support or to discuss policies.

The President gave no thought to what Lincoln would have done in his position. They were mirror opposites. Lincoln's way was to guide people into doing what he wanted while permitting them to believe it had been what *they* wanted. Johnson's way was to bludgeon through. Lincoln worked through other men; Johnson pushed them aside. The self-made man who never learns to depend upon others for anything, Johnson owned a certain opinionated arrogance. Back home they used to say that some people started out high on life's ladder but that Andy Johnson started out underground. It was true. Yet he had gone up and up so that the whole world deferred to him. He was stubborn, with the uneducated man's contemptuous appraisal of matters of which he knew nothing. Tactless in the extreme, he possessed limited knowledge and understanding of either men or geographical sections other than his own. Certainly he did not know or understand the North. Yet he had no doubts of his ability to lead. The United States was at a crossroads. He would show which road was to be taken.

President Johnson made up his mind as to what must be done. He explained his course and his thinking to no one. He would permit his later actions to speak for him.

But it was very dangerous to sit silent while men expounded their views. They assumed that silence meant consent. The President did not know their assumption, or did not care. So he proceeded to act without explanation. The war had been fought to save the Union. The Constitution was the overriding law of that Union. And so the southern states must reenter the Union with all their rights assured. Once more the men of the South were United States taxpayers and citizens and therefore should enjoy the privileges to which they were again entitled.

It had been different during what was already called "the late unpleasantness between the states." * Then there had been actual armed warfare (and even after the surrenders of Lee and Joseph E. Johnston, there was the danger of guerrilla warfare that could go on forever). But now there was no need for any continuing penalties. Johnson had wanted to hang Davis, but government legal experts told him it would be difficult to select a court competent to hear the case because of technicalities of jurisdiction. The President had sought to arrest Lee, but General Grant said that he had given his word of honor to Lee's army at Appomattox that there would be no arrests if the paroled men kept the peace. Thwarted on both counts, Johnson put Davis and Lee out of his mind and went ahead with his policy of bringing the South back into the Union. He told a friend, "We are making rapid progress—so rapid that I sometimes cannot realize it. It appears like a dream."

By then, the late summer of 1865, the President's entire family was with him and he had settled into a routine. Mrs. Johnson spent her days in her little room in the northwest corner of the second floor of the White House. There she sewed,

* The North has generally referred to the conflict of 1861–65 as the Civil War, which implies that the southern states were never out of the Union, or as the Rebellion, which also implies an unbroken relationship between the sections. The South has called it The War Between the States or, upon occasion, The War for Southern Independence, implying that a separate southern republic existed.

121

knitted and read. She rarely came downstairs. In the mornings before going to his office her husband would join her for half an hour. Then she would slowly walk about the upstairs chambers making sure that Sam, the valet, whom he had owned in slavery days, was taking care of him. Eliza Johnson was not interested in the high position the President's rank conferred upon her. "I don't like this public life at all," she told the Presidential bodyguard, William Crook. "I often wish the time would come when we could return to where I feel we best belong." Upon occasions when the President's stoic calm dissolved into a rising anger she was always able to calm him by repeating quietly, "Andrew, Andrew." She dressed for his approval and when he complimented her she would pat his shoulder in thanks. Few people outside the family saw her and everyone looked to Martha Johnson Patterson as the official White House hostess.

Mrs. Patterson and Mrs. Mary Stover, the other daughter, a widow thanks to the war, had five children between them. A tutor was hired to conduct classes. Sometimes in the afternoons their grandfather took the youngsters in a carriage to Rock Creek Park where the children fished, waded and picked flowers. The President silently watched. Sometimes he skipped stones across the stream. Or he would walk for an hour with Crook, the two men exchanging hardly a word. He was, in Crook's eyes, so self-contained as to be "almost somber," the most silent man the bodyguard ever knew.

It was well for the President that the family's arrival forced some recreation upon him, for he was not well, the victim of frequent headaches and a continued languid feeling. Johnson said that he hardly knew how to deal with the work load which demanded that he see dozens of persons each day, but he took no steps to relieve himself. Secretary Welles told him that he was permitting weeks to pass during which he took no exercise at all: "No constitution could endure such labor and close confinement." Welles suggested cruises down the Potomac. Perhaps the fresh air would help the headaches. So on summer afternoons they sailed to Aquia Creek or out into the bay, Mrs. Patterson and Mrs. Stover and the grandchildren coming along. But the President still did not look well. Secretary Seward, slowly recovering from Lewis Paine's murderous attack, took note of the President's pale complexion and unhealthy appearance. Seward urged that Johnson curtail the incessant flow of pardon-seekers crowding upon him.

But the President wanted to see them all. As the summer of 1865 ended, those who watched with disbelief, then horror, thought that they knew why.

Andrew Johnson the mudsill, they said, had been seduced. The one-time bound boy, with the flower of the aristocracy at his feet, had gone over to them. The old plantation high-born, proud and still glorious even in defeat, had come to him, Carl Schurz wrote, and he "could not withstand the subtle flattery of the same aristocrats when they flocked about him as humble supplicants cajoling his vanity." Theirs was, thought Moorfield Storey, who shortly would become Charles Sumner's secretary, "the persuasion of southern men, for whom he held the instinctive respect of one who had held an inferior social position among them."

He must revel in it, men thought, those great-family names of Virginia and South Carolina kowtowing as they sought his royal pardon. The President's amnesty terms spared him from dealing with ordinary pardon-seekers, rear-rank privates in the Confederate army, minor postmasters. But each day he had in a succession of the rich and the grand. The deference of these to the mudsill, wrote the New York politician Chauncey Depew; their flattery offered to the man who had once held their horses and made their clothing, "captivated him and changed his whole attitude towards them."

How else could he have changed so completely and abruptly? Perhaps this man who was believed to be a Nero or a Caligula when he ascended to the Presidency had become unbalanced. Or perhaps he was drunk all day. But he did not in other ways act like a crazy man. And too many witnesses who saw him daily let it be known that the President was no sot. So it must have been that he was seduced by the very men he had cursed throughout his life. He had said treason must be humbled, reflected Whitelaw Reid. They told him they were now humble. He had said traitors must be punished. They had suffered. Loyal men must rule. Now they were loyal.

And perhaps, Reid thought, these southerners promised to gather the votes of their region behind him. Johnson could combine those ballots with the voters of the North who were tired of war and interested only in making money. The two groups could then elect him President in his own right in 1868.

But primarily, men said, it was a glittering bribe, more precious than money, that the South could offer to someone who once had been called poor-white demagogue and the drunken tailor from the mountains. Chauncey Depew said that a group of men called upon Johnson to say that once he was of a class different from themselves and that therefore they had never recognized him socially. But now, according to the rule of all nations, he became the supreme ruler and hence was to be accorded social recognition. Here was their accolade: they accepted Andrew Johnson as their equal.

That summer of 1865 the veterans of the great army of the North put away their arms. They sought new work building the railroads west, expanding the factories, the foundries, the industrial enterprises of the coming Age of Gilt. The war was destined to become sacred in the memories of the Boys in Blue as they met in Grand Army of the Republic encampments. But they held no enmity for the late enemy. Even on the day Lee surrendered, they had offered the former opponent rations and tobacco as they swapped stories.

The majority of the high officers similarly put the war behind them. Like Lee, Grant never again expressed interest in military matters. Sherman lost at once the fire which led him to devastate the South.

It was different for the civil leaders. Unbloodied and personally unexposed to the brutality of war, the political chieftains looked ahead and thought of the greater meaning of the conflict and its frightful outpouring of blood and treasure. They considered many things: railroad rates, high tariffs, bond payments, encouragement of northern industry, revenge, political power and political positions, future elections and, of course, the black man.

These were the things for which they had fought the war. Now a southerner jeopardized everything.

One of the chieftains, the strongest, the shrewdest and the toughest, watched from the home he shared with his Negro mistress of many years. "If something is not done, the President will be crowned King before Congress meets," he wrote in one of his many letters. "I fear before Congress meets he will have so be-deviled matters as to render them incurable."

"Perhaps very low farce was thought necessary amidst so many bloody tragedies," he wrote. And, finally, he said, "Could we collect bold men enough to lay the foundation of a party to take the helm of this government and keep it off the rocks?"

He had not attended Lincoln's funeral but had stood on a hill above where the funeral train would pass on its way to Illinois. Some had said that as the draped cars went slowly by he had failed to raise his hat: Thaddeus Stevens, Republican of Pennsylvania.

6

Clubfooted, never seen to laugh, rasping—Lord Hate-good of the Fair, Old Sarcastic, Caliban, Mephistopheles—Thaddeus Stevens frightened and baffled everyone who knew him. Once during his days in the Pennsylvania Legislature a little boy stared at the grotesque clubfoot that rested on top of Stevens' desk. Stevens shoved it into the child's face. "There, look at it!" he snapped. "It won't bite! It's not a snake!" Yet Stevens told his doctor he would pay him to treat any lame boy or girl whose parents could not afford the doctor's aid.

Once a woman praised Stevens' political views and asked if she might have a lock of his hair. He bowed low, yanked off the wig he had worn since becoming bald years earlier, and put it into her hand. Yet he could be the most understanding and generous of men. When he died bad debts for small sums aggregating one hundred thousand dollars were found among his effects. He had never made any attempt to collect.

In all his mature life Thaddeus Stevens never went to church. "You have heard that I am one of the devil's children," he would say, indicating his cloven hoof, "and this is proof." Yet he gave freely to religious orders. After one of his frequent visits to an all-night faro session in a Washington gambling hall, he was approached in the street by two Negro clergymen seeking donations for their church. He reached in his pocket, took out a bill and gave it to them. They thanked him and walked away, to return a moment later saying that Stevens had by mistake given them too large a sum. He had handed the clergymen a one-hundred-dollar bill, half the month's salary he was receiving as a United States Congressman. "The Lord his miracles accomplishes in wondrous ways," Stevens said, waving them off and clumping away.

He ruled by fear. (In the Pennsylvania Legislature it was said that the other members huddled together or hurried out of his way when he roamed the halls, saying he was like a buffalo who would simply toss them up on his horns.) At Dartmouth he had been disciplined for killing a cow with an ax. As a young lawyer he had been suspected not only of fornication but of murder when a pregnant girl was found lying dead in a ditch. The day of her death she had told people Stevens was the father of her unborn child. Afterward the neighborhood children looked at his hands to see if the blood was still on them.

As a trial lawyer Stevens was brilliantly effective, combining impeccable logic with brutal sarcasm. His cynicism was overwhelming. He liked to point out that he had successfully defended forty-nine out of fifty men accused of murder by pleading them innocent by reason of insanity—and that the man whom the state hanged was really the only one who was crazy.

Stevens was born poor and in effect fatherless, for his drunkard father had vanished not long after his birth in 1792. He grew up in Vermont, a hopeless cripple and thus the butt of other children's jokes. Physically weak, he never strayed far from his mother until he began to show promise in his schoolwork. To provide him with an education his mother worked as a nurse and maid, moving her residence nearer the school so that it would be easier for him to attend. She got him into Dartmouth, slaving for him and neglecting her other less promising children. (So unsuccessful were his brothers in comparison that Stevens' enemies later spread the story that he was really the bastard son of the French Count Charles de Talleyrand, who, also a cripple, had visited America about the time of Stevens' conception.)*

His roommate at Dartmouth detested him as a humorless, harsh man. Stevens himself had contempt for the elect of the college although he envied wealthy students. Determined to become rich himself, he migrated to Pennsylvania after graduation. He found great success in the little town of Gettysburg, becoming in a few years one of the richest men in the county. His methods were not always the most fastidious. Stories of sharp dealings attached to his name. Better authenticated were the descriptions of his activities with women. Determined never to marry—to him the institution was mere "licensed copulation"—he had a series of mistresses whose existence he never denied. He swore, though, that he had never deflowered a virgin: "I vow to God I have never yet learned (except by description) the meaning of maidenhead."

Thaddeus Stevens moved to Lancaster, became active in promoting railroad lines, and an ironmaster with a plant employing several hundred men. He owned thousands of acres over which he used to gallop alone, a startling figure dressed in black. His other entertainment was gambling. Once a man delivering a wagonful of hay came into a room where Stevens was playing cards. The man asked what he should do with his load. "Bet it on the ace," Stevens replied. In Washington he could be found almost each night at one of the elaborate gambling halls along Pennsylvania Avenue. There, in defiance of the law but with the full knowledge of the authorities, men played in luxurious surroundings. Fine foods were available, along with representations of the Old Masters, and, it was said, some old mistresses, too.

In time Stevens maintained two residences, one on Capitol Hill in Washington and the other in Lancaster, with whose other most distinguished citizen, James Buchanan, sometime President of the United States, he was not on speaking terms.

* Most Stevens biographers doubt the likelihood.

At both Stevens residences a particular lady was in charge, the ostensible housekeeper. She had been born Lydia Hamilton and had been married to a man named Smith. When Smith died, she came into Stevens' life. She was black.

Stevens called her "Mrs. Smith" in front of his friends—an unheard-of form for the time of addressing any servant, let alone one who was black. When discussing plans for the Stevens household Lydia Smith always said "we." When Stevens invited cronies for sessions of euchre she bustled about with drinks and food in wifely fashion. Mrs. Smith called Stevens' grown nephews by their first names. They wrote her fondly during the war, during which one of them was to fall at Chickamauga. At Lancaster she was called "Mrs. Stevens" behind her back.

Stevens came late to an important political career. He served with no great distinction in the Pennsylvania Legislature, where he crusaded against the Masonic order. However, to his credit he championed a state free-school system. He went to Congress for a term, made no particular stir, went home. He came back in 1859, aged sixty-seven, Old Thad. The war was just over the horizon. Passions of the type which led Brooks to attack Sumner corrupted the halls of Congress. When two prospective duelists threatened each other in the House, Stevens suggested their proper weapons were dung forks. The thought was typical of his frequent scatological comments, most of which were edited out of the stenographic record.

The outbreak of war did not surprise or frighten him. He had always been against making concessions to the South. His reaction as a freshman Representative to Daniel Webster's compromise speech of 1850 was typically direct: "As I heard it I could have cut his damned heart out." He offered a warning to those of the South who had spoken of justice for the blacks: "Take care that your works testify to the purity of your intentions, even at some cost. Take care that your door posts are sprinkled with the blood of sacrifice, that when the destroying Angel goes forth, as go forth he will, he may pass you by." (Howell Cobb of Georgia, Speaker of the House, listened and said privately, "Our enemy has a General now. . . . He is in earnest. He means what he says. He is bold. He cannot be flattered or frightened.")

Cobb's prediction came true when the war began. Stevens became chairman of the Committee on Ways and Means, the most powerful post a Congressman could hold. He called for wholesale confiscations, no negotiations, emancipation of the slaves, insurrections by the South's blacks. The Confederacy in his eyes was a foreign nation no longer under Constitutional protection. "If their whole country is to be laid waste, and made a desert . . . so let it be." He said he was "tired of hearing damned Republican cowards talk about the Constitution"; that there *"was* no Constitution any longer so far as the prosecution of the war" was concerned.

Stevens came to detest the gentle Lincoln with his talk of erring brothers, of peace without victory. Behind the northern lines he fought his own war with the White House: "I hold that Congress is the sovereign power of this nation, not the President." As the war against the Confederates progressed he became the tyrant of the House of Representatives, his rasping voice demanding fighting generals for the North and hangmen's ropes for the South.

In the South, Lincoln was regarded as an uncouth baboon. Stevens, more respected, was granted the status of devil incarnate. When the Army of Northern Virginia's probing forces marched toward Gettysburg, they detoured slightly in order to take Stevens' Caledonia Iron Works. Three days later Lee himself arrived. He regretted the smoldering ruins which showed where the works had been. That was not Lee's way, but General Jubal Early had enjoyed the fire and was disappointed that he had missed the archfiend himself.

During the course of the war every section of the South suffered, but the destruction of the Caledonia works was one of a mere handful of blows struck at individual northerners. Yet Stevens took it unemotionally, making himself responsible for the care of his employees who no longer had a place to work. He said he would count his loss a cheap price to pay for victory over the South.

He called for Draconian measures, fire and the sword, Negro uprisings which would devastate the enemy behind his lines—and Lincoln spoke in his always-gentle way. The President went to Gettysburg to deliver a speech—"Let the dead bury the dead," Old Thad said. At the Republican Presidential Convention of 1864 Stevens attempted to get Lincoln displaced as leader of the ticket. Failing that, Old Thad supported the President only because he held the Democratic nominee to be a blundering coward and possibly an outright traitor: "Lincoln's election would be a disaster, but McClellan's damnation." He was opposed to the nomination of Andrew Johnson as the President's running mate. "Can't you find a candidate for Vice President in the United States without going down to one of those damned rebel provinces to pick one up?" he asked a man who supported Johnson.

Then came the assassination and the end of the war. Now was the time to assure the perpetual ascendancy of the Party of the Integrity of the Union, Stevens declared. Peace should rightly bring high tariffs, new turnpikes and factories, the enrichment of banker and mill owner, railroad builder and ironmaster, those titans of the coming great age which would see the United States take a premiere place in world affairs. Never again must the nation seek its strength in agriculture or be dependent on Europe for its manufactured goods. The South, which thought in those terms, was prostrate. It must remain so.

A month after Johnson was sworn in as President, Stevens wrote to him from Lancaster to suggest that he suspend all Reconstruction measures until Congress met. Johnson did not answer. Stevens wrote again. He had warned Lincoln against too easy a peace. Now he must make the same appeal to Johnson. "Can you not hold your hand and wait the action of Congress?" he asked. Johnson again ignored Stevens, pouring out fourteen thousand pardons in six or seven months. In early October, Stevens spoke in Lancaster. The number of pardons being issued was so great, he said in his deadpan fashion, that mere humans could not produce them quickly enough. Therefore, he understood, a machine had been invented to crank them out as fast as light. When all the pardons were finished, he went on, they would be joined together to build a throne for Andrew Johnson.

In Washington the President did not take note of Stevens' remarks. He continued to pardon the southern gentry, occasionally reminding them of the "taunts, the jeers, the scowls, with which I was treated" in the past. That was wonderful sport for him, people said, but were all the Confederacy's sins to be put aside so that one man could gratify himself?

Johnson did not listen. Once the wife of former Confederate Lieutenant General Richard Ewell came to seek a pardon for her seriously wounded husband. The woman owned the home in which the President had stayed for a time while Military Governor in Nashville, and she had married since last seeing Johnson. The President was ill that day but ordered that Mrs. Ewell be sent up to his room. "Couldn't you find anybody better to marry than a one-legged man?" Johnson asked. She remained silent. He asked her to hand him a comb on the table near his bed. His daughter Martha was in the room and could have performed the service, but Mrs. Ewell thought of her husband's pardon and reached for the comb. Johnson began combing his hair while denouncing the South's leaders. But he must have been thinking of the past even as he lectured the petitioner, for he remembered one of her favorite beverages from Nashville days. "Have some green tea for Mrs. Ewell," he said to his daughter. "She will stay to lunch." Soon General Ewell had his pardon.

In November, Mrs. Clement Clay came to see what could be done for her husband, a former U. S. Senator from Alabama who was imprisoned with Jefferson Davis at Fortress Monroe. Clay had been named in the President's reward proclamation as one of the Confederate leaders implicated in Lincoln's assassination.

Once very rich, Mrs. Clay had been impoverished by the war. She was in Washington only by virtue of a one-hundred-dollar gift from a Huntsville, Alabama, merchant who also gave her material for a silk gown to be made up when she arrived in the capital. So worried about her finances that she was even concerned over the price of a hack to take her to the White House, Mrs. Clay went there and ran into the widow of Senator Stephen A. Douglas of Illinois. The two women had been friends in prewar days. Adele Douglas volunteered to accompany Mrs. Clay into the President's office.

Mrs. Clay stood before a self-contained, composed man with whom she had, of course, never mixed socially, and asked if she could at least visit her husband in Fortress Monroe. Johnson was noncommittal, indicating the matter was in Secretary of War Stanton's hands. Mrs. Douglas joined in her pleas and then, bursting into tears, fell on her knees before the President. Mrs. Clay looked down at the kneeling figure of her friend and thought to herself that it was a monstrous wrong that this man should have her husband's life and death under his control. *She* would not kneel to Andrew Johnson, even to save her husband's life. The two women departed. (Later, for reasons known only to Johnson, the President let Clay go free.)

By then there were virtually no prisoners left save for Jefferson Davis. Granted pardons, men who had held high positions under the Confederacy made bids for similar offices in the United States Government. Almost without exception the men elected to Congress in the elections held by the South's speedily organized "Johnson governments" were important ex-Confederates. They included Davis' former Vice President, Alexander Hamilton Stephens, now Senator-elect from Georgia, six former members of the Confederate cabinet and four ex-Confederate Generals.

It was madness, said Bluff Ben Wade. Were he and other loyal men to greet as equals in the Thirty-ninth Congress men who had been fighting the United States when the Thirty-eighth Congress adjourned? It was like a prisoner at the bar getting up on the bench to sit next to the judges. "Did ever a nation on the face of the earth which had been so merciful as to save the lives of traitors that sought to destroy it, on the very next day after wrenching the arms out of their hands, invite them into its councils to participate in its deliberations? Would a man who was not utterly insane advocate such a thing?"

Congress was scheduled to convene on December 4, 1865. By then every Confederate state with the exception of Texas had complied with Johnson's requirements for reentrance into the Union. The newly elected southern Senators and Representatives were on hand for the swearing-in ceremonies.

On Saturday, December 2, Charles Sumner called upon the President. They sat down alone. Evening had come; it was dark outside. Sumner plainly told the President that he was throwing away the fruits of the victories of the Union army.

The President asked for specifics. Sumner talked of insults to the ex-slaves by southerners, rapes and murders and mutilations. He had a whole sheath of letters from the South telling of whippings and ear-cuttings. On a Mississippi River steamer a well-dressed black couple had asked for a stateroom. The captain answered, "God damn your soul, get off this boat!" Behind him passengers were yelling, "Kick the nigger! He ought to have his neck broke!" The captain said, "They can't force their damned nigger equality on to me!" The captain would have been one of that great mass of southerners who were sending ex-Confederates to Congress. Was the Negro the captain threw off his boat to be represented by such men?

In Mississippi, Governor Humphreys of the "Johnson government" had said in his inaugural address: "Ours is and it shall ever be, a government of white men." The Louisiana State Democratic Convention resolved: "We hold this to be a Government of White People, made and to be perpetuated for the exclusive political benefit of the White Race." Was it conceivable, Sumner asked the President, that such people should be permitted to come back into the Union with no safeguards, no penalties? An avenging God would not sleep if such a monstrous wrong were permitted.

But as he talked of outrages and insults to the blacks it seemed to Sumner that the man before him was no longer the sympathetic and kindly listener of the days immediately following his accession to the Presidency. His manner seemed to be that of a man with southern sympathies, Sumner thought. His voice sounded harsh and petulant to Sumner, and he appeared uninterested in the troubles of the southern Unionist, white or black.

"Are there no murders in Boston?" the President asked.

"Unhappily, yes, sometimes," Sumner replied.

"Are there no assaults in Boston? Do not men there sometimes knock each other down, so that the police is obliged to interfere?"

"Unhappily, yes."

"Would you consent that Massachusetts, on this account, should be excluded from Congress?"

Sumner got up to leave. The man was ignorant, he thought to himself, pigheaded, perverse. The Senator reached down to take his hat, which he had put on the floor, to discover that the President had absent-mindedly used it as a spittoon. Sumner went away thinking to himself: The President's soul is set as flint against the good cause. With the assassination of Abraham Lincoln the rebellion had vaulted into the Presidential chair. *"Jefferson Davis,"* he would say later, *"was then in the casements at Fortress Monroe, but Andrew Johnson was doing his work."*

The Chief Clerk of the House of Representatives, Edward McPherson, began to read the roll of the members. The hall had recently been redecorated with a new Brussels carpet of cheerful colors; the galleries had been handsomely refurnished.

McPherson was the son of one of Old Thad Stevens' dearest friends and neighbors. As he droned out the names of the members he omitted those who came from southern states. Horace Maynard of Tennessee jumped up when McPherson passed over his name. He waved his "Johnson government" certificate of election over his head. "Mr. Clerk," he shouted, "I beg to say that in calling the roll of members—"

McPherson rapped his gavel. "The Clerk cannot be interrupted during the roll call," he said. Maynard sat down.

When McPherson finished calling the names of the northern Representatives, Maynard got up again. "The Clerk cannot be interrupted while ascertaining if a quorum is present." Maynard sat. McPherson announced a quorum was present. Maynard was on his feet.

"Mr. Clerk—"

"The Chair cannot recognize as entitled to the floor any gentleman whose name is not on the roll."

Maynard tried to say something. Stevens called him to order. Did the gentleman not understand that a nonmember could not speak on the floor of the House?

The Democratic leader, Representative James Brooks of New York, arose to ask when the matter of admission of southern members would be considered. ʼ

"At the proper time," Stevens answered.

Maynard again got up and said, "I appeal to the gentleman from Pennsylvania to listen to me for a moment."

"I cannot yield to any gentleman who does not belong to this body—who is an outsider," Stevens answered.

Brooks cried, "Why, this is not parliamentary propriety, if it is even decency."

Stevens waved his hand in dismissal. He would have more to say shortly about "impudent claimants" for congressional seats. Moments later Stevens offered a resolution for the creation of a joint Senate-House committee. Its purpose would be to examine the qualifications for membership of the would-be southern Senators- and Representatives-elect. The resolution was voted on and passed—as a menacing Stevens had made certain it would be in a Republican caucus the previous night. In the Senate the same resolution, sponsored by Charles Sumner, also passed.

Thus the Committee of Fifteen, the Committee on Reconstruction, was born, with Thad Stevens as its guiding spirit. The southerners could guess in advance what result the Committee's leisurely deliberations would bring. There was no point in remaining in Washington. One by one the ex-Confederates went home, leaving Old Thad to define them and the region they had hoped to represent in the halls of Congress. "Dead men cannot raise themselves," Stevens said. "Dead states cannot restore their existence."

Three days after Congress convened, Sumner called upon Secretary of the Navy Gideon Welles. The Administration's policy was the "greatest and most criminal error ever committed by any government," Sumner said. Welles noted that Sumner had apparently read up on the subject, from the works of Plato to the latest French pamphlet. The Senator from Massachusetts had concluded that all Johnson was doing was totally wrong, and that he, Sumner, was "beyond peradventure right." In not opposing Johnson's sinful progress, Welles, Sumner said, was "foully, fatally culpable."

Johnson fought back. Two weeks after the congressional session opened he sent the Senate a report written by General Grant. The General had toured the South and found that everything seemed to be in order. There was no resentment against the Union forces, no thought of reinstituting slavery. By and large, Grant said, southerners "accepted the situation."

But Sumner, so quixotic, fervid, impractical, so much the crusader, could yet upon occasion be the clever tactician. General Carl Schurz had also been asked by the President to report on conditions in the South and Sumner had made Schurz an ally. He had made it possible for Schurz to write articles for a Radical Republican paper while settling some financial problems for Schurz. Word of this sponsorship must have reached Johnson, for when Schurz came to report the President was not able to see him. Schurz came back the next day. He was told the President was busy. Schurz said he had just returned from a three-month trip and would be obliged if the President would make known whether he would be received. The message was sent in. After an hour's wait, Schurz was told to come into the President's office.

They greeted each other. Schurz said he was ready to offer information on conditions in the South. There was a moment's silence, broken when Johnson asked after Schurz's health. Schurz thanked him for the inquiry and expressed the hope that Johnson's health was good. Johnson said it was. Another silence ensued. Schurz said he would be submitting an elaborate report on his southern tour. Johnson said he need not trouble himself. The General said that it was his duty to do so. Johnson was silent. Schurz bowed himself out.

In his report Schurz wrote that the South was unpenitent and that "rebeldom" had not changed its prewar views. To himself the General reflected that the once-wealthy southerners who flocked to Johnson as "humble suppliants cajoling his vanity" had managed to destroy the President's ability to see the South as it really was: a people who had not been convinced they had done anything wrong in making the war.

At Sumner's request Schurz's report was offered to the Senate on the same day as General Grant's. Sumner asked that Schurz's be read aloud, explaining it was needed as a counterbalance and a refutation of the "whitewashing" in which the President was indulging. The word jolted several Senators, who rose to say Sumner had spoken too harshly. He replied he had "nothing to retract, nothing to modify, nothing to qualify." From then on Johnson always had something to say about Sumner when black delegations came to the White House. The President told one group he did not like being criticized by someone who could deal in rhetoric but had never risked his life, liberty or property for blacks. He asked another group if Sumner was their God.

By then Thad Stevens was referring to "that man at the other end of the Avenue" as someone who had done worse things than those which cost Charles I his head. Sumner was now denouncing the President with such vehemence as to make Senator Edwin Morgan of New York think him "demented." Sumner would not have denied that he spoke strongly. But any moderation, he added, was out of the question.

"It is not I who speak," he said. "I am nothing. It is the cause, whose voice I am, that addresses you." He read the Senate extracts from letters he said he received daily from the South.

"'The former masters exhibit a most cruel, remorseless, and vindictive spirit towards the colored people. In parts where *there are no Union soldiers, I saw colored women treated in the most outrageous manner. They have no rights that are respected. They are killed, and their bodies thrown into ponds or mudholes. They are mutilated by having ears or noses cut off.'*"

Sumner went on with descriptions of hangings, beatings, people tortured by firebrands held in the hands of southerners who were " 'loud in their praise of President Johnson for his wholesale manner of dispensing pardons.' " Men with kind feelings for the blacks could expect to be shot down from behind; if the killer was caught he could expect acquittal from a jury. Now that he had been freed the Negro was worse off than before. Under slavery, the master protected valuable property. Now the black was everyone's prey.

From Mississippi: *" 'After a great step and a mighty victory you are expected by the President to withdraw your protection from this people and turn their destiny over to those who for centuries have ground them into the dust.' "*

A Texan wrote Sumner that Johnson's course would soon restore the old order to power. *" 'For heaven's sake preserve us, if you can, from this calamity!' "*

The North could not permit the South to do what it wished with the Negro, Sumner told the Senate. The Negro must be given equality, backing and, most important, the vote. The Constitutional injunction that the states must individually determine voting rights was not important. "Nothing can be unconstitutional which is against slavery."

Cato held, Sumner said, that if his belief in the immortality of his soul was an error, it was an error he loved. He regarded, Sumner said, his own feeling for real liberty and equality in the same way. In *Pilgrim's Progress*, "Doubting Castle" locks were opened by faith. William Tell had said, "I do not know whether it is possible, but I know that it must be attempted."

He ended with an appeal to Andrew Johnson: "If you are not ready to be the Moses of an oppressed people, do not become its Pharaoh."

Christmas of 1865 came, the first Christmas of peace. All through the summer and fall the blacks of the South had told one another that on Christmas Day the land would be distributed. They had heard that in Washington there was a club-footed old man who had said that even as the Russian Czar Alexander II had given land to the serfs when he freed them, so must the United States distribute land to those who had been slaves. "Strip a proud nobility of their bloated estates," Stevens said. "Drive out the present rebels as exiles."

The hopes of the blacks, and those hard words from Washington, bred in the whites of the South a great terror, for it seemed to them that December 25 would bring insurrection, burning, seizures. Under the lead-gray skies of that day a battered land, its youth dead and wealth gone, waited. Christmas ended. There was no distribution of land. Nor did the blacks rebel.

The Negroes knew, then, there would be no more Jubilees, no miracles. The greatest number of them settled down to farm work. Some of the blacks, understanding the situation and reading the future, sought an education from the volunteer teachers who came down from the North. The whites talked about putting in a spring crop if money could be borrowed to buy the seed. And they harked back to the great days with Stuart or Jackson, to Bull Run, Chancellorsville, Brandy Station.

In the large southern towns the Union officers garrisoned locally were not invited to people's homes for Christmas dinner as they would have been in the North. The officers derived grim amusement in seeing how ladies stepped off the curb to avoid walking under the American flag hanging from army-commandeered buildings. Here were the people who were unable to understand why their elected representatives were not welcomed to the Halls of Congress.

In Washington, on January the first of the new year of 1866, President Johnson held his first great reception. During the eight months of his administration Martha Johnson Patterson had transformed the worn and dreary White House of the war years. New gilt moldings adorned the sparkling rooms, and there was elegant new furniture and fresh flowers. At eleven in the morning the foreign diplomats came in court dress, followed by the Justices of the Supreme Court, Congressmen, army and navy officers and their ladies in morning costume. By noon the dignitaries had all passed through the Blue Room, where the President waited with his daughters. Mrs. Stover wore a rich black silk dress with a basque of the same material, each embroidered with violet-colored wreaths. Mrs. Patterson was in black velvet with a single white japonica in her hair and laces around the throat over a high corsage.

When the notables departed the public was admitted so that those who wanted to might shake the hand of the seventeenth President of the United States. Studying the people, Secretary Welles was struck by the high proportion of former Confederate sympathizers among them.

Old Thad was not in attendance. Charles Sumner did not come.

7

All through January and on into the spring the Joint Committee on Reconstruction conducted its hearings into the admissibility of the former Confederate states into the Union. Only picked witnesses came before it. One testified that southerners had plowed up a Union army graveyard and destroyed the markers. Andrew Johnson had known all about it, the witness added, but had done nothing. Another witness said it was commonly believed in the South that Robert E. Lee would be the next President. Mrs. Lee, said a third, was under Johnson's sponsorship well on the way to regaining her commandeered estate at Arlington. Her first act would be to dig up and get rid of the many Union soldiers buried there. A similar action was planned by the Johnson-pardoned owner of the land which had contained Andersonville, the notorious prison camp.

Other witnesses spoke of how southern Unionists were shot down by their neighbors while schools for the freedmen burned to the ground. General George A. Custer testified that weekly, if not daily, murders of freedmen took place. Clara Barton spoke of treating a young Negro girl who was flogged for not spinning wool to her employer's satisfaction. The gashes in her back were eight to ten inches long and the flesh had been completely cut out for most of the length of the wounds.

As the hearings continued, both houses considered the bill for the extension of the Freedmen's Bureau. The Bureau had been created for a one-year period to deal with the flocks of Negroes who came under Union army control during the war. The one-year period was almost over; an extension was sought. Headed by an idealistic officer, General Oliver O. Howard, "The Fighting Christian," its ranks included opportunistic and sincere New England schoolteachers, swindlers and God-fearing crusaders. It was the best hope the new-freed blacks owned; it was also a patronage heaven largely Radical in outlook.

The Freedmen's Bureau extension bill included provisions for additional as well as continuing aid to the blacks. The bill also stipulated that Bureau agents had the right to intercede in court cases in the South when the agents suspected that blacks had not been given equal treatment. The Bureau agent alone would decide if someone suing or prosecuting a black was violating the Negro's civil rights.

Here was a curious bill, remarked the eminent New York lawyer David Dudley Field. It took the blacks under the protection of the federal government, as if they were not able to take care of themselves. At the same time, Field added, those most vociferous in support of the bill were also "the most clamorous to give this same dependent population a large share in the government of the country by granting them the right to vote."

Similar thoughts came into President Johnson's mind. He said that if too much aid was given to the freedmen they would stay idle forever and never work for their own betterment. Then there was the question of the rights of southern white persons who might bring a court action against a black. A Bureau agent could simply charge the white petitioner with violation of the black's rights. No jury or judge could rule on the matter; it would be accepted. How would the rights of the white petitioner be protected in such a case?

But what concerned Johnson above all was the fact that Congress was legislating when eleven states of the Union were not permitted to take part in the deliberations or cast votes.

The bill came to him on February 6. On February 19 he sent it back with his veto. His listed objections emphasized the absence of the eleven southern states. He appeared to be saying that any bill Congress passed without their presence was illegal, in effect that Congress was not a legal body.

The British Minister, Sir Frederick Bruce, was in the Senate when the veto message was read aloud. He looked at Charles Sumner and saw what he thought was a picture of "venom and defeat." Sir Frederick thought to himself, A dangerous man with no human sympathies, a man who would prove remorseless in carrying out his doctrines. "I should judge him to be very like Robespierre." That thought had occurred to others. In fact, the Radical Republicans were frequently called The Jacobins, after the most violent of the groups who had overthrown the established order in France and made the Revolution and the Terror.

Bluff Ben Wade got up to speak when the reading of the message was finished. Johnson had not lived up to his promise to punish traitors, Wade said. He himself must be a traitor at heart.

Less than a year had passed since the time when Johnson was thought to be a hangman.

Sir Frederick Bruce was not alone in looking at the Radicals and thinking of the French revolutionists. Secretary of the Navy Welles viewed the Freedmen's Bureau extension bill as being like a decree from a despotic power, not a legislative enactment from representatives of a republic. According to Welles, Stevens was the whipmaster of Congress, "dark, revolutionary, reckless, vindictive and passionate." Lincoln's old Postmaster General, Montgomery Blair, described Stevens as a "root and branch man," who would spare nothing of the government but the Congress, and that he would turn into a revolutionary club.

144

President Andrew Johnson:
"I am right. I know I am right."

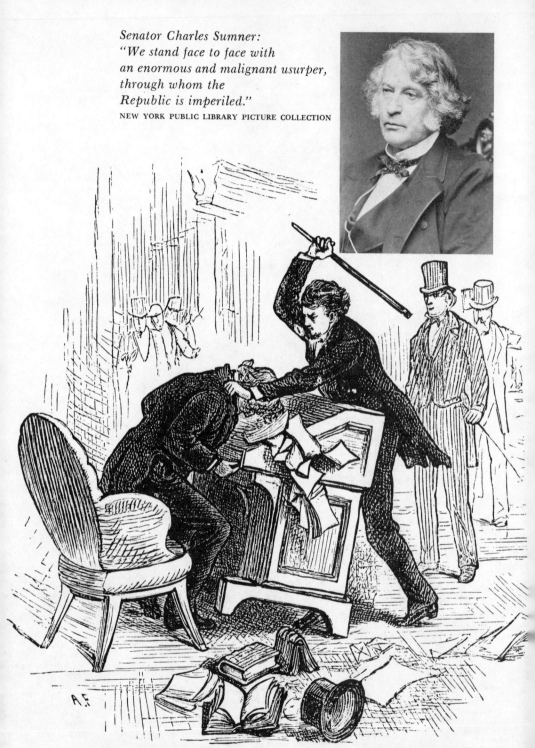

"Mister Sumner," Representative Preston Brooks of South Carolina
said. When the anti-slavery senator looked up from his desk, Brooks
slammed a cane on his head again and again. Four years passed before
Sumner was well enough to resume his Senate duties.

Representative Thaddeus Stevens: "If you don't kill the beast it will kill you!"
LIBRARY OF CONGRESS

Secretary of War Edwin M. Stanton. When the President attempted to remove him from his office, an impeachment trial was made inevitable.
NEW YORK PUBLIC LIBRARY PICTURE COLLECTION

Eliza McCardle Johnson, who took an illiterate husband of nineteen and taught him to read and write. An invalid when her husband became President, she was miserable in the Executive Mansion. "I have not had a happy moment since I came to this house," she said.
NEW YORK PUBLIC LIBRARY PICTURE COLLECTION

The President's daughter and official hostess, Martha Johnson Patterson.
NEW YORK PUBLIC LIBRARY PICTURE COLLECTION

The tailor-President's first shop, Greeneville, Tennessee. On his deathbed Johnson did not speak of his time in Washington, but only of the days he had spent in this tiny building.
LIBRARY OF CONGRESS

"VERDICT","HANG THE D— YANKEE AND NIGGER."

The Ku Klux Klan. Johnson's enemies said
he was its secret leader.

THE FREEDMAN'S BUREAU!

AN AGENCY TO KEEP THE **NEGRO** IN IDLENESS AT THE **EXPENSE** OF THE WHITE MAN.

TWICE VETOED BY THE **PRESIDENT**, AND MADE A LAW BY **CONGRESS**.

SUPPORT CONGRESS & YOU SUPPORT THE NEGRO.   SUSTAIN THE PRESIDENT & YOU PROTECT THE WHITE MAN

For 1864 and 1865, the FREEDMAN'S BUREAU cost the Tax-payers of the Nation, at least, TWENTY-FIVE MILLIONS OF DOLLARS.   For 1866, THE SHARE of the Tax-payers of Pennsylvania will be about ON? ?ON OF DOLLARS.   **GEARY** is FOR the Freedman's Bureau.   **CLYMER** is OPPOSED to it.

One view of the Freedmen's Bureau, the agency set up to aid the newly emancipated blacks of the former Confederacy.   LIBRARY OF CONGRESS

A different estimation of the Freedmen's Bureau.   LIBRARY OF CONGRESS

The slaughter of more than two hundred persons in a New Orleans race riot, nearly all of them blacks or "carpetbagger" northerners, was laid at the President's door by his enemies.

The famed cartoonist Thomas Nast portrays His Accidency, King Andy the Indecent, as Nero watching the slaughter of innocents in the Roman Colosseum. The cartoonist likened the massacred victims to those who died at New Orleans.

During Johnson's "Swing Around the Circle" he attempted to rally support for his policies in the eastern and midwestern states. But the crowds were more interested in viewing the President's increasingly unhappy fellow-voyager, Ulysses S. Grant, seen smoking one of his inevitable cigars as the President futilely shouts at his listeners.

An anti-Johnson cartoonist depicts the tour as a drunken orgy undertaken with the connivance of Secretary of State William H. Seward.

6. *The President received by New York. He leaves the Constitution* HERE.

7. *He is supported by Mr. Seward, on all occasions*

The President's chief defense lawyer, William M. Evarts.

The principal spokesman for the House of Representatives' board of managers, Benjamin F. Butler.

Ross of Kansas, whose vote would decide all.

Had things gone differently, he would today be remembered as the eighteenth President of the United States, Benjamin F. Wade.

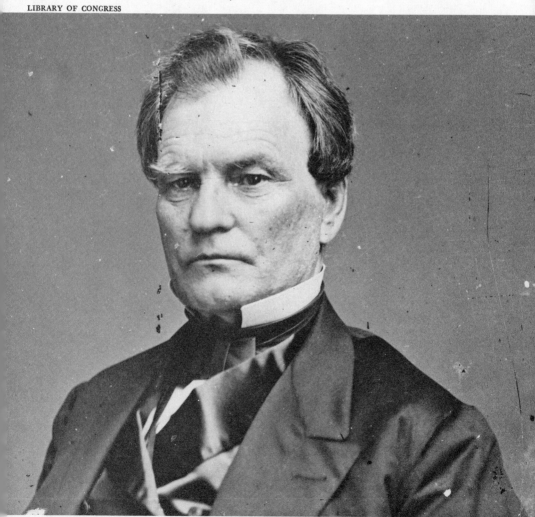

Old Thad Stevens presents the articles of impeachment to the House of Representatives.
LIBRARY OF CONGRESS

Too weak to walk, Stevens is carried into the Senate Chamber for the trial.
NEW YORK PUBLIC LIBRARY
PICTURE COLLECTION

The House of Representatives' board of managers for the impeachment trial. Standing from left: James F. Wilson, Iowa; George S. Boutwell, Massachusetts; John Logan, Illinois. Seated, from left: Benjamin F. Butler, Massachusetts; Thaddeus Stevens, Pennsylvania; Thomas Williams, Pennsylvania; John A. Bingham, Ohio.

The Senate sitting as the court of impeachment for the trial of Andrew Johnson.

"He wants a revolution . . . to reign on its scaffold and ply its axe."

The President himself was coming to believe that Stevens and Sumner and their followers intended to take the government into their own hands. It was an "unmistakable design," he told Welles. They would declare Tennessee out of the Union and so get rid of him, and then set up a Directory based on the French Revolution's model. Lincoln in his time had thought of Charles Sumner as a man willing to tear asunder the fabric of the government and the character of American political processes because of his feeling for the downtrodden, and now Johnson saw no reason to think that his predecessor had exaggerated.

The President's fears were confirmed, at least in his own mind, when the morning after his veto of the Freedmen's Bureau extension bill Stevens told his Joint Committee on Reconstruction that he had changed his mind about admitting Tennessee, which hitherto he had thought to be the most worthy of representation of all the southern states.* That afternoon Old Thad put through the House a resolution saying no state was automatically entitled to representation in Congress. Congress must specifically declare the state to be so entitled.

On February 22, two days later, the country would celebrate Washington's Birthday. On the morning of the holiday Secretary of the Treasury McCulloch read in his newspaper that a group of well-wishers were expected to march from Glover's Theatre to the White House, where they would greet the President. McCulloch had heard dozens of Andrew Johnson's impromptu addresses to callers during the weeks when the President had worked out of the Treasury. *There must not be a speech,* McCulloch thought to himself. He went to the White House and bluntly told the President not to address the crowd. To do so might widen the breach between himself and his sometime allies. He might say things his supporters would be sorry for.

* The number of Tennessee Unionists who fought in the Union army was equal to the number of Tennessee rebels who fought for the Confederacy.

"Don't be troubled, Mr. Secretary," Johnson replied. "I have not thought of making a speech and I shan't make one. If my friends come to see me, I shall thank them and that's all."

The President went out on the balcony to salute the crowd. They shouted that they wanted a speech. He said a few mild words of greeting. They shouted. He spoke some more. Looking on, the Presidential bodyguard William Crook thought to himself how strange it was that a man so somber and reticent as the President could rouse himself to offer so vibrant a response. And as Crook listened, the calm and dispassionate manner began to evaporate and the President became again Andrew Johnson the mudsill bound boy of the years of stump oratory. What a world of trouble the President would have escaped had he been stricken dumb when elected Vice President, Secretary McCulloch said later.

For the President began to harangue what was essentially a random crowd hardly better than a street mob.

"I fought traitors and treason in the South," he yelled. "I opposed the Davises."

They roared. It was a holiday, a day off from work.

"Now when I turn round," he called out, "and at the other end of the line, men, I care not by what name you call them, are still opposed to the restoration of the union of these states, I am free to say to you that I am still in the field. I am still for the preservation of the Union. I am still in favor of this great government of ours going on and on, and fulfilling its destiny."

People were shouting back, some in approval, some in derision. "Tailor!" someone yelled.

"Yes," the President shouted back, "I did begin as a tailor, and that suggestion does not discomfit me in the least, for when I was a tailor I had the reputation of being a good one, and of making close fits, and I was always punctual to my customers, and did good work."

He began to talk again of the men who opposed him, the men he was fighting as he had fought Jefferson Davis.

"Name them!" someone in the crowd shouted. "Who are they?"

"You ask me who they are," he replied. "I say Thad Stevens of Pennsylvania is one. I say Mr. Sumner, of the Senate, is another."

There were cheers, whistles, boos. Standing in front of an unruly holiday crowd in the process of becoming a mob, the President had compared the two most powerful men in Congress to the leader of the late Confederacy languishing in a federal prison. He alluded to Stevens' remark that he, Andrew Johnson, was comparable to Charles I, and to Sumner's use of the term *whitewashing*.

"It had been declared elsewhere," he called out, "that I was guilty of usurpation which would have cost a king his head, and in another place it has been alleged that I had been engaged in whitewashing, meaning that I had attempted skillful deception. When and where did I ever whitewash anything or anybody?"

He was shouting at the top of his voice. "I have been an alderman of a town, I have been in both branches of the legislature of my state, I have been in both houses of the national Congress, I have been at the head of the executive department of my state, I have been Vice President of the United States, and I am now in the position which I occupy before you, and during all this career where is the man and what portion of the people is there who can say that Andrew Johnson ever made a pledge which he did not redeem, or that he ever made a promise which he violated? None!"

It was all wretched, Secretary McCulloch thought to himself, bad in substance and bad in style. "Men may talk about beheading and usurpation, but when I am beheaded I want the American people to be the witnesses!" Johnson cried out. He was waving his arms as he shouted. It was impossible not to think of another of his public orations, the speech he made upon his inauguration as Vice President. The next day the papers would say that his remarks had about them the aroma of Old Bourbon.

He went on and on, occasionally interrupting himself to say, "I have already spoken to you longer than I intended when I came out," and then talking some more before saying,

159

"My fellow citizens, I have detained you much longer than I intended." Then he roused himself for the rolling peroration:

"In conclusion, let me ask this vast concourse here today, this sea of upturned faces, to come with me, or I will go with them, and stand around the Constitution of our country. Let us stand by the Constitution of our fathers, though the heavens themselves should fall, though faction may rage, though taunts and jeers may come, though abuse and vituperation may be poured out in the most virulent form. I mean to be found holding to the Constitution as the chief ark of our safety. Yes, let us cling to it as the shipwrecked mariner clings to the last plank, when the night and the tempest close around him!"

Finally he was finished. In every way the speech was a disaster. "Your speech made me feel mortified," William Crook heard a supporter tell the President. In New York a friend told George Templeton Strong that the President reminded him of the Daughter of the Regiment, whose aristocratic relatives raised her from low estate to train her in the ways of the great world. Then one day she hears the music of the soldiers' band and rushes to join the marchers, forgetting the aristocratic life she had been taught. So it was with Andrew Johnson. A stump orator by profession, he had accidentally been made President. Now faced with the call of a mob he forgets official dignity and goes back to his old ways. Another friend said to Strong, "When he dies there will be one comfort. Judas Iscariot will not be quite so lonesome." Still another declared, "It's bad enough to have a tailor for President, but a drunken tailor and a drunken Democratic tailor, is beyond endurance."

In Washington the newspaperwoman Emily Edson Briggs wrote that in the speech the President had thrown away the cloak which concealed his true motives and had shown that he, the First Tailor of the Land, was now in the business of making new garments for returned rebels. She said southern sympathizers in the capital now felt free to put up pictures of Robert E. Lee. The Confederate chieftain had taken Washington at last. Next: pictures of Lincoln and Booth side by side.

Senator William Pitt Fessenden of Maine counseled a

moderate reaction. "I do not know how gentlemen around me may feel," he said. "They may be in a state of excitement and wrath which prevents their speaking and acting calmly. For me, I am too old a man not to be able to get over excitement of that sort." But certainly no more than half the Senators accepted his advice. Among those who did not was Sumner, who pronounced the speech a series of "foul-mouthed utterances which are a disgrace to human nature."

It was Old Thad who gave the most effective answer to a President who compared him to Jefferson Davis. "I must apologize to the House for the tameness of the remarks I am about to make," he mumbled. His listeners were already suppressing laughter. In a rambling way, seemingly talking to himself, Stevens spoke of the special attributes of the President. Here was a man of principle. Who could not admire such a paragon of integrity, patriotism, courage, good intentions? Nothing could be said that was too complimentary of the President.

Representative Hiram Price of Iowa, primed, interrupted to ask in mock astonishment if this was really Thaddeus Stevens speaking, the same Thaddeus Stevens referred to by the President in a certain recent speech?

Stevens said he did not comprehend the question. "Does the learned gentleman from Iowa suppose for a single moment that that speech, which he refers to as having been made in front of the White House, was a fact? I desire at this time to put the gentleman right." He explained that there had been no speech. It was all a newspaper hoax. The President had never uttered the words attributed to him. To say that he did was to fall in with the plots of the President's enemies, who had been persecuting him ever since he took the oath of Vice President.

Stevens waved a newspaper clipping. Here was an example of the persecution which the good President had to endure. He requested the Clerk to read aloud the editorial from the New York *World* which appeared the day after Johnson's Vice Presidential inauguration speech. "Let the Clerk read that vile slander."

161

The Clerk read: *"The drunken and beastly Caligula, the most profligate of the Roman emperors, raised his horse to the dignity of consul. . . . The consulship was scarcely more disgraced by that scandalous transaction than is our Vice Presidency by the late election of Andrew Johnson. . . . To see it filled by this insolent, drunken brute, in comparison with whom even Caligula's horse was respectable! . . . This insolent, clownish drunkard!"*

What lies, Stevens cried when the Clerk finished. What persecutions! And so it was with the President's speech given on Washington's Birthday. "We all know he never did utter it. It is not possible, and I am glad of this opportunity to relieve him from that odium."

As Stevens sat down the roar of laughter engulfed him. But he and the Radicals needed more than derision. They needed votes to overturn any future Presidential vetoes. Stevens could control the House of Representatives, but the Senate was unreliable. Yet a change of only one or two votes there would give the Radicals the two-thirds majority needed to overturn vetoes.

The Radical Republicans looked at the Senators. There was John Stockton of New Jersey, a Democrat. A technical protest had been filed against Stockton when he had been elected to the Senate by the New Jersey Legislature * the previous year. It was that he had been chosen by a majority of the entire legislature present, not a majority of the entire legislature. The protest had been disallowed by the Senate Judiciary Committee. Now, however, New Jersey had a Radical legislature. Any replacement the new legislature sent to the Senate would certainly be a Radical.

One Judiciary Committee member, Daniel Clark of New Hampshire, had never signed the report recommending that Stockton be seated. Clark was persuaded to open the issue by offering a resolution for Stockton's expulsion from the Senate. Before a vote was taken, Senator William Wright of New Jersey, ill and returning home for treatment, arranged a

* There was no direct voting on Senators.

162

pair on the question with Senator Lot Morrill of Maine. By the pair Morrill was pledged not to vote on the Stockton matter. But what was a promise compared to the duty Morrill owed his colleagues and the country? Such was the question propounded by Senator Charles Sumner in private talks with Morrill. Stockton must go, Sumner said. The Radicals must command enough votes to thwart the President. The future of the country was at stake.

The voting began on the proposed expulsion. Morrill's name was called. He hesitated, thinking of his promise. But the Senate Chamber was alive to the sounds of men urging him to respond. Above all the others could be heard the roars of Sumner: "Vote! Vote! Vote!" Morrill gave in and voted against Stockton. Enraged, Stockton then committed a breach against propriety by voting in his own support. That carried the vote in his favor, 22–21, but Sumner thundered that Stockton outraged all decency in voting for himself. He had insulted the Senate. Stockton quailed under the lash of that sonorous voice, and withdrew his vote. That left the matter at an impasse. They agreed to vote again a few days later.

On the appointed day there was no pair for the still-absent Senator Wright, or for another non-Radical Senator who, also ill, was not present. Friends of Stockton asked for a forty-eight-hour delay. They were ignored. This time the vote went against Stockton and he was unseated. The New Jersey Legislature replaced him with a Radical.

On the day of the vote, March 27, 1866, President Johnson sent a message to Congress concerning the Civil Rights Bill of Senator Lyman Trumbull of Illinois. Trumbull's bill was intended to counter and make illegal the Black Codes of the "Johnson government" southern legislatures. Its sponsor had discussed his bill with the President, saying that although the slaves were free they must be guaranteed civil rights. Otherwise their freedom was a cheat and a delusion. Johnson listened to Trumbull and said nothing.

He did not say, as he might have, that he thought the bill unconstitutional in its detailing of a thousand actions which were suddenly to be made crimes, tyrantlike in its substitution of federal for state rulings, and that, finally, it would be destructive for any hopes of good feelings between blacks and whites in the South.

Silent, he let Trumbull leave thinking the President approved of the Civil Rights Bill. The silence was followed by a Presidential message that he was vetoing the bill.

Trumbull, formerly a supporter, threw up his hands. Senator John Sherman of Ohio, also a supporter until that moment, wrote his brother, the General of the Army of the West, that Johnson was an insincere deceiver. Senator Fessenden wrote a friend, "I have tried to save Johnson. But I am afraid he is beyond hope."

The Senate gathered itself. No important Presidential veto in history had ever been overturned. The Senators decided to vote. As with the Stockton matter, the question of postponement arose because of the illness of two Johnson supporters. Bluff Ben Wade got up to answer the request for a delay by saying, "I will tell the President and everybody else, that if God Almighty has stricken one member so that he cannot be here to uphold the dictation of a despot, I thank Him for His interposition."

The Senate voted. And burnt the bridges between the executive and legislative branches of the government. For the veto was voted invalid by a vote of 33 to 15. Cheers rang through the chamber.

That night General and Mrs. Grant held a scheduled reception at the Washington home which admirers had given Grant. The General's support was important to any campaign against the President, and so a group of Radicals went to the party. Stevens came unaccompanied. (He could hardly bring his Negro housekeeper-mistress.) He went in, clumping, to find the President standing between the host and hostess. Calm and cordial as always when away from the stump, Johnson shook hands with Old Thad and presented him to Mrs. Grant. The former Vice President of the Confederacy, Alexander H. Stephens, looked on, as did an ex-Union army officer serving his first term in the House of Representatives, Rutherford B. Hayes. A happy gathering, Hayes reflected. The President was behaving very well.

Others reflected that it would be possible to make the President more compromising, more accommodating. Representatives Shelby Cullom and Godlove Orth decided to go see the President and advise him somehow to smooth over the differences between himself and the Radicals. "I will never forget that interview," Cullom wrote later. "He gave us to understand that we were on a fool's errand and that he would not yield. We went away, and naturally joined the extreme Radicals in the House, always voting with them afterwards."

The President said then, as he had before, that the North had fought so that the South would stay in the Union. The Union, indivisible, could not be split asunder. The three hundred thousand who fell in its cause proved that. The Radicals were doing more than locking the door after the horse was stolen. They were barring it against the horse's return.

His duty was clear, he said. Individuals might be punished, but never states. Charles Sumner could say that Massachusetts might instruct Georgia, that it was Massachusetts' duty to lead and show the true way, but the President in the Executive Mansion—the Nation's House—could never agree to that. Above all there stood the Constitution, which held there were no classes of states, that all states were equal. There could be no other law than that of the Constitution.

The President could not be called a religious man, his secretary Frank Cowan thought, but perhaps he had substituted something else for the Bible: the Constitution.

But the Constitution could be interpreted in a multitude of ways. Yet, even above the Constitution, there stood a man's personal concept of what he owed himself and his country. The highest duty Johnson knew—the very essence of his being—was service to that entity called the People. Politicians always aver their devotion to that abstract word, but in Johnson's case something more than pious lip service was involved. Narrowly educated, unsubtle, he saw the poor and unprivileged—the People—as those whose interests he must serve. The rich could look after themselves.

A willing servant of the People, a worshiper at the throne of democracy as he saw it, he had spent his life fighting those who he thought would exploit the poor. A southerner, he had seen the King Cotton aristocracy, the men who lived in the plantation Great House, as the enemies of those he wished to serve. They had insulted him in his youth. They had snubbed him in his maturity. They had fought him during the desperate days at Nashville when he was Military Governor. When he became President he had no guarantee that they would not carry out an endless guerrilla war.

Then, as President, he had seen them in their new position as petitioners for his pardon. The bogeymen took off their masks. Revealed were the ravished features of those who had seen their world shattered. The slaves were free. The sons of the Great House were dead on the field of battle. Money, glory, position, all were gone forever.

But nature abhors a vacuum. And so it seemed to Johnson that into the void were moving the new aristocrats of the North, who did not talk in a Cavalier, Sir Walter Scott fashion, but instead spoke in the language of a new concept of government for the benefit of business and industry. Railroads, corporations, steelmasters, the proprietors of giant commercialized agricultural empires, stock and bond speculators—these were the new enemies of the People, Johnson decided. They did not trust the South to govern itself; they did not want the laboring men of the North to have a real say in important matters. They were the antithesis of the yeoman farmer for whom Johnson had designed his Homestead Bill. They looked to Alexander Hamilton as their prophet—and Hamilton had seen the rich and capable as the legitimate overseers of the country. For Johnson the teachings of Thomas Jefferson and Andrew Jackson took precedence. Temporarily yoked into line with the North's titans for the purpose of winning the war, he had nothing in common with them once the war was over.

In his own mind he had been consistent. There had been

no sudden reversal of course. If it were the last act of his life, he said, he would have hanged Jefferson Davis. That had proved impossible because of the legal technicalities involved. So reluctantly he shelved the appealing prospect of seeing the Confederate leader swing at the end of a rope. But never had he said that he would hang the entire South. For he knew that the Confederate army was made up of little farmers, plain workingmen. Only a tiny fraction were Cavaliers. Now the great and mighty of the North sought to crush those farmers. He could not permit that. For Johnny Reb, as the President saw him, had been simply a misguided, tricked citizen of the United States.

Johnson knew the South. A man largely mired in the static world of his youth, he was incapable of visualizing the black man as the political and social equal of the white. To exalt the black man was to cheat and push downward upon the white, he thought. And he knew the South of the post-Civil War period would never accept what Charles Sumner had in mind. Bayonets could compel a sullen obedience, but bayonets could not change men's minds. One day the federal troops would have to be withdrawn. What then? He questioned too the purity of motive of those who marched in Sumner's wake. Sumner was sincere, but what of the men who saw the war's victory as a license to make money? They would grind down the whites of the South by using the blacks as a weapon, but with what aim in mind? To create a money aristocracy. And the future conduct of that money aristocracy? "It goes for the last dollar the poor and helpless have got," he said. "And with such a vast machine as this government under its control, that dollar will be fetched. It is an aristocracy that can see in the people only a prey for extortion."

A Populist before the word was known (and the later Populists of the turn of the century imitated Johnson in paying scant attention to the plight of the Negro), the President set himself to do what he had always said he would do: help the little man. Forty years later, looking back, the eminent historian James Ford Rhodes can almost be heard sighing as he took up the case of Andrew Johnson. "Johnson stood for some correct principles," Rhodes said, "but he had the knack of doing even right things in the wrong way."

Lincoln would have conciliated, compromised, talked enemies around. Johnson could only bludgeon. He did not think of other men's views; still less did he dwell on how to change them. One afternoon he sat with his aide Colonel William Moore. They had been together since Nashville and the defense of the city against the rebels. He had sworn then he would burn the city before surrendering it. Now he and Moore sat sharing a glass of wine in the President's bedroom. Andrew Johnson walked up and down, then stopped pacing. "Sir," he said to Moore, "I am right. I know I am right. And I'm damned if I don't adhere to it."

8

Charles Sumner of Massachusetts went calling upon his fellow New Englander, Secretary of the Navy Welles of Connecticut. In serving Andrew Johnson's policy, Welles was betraying their section of the country, Sumner said. "Atrocious wrong" and "monstrous error" and "greatest mistake which history has recorded" were phrases that punctuated the Senator's conversation. Welles did not agree, but other Cabinet members did. Half the men were moving closer to the Radicals. Welles said to the President that Lincoln had been dead almost a year now, but that the Cabinet he had left behind was strengthening the hands of Stevens and Sumner. The time had come for certain department heads to leave.

Welles was not the first man to speak to Johnson on the matter. Lincoln's old friend Orville Browning of Illinois told Johnson it was most important to have a Cabinet in agreement with its chief's policies. The President replied that in the Cabinet, as in a church, there ought to be unity on essentials, but that in nonessentials one could permit the greatest liberty and latitude. By then Johnson was finding anonymous letters in his mail:

"In the name of God Almighty do you intend to let this fellow Harlan remain in your Cabinet? Also, Otto, his assistant secretary, who, when the 'Veto' was passed over your head, shook hands with the Radicals, made FUN OF YOU."

It was indeed "indecent" of James Harlan to remain in the Interior Department, Johnson said to Browning, and if he had any sensibility he would resign. But to throw him out would be unpleasant. Perhaps he would leave voluntarily.

Harlan and Attorney General Speed and Postmaster General Dennison were annoyances, but Secretary of War Stanton was becoming a mortal danger. He was indiscreet, saying to Radical friends he was their ally. He told the Radical Congressman Samuel Shellabarger of Ohio he was for the Johnson who had spoken of hangings. Now that Johnson of the past had been replaced by an apostate in sympathy with traitors. But he would remain in the Cabinet, Stanton told Shellabarger. Someone had to thwart the President's evil aims.

Spring of 1866 came to the South. With the appearance of the first blooms, plans were made to decorate the graves that held soldiers of The Lost Cause. In the North the Radical papers said the Ladies' Aid and Remembrance associations were another sign the South was still rebellious. But soon there was something far more serious for the "SOUTHERN OUTRAGES" columns.

In Memphis, Tennessee, a group of Negroes who had served in the Union artillery were waiting to be given their mustering-out pay. A policeman got into an argument with one of the former soldiers. Someone tripped the officer. Three days of rioting followed. The police burned, pillaged and freely used their guns. More than forty blacks, including women and children, died.

On the day the riots began, the Committee of Fifteen, the Committee on Reconstruction, offered recommendations for the wording of the Fourteenth Amendment. The Thirteenth had freed the slaves. The Fourteenth would make them truly whole American citizens with full protection under law. Many years later, its principal framer under Stevens, Representative John Bingham of Ohio, would say he intended the Fourteenth Amendment to apply also to the burgeoning corporations of the North, protecting them from any interference in their quest for greater riches. But what the public understood was that a series of measures had been introduced in Congress which would limit the power of the South. One measure stated that no one who had ever held an office requiring an oath of allegiance to the United States could hold any other public office if he had given aid and comfort to the late rebellion and thereby violated his original oath of allegiance. It would take a special act of congressional forgiveness for such a person to return to any position, civil or military, state or federal, legislative, judicial or executive. That meant the end of thousands of southern careers. It also meant the South would be run as a foreign holding is run by an empire, with administrators sent out from the homeland. A swarm of office seekers at once headed south. They would arrive, or so the quick legend had it, carrying all their worldly goods in a satchel made of a cut-up rug: carpetbaggers.

These northern newcomers, even the best of them, had an interest in proving to the freedmen that they were the friends of the blacks, as opposed to the native whites. In July a northern dentist, Dr. A. P. Dostie, who had migrated to New Orleans, spoke to a group of freedmen about a larger Radical meeting to be held a few days following. Its purpose was to establish long-lasting Radical government in Louisiana. "On Monday I want you to come in your power," he cried. "I want no cowards to come. I want only brave men to come, who will stand by us, and we will stand by them. Come, then, in your power to that meeting, or never go to another political meeting in this state. We have three hundred thousand black men. Also one hundred thousand good and true Union white men, who will fight for and beside the black race against the hell-bound rebels.

"There will be no puerile affair as at Memphis, but, if

interfered with, the streets of New Orleans will run with blood! . . . Though you have the traitor, Andrew Johnson, against you!"

The meeting was scheduled for July 30 at noon. Early that morning it was already apparent trouble would ensue. Groups of men and boys, many bearing weapons, gathered on street corners. The local authorities requested that United States troops be sent to the area of the building where the meeting would be held. General Absalom Baird, commanding the local garrison during the temporary absence of General Philip Sheridan, telegraphed Secretary of War Stanton to ask if it was the President's wish that federal troops should be involved in dealing with a local political meeting.

Stanton took the telegram, read it and put it in his desk.

At noon about one hundred Negroes came marching down Burgundy Street, headed for the Mechanics Institute, where the meeting was to be held. They had a drummer and a fifer, and a man to carry the American flag. Mobs crowding the sidewalks shouted a constant stream of abuse.

The marchers crossed Canal Street. One of them shoved a young boy on the curb. There was a scuffle. A black marcher fired a gun, and suddenly the streets were filled with running men and the sound of shots.

The Negroes broke for safety as the police and the mob closed around them. They made it into the Mechanics Institute where they hung a white flag out of a window. The police accepted the flag as a signal for surrender and began to enter the building. As they did, someone inside fired.

In one of the great cities of the South, Negroes and Radicals had fired upon ex-Confederates. The mob surged forward, screaming it would take no prisoners. Most of the police joined in. Some of the officers tried to prevent the slaughter of the outnumbered people inside the Institute, but there was no chance of success. On the other side of the city United States troops lounged in their quarters while the mob swept into the building, caught Dr. Dostie and hacked him to pieces. More than two hundred other persons, almost all Negroes or Radicals, died in what the northern newspapers immediately called the Saint Bartholomew's Day * of New Orleans.

The reaction in the North was a combination of horror at the butchery and rage at a Commander-in-Chief whose troops had not been ordered to the scene. Fear was present too. Perhaps the riot meant that the war was going to begin again.

That Stanton had never shown Johnson the telegram from General Baird was not known. The Secretary of War himself told Sumner that Johnson was the "author" of the massacre. There was hardly a northern publication that did not echo his charges. The New York *Tribune* declared Johnson had committed "cold-blooded murder." *Independent* Magazine said, "This man aided and abetted the New Orleans mob. He doubly inspired the murderers."

Secretary Welles countered by saying the Radicals had fomented the massacre to prove that the late rebels could not be trusted with place or power, and an advertisement was placed in anti-Radical papers: *Wanted: Southern riots to help the Radicals. . . . A number of riots are desired at various points in the South. . . . If twenty or thirty Negroes, martyrs of liberty, can be killed at each of these places, so much the better for the Radical cause. For further particulars, terms of compensation, etc., apply to Old Thad Stevens.* But for most of the North what Charles Sumner told a Boston meeting seemed to have the ring of truth:

"Witness Memphis. Witness New Orleans," Sumner cried. The South was now the sepulcher of human rights. "Who can doubt that the President is the author of these tragedies? Charles IX of France was not more completely the author of the massacre of Saint Bartholomew. Andrew Johnson is the author of these recent massacres which now cry out for judgment.

"History records that the guilty king was pursued in the silence of the night by the imploring voices of murdered men, mingled with curses and imprecations, while their ghosts stalked through his chambers until he sweated blood from every pore;

* After the massacre of the French Huguenots on the saint's birthday in 1572.

and when he came to die, his soul, wrung with the tortures of remorse, stammered out to his attendant: 'Ah! nurse! My good nurse! What blood! What murders! Oh! what bad councils I followed! Lord God pardon me! have mercy on me!'

"Like causes produce like effects. The blood at Memphis and New Orleans must cry out until it is heard, and a guilty President may suffer the same retribution which followed a guilty king."

Johnson's term had more than two years to run. He had lost the leaders of the Republican party. Those Republicans more moderate or conservative than Radical supported him at their peril. The lash of party obligations would come down upon their backs if they deviated from what the Stevenses and Sumners and Wades decreed was party policy.

The President knew he could never go back to the Democrats, for they represented the rebellion and the Copperheads, those northerners deemed to have been, at best, only lukewarm in their support of the war.

If he was to have any backing in the future Congresses of his Presidency, he must organize a new party for the 1866 fall elections. This new party would occupy the middle ground between the Radicals and the die-hard ex-Confederates. He canvassed the members of his Cabinet for their reactions; and Attorney General Speed, Postmaster General Dennison and Secretary of the Interior Harlan showed their views by resigning and openly endorsing the growing Radical group in whose eyes the President was His Accidency, King Andy the First. Stanton wrote a fiery letter to the President which Mrs. Stanton urged him to send. But the act would have to be followed by his resignation. He finally decided not to send the letter, explaining to his wife that he owed it to the memory of those who had died in the war to stay. Yet, he told his friends, it was agony for him to be part of such an Administration. Only duty kept him at his post.

The National Union party—such was the name of the new organization, borrowed from the heading under which the

Lincoln-Johnson ticket had run in 1864—scheduled its convention in Philadelphia on August 14. There was very little time to get matters in order, and doing so was not going to be an easy job. In Warrensburg, Missouri, Montgomery Blair's brother Frank called a meeting to speak of the aims of the new group, to say that it would save the country from the extremists of both North and South. A man in the audience got up and menacingly called Blair a liar. A friend of Blair's grabbed the man, but Blair indicated the man should be permitted to come forward. "I'll take care of the son of a bitch," he promised, fingering a pistol in his pocket. The man's son yanked out a knife and started forward, and another Blair supporter leaped forward with his own knife. The son died; the speakers' platform collapsed. In Massachusetts, the President's predecessor as Vice President, Hannibal Hamlin, resigned his job as collector of customs for the Port of Boston. Hamlin announced he did so to protest the formation of a party "consisting almost exclusively of those who actively engaged in the late rebellion and their late allies who sought by other means to cripple and embarrass the government. Did we fight down the rebellion to give the South more power?"

By then the *Harper's Weekly* cartoonist Thomas Nast was regularly picturing Andrew Johnson as Nero in his toga watching the slaughter of innocents in the Roman Colosseum, with the slaughtered people in the arena likened to the victims of the mob at New Orleans. Or, wearing the robes and crown suitable for King Andy the Indecent, the President was depicted handing down orders for the guillotining of Charles Sumner, as Liberty and Columbia, in chains at the foot of the throne, wept. Radicals mobilized crowds of blacks to break up rallies hailing the new party, and there were street battles in Philadelphia as the time for the convention approached.

The convention opened on the note that no one had any right to oppose the Union, either by secession or exclusion. The new Postmaster General, Alexander Randall, called the ten thousand persons in attendance to order and "The Star Spangled Banner" and "Dixie" were played. A door opened and the delegates marched in two by two. They were led by Governor James Orr of the "Johnson government" of South Carolina, who walked arm in arm with Major General Darius Couch of Massachusetts, the former commander of a Union army corps. That former enemies could meet now on a better plane of understanding, declared Senator James R. Doolittle of Wisconsin, was a sight noble enough to bring tears of happiness. His words were telegraphed to newspapers throughout the country, to be lambasted by the Radicals, who thereafter called the Philadelphia gathering The Tearful Convention, The Jeff Davis-Andy Johnson Convention and The Noah's Ark Convention.

When the National Unionists, who themselves called the meeting The Arm-in-Arm Convention, had finished, they went to Washington, where the President received them with General Grant standing at his side. Johnson thanked the delegates for coming and said it would be the task of the new party to change the mood of a Congress which, he said, was not really a true Congress because it represented only a portion of the states, the others having been excluded. "Hanging on the verge of government," he said, Congress was attempting to make disunion between the states a permanent condition.

A few days later the President left Washington. Ostensibly he was traveling to Chicago to dedicate the new Stephen A. Douglas monument. Actually he was going out to fight for his policy and for those congressional candidates who would support it.

Nothing like the tour he outlined had ever been attempted by a previous President. It was to be what he called "a swing around the circle." It would take him through almost every northern state save for those of New England. Welles, the Secretary of the Navy, and Seward, the Secretary of State,* would accompany him. Seward's worries about the safety of the Presidential train were relieved when General Grant also

* Although one side of the Secretary's face was permanently disfigured by Lewis Paine's knife, Seward had survived the assassination attempt with no other ill effects.

consented to make the trip. Grant's presence, Seward thought, would be a deterrent to any fanatic who might decide to fire on the party or dynamite the Special off the tracks.

Grant himself was not looking forward to the trip, and had agreed to go only when the President pointedly invited him just after signing promotions for a number of officers the General favored. Grant's political views were still an enigma. Everybody sought his backing, but he silently smoked his endless cigars and talked about horses. It was rumored that the President had asked Grant's backing in an armed coup d'etat which would dissolve Congress, and parallels were made to Cromwell's dispersal of the Long Parliament and Napoleon Bonaparte's breakup of the Council of Five Hundred. But no one knew if the rumors were correct, still less what Grant's answer had been.

On August 28, 1866, two weeks after The Arm-in-Arm Convention was called to order, the President went stumping for its candidates. Even as he left, other conventions were being held to counteract the one he had backed. "The rich traitor is caressed and the poor Unionist butchered with the connivance of Andrew Johnson," Roscoe Conkling of New York told the Loyal Union Convention. If, said Benjamin Butler of Massachusetts, the President managed to make the army his tool and called upon it to support him, the country's Union veterans would rise up and "sweep it away like cobwebs."

Johnson had not written out a great number of set speeches, and Secretary of the Treasury McCulloch and Orville Browning, who would soon be replacing Harlan in the Interior Department, warned him not to improvise. They had not forgotten the Washington's Birthday speech from the White House balcony. Senator Doolittle agreed, writing the President not to say anything extemporaneous beyond offers of simple acknowledgments for a kind reception.

Before noon on August 28 the four-car Special reached Baltimore, where the President was met by an enthusiastic crowd of one hundred thousand cheering people. But Baltimore had always been a pro-secession city. Lincoln had been told he would be killed if he openly went through the streets when coming to Washington for his first inauguration just before the war. Northern troops passing through Baltimore had been attacked by the city's citizens. (Bluff Ben Wade said the place should have been burnt to the ground.) Of all the cities north of Washington there was none less likely to have welcomed the Andrew Johnson of pre-Presidential days. The applause for him now was deafening. He did not speak.

The President continued on to Philadelphia where he spoke that night in a hotel ballroom. "Forget that we have been divided into parties," he cried out. "Let the interests of the great mass of people be promoted, and let parties sink into insignificance." The next day Johnson traveled up to Jersey City, where a chartered ferryboat took him and his party to Manhattan's Battery. There carriages brought them up Broadway to the sound of roaring cheers. John A. Rawlins, Grant's closest adviser, rode with the General of the Army and thought to himself that such an ovation had never before been heard in the country. Perhaps the cheers were really for Grant and Admiral David Farragut rather than the President, Rawlins decided.

But up ahead, behind the marching militia units, the President was bowing to the crowds. He made George Templeton Strong think of a basso called before the curtain. He was too assiduously doffing his hat, Strong thought. Because of this man going up Broadway, Strong believed, the events of 1861–65 might well be remembered as The First Southern War. The second would ravage the North as well as the South, Strong told himself.

They went up Broadway and came to Delmonico's at Fourteenth Street. A reception stand was on the Fifth Avenue side of the building. There the President reviewed twenty regiments. The cheering for him seemed enthusiastic. "What do you think of that, sir?" Welles asked. The President said it was wonderful. That night at a banquet he said again, as in the past, that the South had never been out of the Union, for that was impossible. Therefore, it could not be treated as a conquered country. "They are our brethren. They are part of ourselves. They are bone of our bone, and flesh of our flesh."

Let them be welcomed back into the heart of the great country, he said, not debased and degraded. If he could bring them back, he said, then with Simon of old he would cry, "I have seen the glory of thy salvation, let thy servant depart in peace." And he would die happy. "I would rather live in history in the affections of my countrymen, as the one who had consummated this great result, than be President of the United States forty times!"

The President stepped onto a balcony overlooking the crowds in the street. From there he denounced the Radicals who said he was a would-be dictator. "What have I got to gain now? From the office of alderman up to that of President of the United States, I have filled all positions." The next day he went up the Hudson to review the corps of cadets at West Point and then to Albany and more speeches. Then Schenectady, Utica, Syracuse, Seneca Falls, Canandaigua, Rochester, Lockport, Niagara Falls and Buffalo, shouting at each stop that he had begun as an alderman but was now the President, that he was a humble individual but he stood for a great thing: the Constitution. Grant turned fidgety listening to the repetition of the same theme. Often the General hid in the baggage car, smoking, until the train halted and he had to acknowledge the cheers offered the hero of the war. He did not say one word publicly.

The President's party headed toward Ohio, Bluff Ben Wade's state, Stanton's birthplace. Hecklers were starting to appear in the crowds. At one whistle-stop Johnson said that time did not permit him to make a speech. "Don't!" someone shouted. "Keep quiet until I have concluded!" the President shouted back.

Entering Cleveland, he denounced Congress as an illegal assemblage because it denied representation to eleven American states. The crowds were growing uglier and there was derisive laughter when he made his usual remarks about com-

mencing as an alderman. He did not seem to realize the newspapers had reported his earlier speeches. Ohio's Governor did
not come to greet the Chief Executive.

At the hotel Secretary Welles looked at the people outside and said it would be a mistake for the President to try to
address them. Johnson must have agreed, for he came onto the
hotel balcony and said he would not make a speech. But the
Radical papers had reported all through the trip that this was
his inevitable promise before launching into a full-blown oration, and so loud laughter greeted him.

He began to defend his policies again, talking of how
the two sections of the nation must unite and stand up for the
Constitution. Almost from the start listeners shouted insults.
Those who looked on thought a concerted effort was being
made to make him lose his temper.

The interruptions seemed almost continuous, and the
President dropped his train of thought when someone yelled,
"How about New Orleans?" He began to say the riot was the
work of the Radicals. Yells and groans drowned him out.
"Traitor!" someone screamed. The President yelled back, "I
wish I could see that man. Show yourself. Come out here where
I can see you. If you ever shoot a man, you will do it in the
dark." He went back to his speech, shouting that "the powers
of hell, death and Stevens" might combine against him but that
he would do what he thought was right, that they could not
deter him. "It's a lie!" people were yelling. He stopped speaking and went into the hotel.

In the view of the Radical papers, it was Washington's
Birthday and Inauguration Day all over again. A turncoat
demagogue was showing his coarseness in vulgar harangues
directed at voices shouting from the darkness. The whole trip
was a continual drunken orgy.

They went on to Indiana. The Governor of the state
did not appear to greet a President the newspapers said was
"reeling" to Chicago. Several times he was shouted down by
people yelling they had come to see Grant and Farragut, not
Andrew Johnson. At Ann Arbor people cheered for Grant

throughout the President's speech about how he was a humble individual who had begun as an alderman but now stood for the Constitution. Radical papers ran stories of the trip under headlines reading simply *I, ME,* or *MY.*

In Chicago he spoke at the Douglas monument dedication and then visited Lincoln's tomb at Springfield. Neither the Governor of Illinois nor Lincoln's widow met with the President. Mary Lincoln had written a friend (as she had before and would again) that she would go to her grave believing Andrew Johnson had something to do with her husband's assassination.

In southern Illinois there were continual shouts of "Liar!" People held up signs: NEW ORLEANS. At Bloomington someone screamed, "We don't want traitors hunting bread and butter at the home of Lincoln." Because of the uproar the President was unable to finish his speech. His prepared talk at a St. Louis banquet was followed by an extemporaneous address to the crowd outside the hotel. "Judas, Judas!" someone shouted from the darkness, and it became a drawn-out chant: "Judas, Judaas, Judaas." Senator James Doolittle had declared that every word the President said in public should be as carefully considered as if it were to be included in a state paper, but now Johnson responded to the chanting voices by shouting, "If I am a Judas, who is the Jesus Christ? Is he Thaddeus Stevens? Is he Charles Sumner?"

The crowd was screaming and hooting; and he, lost to logic and restraint, yelled into the darkness, "These are the men that compare themselves with the Saviour! And anybody who differs with them is denounced as a Judas!"

"Impeach him!" someone cried out, and the President shouted back that Congress might well try if the Radicals were not defeated in the coming elections. "But as we are talking about this Congress, let me call attention to this immaculate Congress. . . . Oh, yes, this Congress that could make war upon the Executive . . . because he stands for the Constitution and vindicates the rights of the people . . . exercising the veto power in their behalf. . . . Because he dared to do this . . . they clamor and talk about impeachment. . . . So far as offenses are concerned . . . upon this question of offenses . . . let me ask you what offenses I have committed."

"Plenty, here, tonight!" someone shrieked, and the President tried to answer the shouts by saying that the country's appointed officials had been corrupted by the Radicals.

"Kick 'em out!" someone yelled, and the President shouted back, "I will kick them out just as fast as I can." The crowd responded with cheers and insults. General Grant said to his aide John Rawlins that he had had enough, that he did not care to accompany someone who was digging his own grave. The two men concocted a story that Grant was anxious to visit his father in Cincinnati. Irritated by the whole business, Grant had been drinking, and, drunk, he departed. Surgeon General Barnes said he would take the General's pulse before he left. Also intoxicated, Barnes ended by falling over the patient. The tour went on, people calling for the departed Grant so regularly that the President was often unable to make himself heard.

In Indianapolis he tried to speak but was halted by shouts of "Shut up! We don't want to hear from you!" He tried again but finally was forced inside as fighting broke out. A man was killed.

Booed and hissed off the platform several times on the return trip through Ohio, he kept shouting about the Constitution, responding to demands that he hang Jeff Davis by asking if he should hang Thad Stevens too. It was all fatal, Senator Doolittle wrote the newly appointed Secretary of the Interior, Orville Browning.

But the President would not stop. In Pittsburgh a Radical band paraded, and the crowd kept yelling for Grant and Farragut whenever the President opened his mouth. "I bid you good night," he said when it was finally apparent that they would not let him speak. Earlier the mayor had left town, saying he did so "to preserve my self-respect."

Johnson went on with his doomed trip, arousing in some a head-shaking respect for a President who endured such calumny in an attempt to make clear his beliefs. One whose respect grew was Seward. So urbane, so well-mannered and perpetually pleasant, the Secretary of State seemed unable to become angry with anyone. Though Seward would have handled things differently, his viewpoint was essentially the same as the President's. Thad Stevens sometimes wondered if Seward was the real cause of the predicament they all found themselves in. Johnson had had good ideas earlier in his career when he was "clothed and in his right mind," Stevens said. Then Seward had "entered into him and ever since they have been running down deep places into the sea." Albert Riddle, Bluff Ben Wade's friend and biographer, found Stevens' bitterness shocking when, referring to Seward's attempted assassination, he snarled, "What a bungler Paine was!"

In Harrisburg, Seward fell gravely ill. Cholera was suspected. Doctors ordered him to remain behind in one of the train's sidetracked coaches where the President and Secretary Welles came to visit him. Seward raised his head and whispered, "My mind is clear, and I wish to say that your course is right, and that I have felt it my duty to sustain you in it; and if my life is spared I shall continue to do so.

"Pursue it for the sake of the country. It is correct."

The President continued on to Washington, reaching the city on September 15 at seven in the evening. He stopped at City Hall to make his usual remarks, then continued to the White House, where he spoke again for the last time on the Swing Around the Circle. He had made more than one hundred speeches in the nineteen-day journey. The humorist David R. Locke, who wrote under the name of "Petroleum Nasby," devastatingly summed up:

✛ He who now addresses you is a Humble Individual.

✛ I have filled all the offices which the nation has to bestow, from Alderman up to the President of the United States. I leave the Constitution in your hands.

✛ I am no traitor; Mr. Seward is no traitor; nobody that supports My Policy is a traitor.

✛ The members of Congress who oppose My Policy are all traitors; everybody who opposes My Policy is a traitor. I leave the Constitution in your hands.

❖ Seward is my friend and I am Seward's friend; Seward likes me and I like Seward; Seward is a good fellow and I am a good fellow; we like each other. We leave the Constitution in this town.

❖ I have served my country in all capacities. I began life as an Alderman, was a Mayor during my infancy, was State Senator in my childhood, became a Representative in my early youth, attained my majority in the Senate of the United States, and now, in the prime of my manhood, I am President.

❖ Who wants niggers to vote? If the northern states want niggers to vote, why don't they let them vote at home? Niggers shan't vote; I desire them to have the same chances as white men.

❖ The Congressmen who voted for the Freedmen's Bureau Bill and the Civil Rights Bill are all fools. I should like to fight the whole one hundred and eighty-two of them. I won't leave the Constitution with nary one of them.

❖ I repeat Seward is a good fellow; he stands by me and I stand by him; I am not afraid of a subsidized and mercenary press; all loyal people may go to the devil; Douglas was a friend of mine; I am going to erect a monument over him; I am not upon an electioneering tour; I have not punished any southern traitors, but I mean to make it up punishing lots of northern traitors; every man who does not go for me is a traitor; I can't be a traitor, because I have been an Alderman, then a Mayor, then a State Senator, then a Representative, then a member of the United States Senate, and then President.

Charles Sumner roared that the President had done more evil in the time he had ruled than anyone in history and was "the author of incalculable woe to his country." Stevens was more subtle. His doctor, Old Thad told a crowd at Lancaster, had ordered that he take the summer off, do no thinking, speaking or reading. He had followed the first injunction, he said, and did not permit a thought to enter his mind. Now it was true that he was being seduced into this one small speech. As for reading, "I have amused myself with a little light, frivolous reading. For instance, there was a serial account from day to day of a very remarkable circus that traveled through the country, from Washington to Chicago and St. Louis, and from Louisville back to Washington. I read that with some interest. . . . I expected great wit from the celebrated character of the clowns.

"One in particular was interesting. He had been a tailor. I think he did not say drunken tailor. He had been a constable. He had been city alderman. He had been in the legislature. God help that legislature! He had been in Congress; and now he was President. He had been everything but one. He had never been a hangman, and he asked leave to hang Thad Stevens."

Rumors circulated throughout the country that cars of Johnson's train had become traveling barrooms, that the President had failed to pay for liquor ordered in half the towns he visited, that he was, as the White House guard William Crook noted, "almost a monster." Shortly after the trip the President told Orville Browning that "he had no doubt there was a conspiracy afoot among the Radicals to incite another revolution, and especially to arm and exasperate the Negroes." He then asked Secretary of War Stanton how many troops were available to quell disturbances in Baltimore. Fifteen hundred men, Stanton replied. Johnson ordered that additional detachments be sent into Maryland. The Radical press speculated that troops were being assembled near Washington so that the President could stage a coup d'etat if the elections went against him. At the same time General Solomon Meredith of Indiana was told by the Governors of Illinois and Missouri that if the voters went against Johnson in the elections, the Radicals would immediately depose the President and set up a military dictatorship. The only question at issue was who would be the country's new leader. Grant and Sherman had been judged unreliable, Meredith reported to Orville Browning. It would have to be someone else.

Perhaps the two Governors did not know that a coolness had developed between the President and the General of the Army. With no knowledge of politics, interested mainly in horses and, as his confidant John Rawlins said, only good for fighting, Grant had concluded that Johnson was planning some sort of revolution. He wrote Philip Sheridan that no one loyal during the war had influence with the President, "unless they join in a crusade against Congress, and declare the body itself illegal, unconstitutional and revolutionary."

After the Swing Around the Circle, Johnson told Grant he would like him to travel to Mexico to look into the affairs of the Mexican Emperor Maximilian. Hopefully for American interests, Maximilian would soon be toppled from power. Grant replied he did not care to go. Later, sitting in at a Cabinet meeting, the General was startled when he heard the President say that he was leaving for Mexico.

"You know," Grant said, "I told you that it would not be convenient for me to go to Mexico." Perhaps the General believed that he was being sent away so that the President's coup d'etat could be carried out more easily.

Johnson stood up at the head of the Cabinet table and banged his hand down. "I would like to know if there is an officer of the army who will not obey my orders!" he snapped. Perhaps it was in Johnson's mind that Grant was reluctant to be out of Washington when the threatened Radical coup took place.

Grant took his hat and stood up. "I am an officer of the army, but I am a citizen also," he said. "The service you ask me to perform is a civil service, and as a citizen I may accept or decline it, and I decline it." Sherman was sent in his stead.

Meanwhile the Radical leader William G. ("Parson") Brownlow was saying a new war with the South was inevitable. The North, he suggested, should fight with three units: the first "to do the killing," the second "armed with pine torches and spirits of turpentine" to do the burning, and the third with surveyors' chains and compasses to divide the land and give it to those loyal to the North.

After the most intensive campaigning ever seen in a non-Presidential year, the people went to the polls—and the Radicals won.

9

Despite the fact that at seventy-four he was on occasion unable to speak more than a sentence at a time before halting for breath, that his Negro mistress worried over his health and his associates asked themselves how long he could carry on, Old Thad, his wig awry, seemed happy when he came back to Washington for the new session of Congress, which began in December. He remarked sardonically that he had the votes now. In the previous session he had been a mere conservative. Now he was going to be a Radical.

Looking back years later, Carl Schurz compared Stevens to a charged electrical wire in his determination to prevail over Andrew Johnson. A fellow Representative discussed a contested election with Stevens, contending both contestants were rascals. "Which is *our* rascal?" Stevens asked. Schurz decided Old Thad would have seated Beelzebub in preference to the Angel Gabriel if he thought the former more likely to aid him in beating the President's policy.

Brutal in the way he addressed people, telling those Congressmen who questioned his dictates that they had better vote as he ordered or confess themselves cowards, Stevens spun his web around the President and the South. Before the session was an hour old Charles Sumner introduced a bill to give votes to the Negroes of the District of Columbia. Both houses approved the measure within two weeks. The President sent it back with a veto message reminding the lawmakers that less than two years earlier a referendum had been held on the question and that only thirty-six District voters out of seven thousand had cast affirmative ballots. European white immigrants were excluded from the franchise until they had been in the country for five years. Even then these white citizens had to furnish evidence of good character. Was it prudent to give the vote to a mass of totally uneducated people who only yesterday were bought and sold in the same manner as cows and mules?

Privately the President told his intimates that this was one more wedge by which the Radicals would assure themselves permanent political dominance. They would extend the Negro ballot from the District to the late Confederate states where the blacks would vote precisely as they were ordered by their Radical overseers. They would be told the heavens would fall and the skies turn red if they did not vote for the right people, and they would believe it. The result would be the setting of one race against another, he said. The consequences could only be chaos and horror.

The suffrage veto was overridden the day the Senate received it. The House followed suit the next day. Later that month, January, 1867, Congress gave Negroes the vote in the Territories of the United States. That meant that in all areas under direct congressional control the black had become peer of the white man at the ballot box.

But of course it was the South which most concerned Stevens. "Some proper pain must be inflicted on the people who constituted the 'Confederate States of America,' " he said. They had waged an unjust war against the United States, "a rebellion only less guilty than that of the devilish angels." Now they were unrepentant in defeat. They had arrogantly tried to inject traitors into the Congress. Although they had failed in Washington they had succeeded in the same design on the state level, putting the rebels into office under the "Johnson governments."

Was the North to accept, Stevens asked, these "Johnson governments" seeking to perpetuate the old ways of prewar? Here were high criminals who had not been punished as they deserved, but had "simply exchanged forgiveness with the President and been sent on their way rejoicing." These state governments and their creator, the President, must be bypassed.

Let there be no talk about that "morbid sensitivity, sometimes called mercy, which affects a few of all classes, from the priest to the clown, which has more sympathy for the murderer on the gallows than for his victim." Let a mailed fist come crashing down, Stevens said. Congress stayed in session day and night. Under Old Thad's direction an act was rushed through the House and Senate that put the entire former Confederacy under the rule of the United States Army. The war had been over for two years.

Under the terms of the act the South was divided into five military districts. Each district was ruled by a commanding officer, who had the power of a viceroy. He might permit the "Johnson governments" to exercise some authority if he wished, but he was empowered to step in whenever he felt any error had been made. He could set up military tribunals to try cases, he could suspend the power of any police official, he could punish or decree punishment as he saw fit. He commanded an army of occupation in hostile territory. These were the facts. Let the South accept them. Let true Reconstruction begin.

In the opinion of Navy Secretary Welles, military Reconstruction meant substituting the decisions of soldiers for all the enactments and laws of eleven American states. It meant overthrowing Constitutional provisions about self-government with as little concern as though they had been resolutions of last year's party convention. It meant condemning American citizens by means of ex post facto law. The organic structure of the country was less binding than the will of Congress. And Congress, Welles said, was essentially one evil old man.

Johnson himself protested that to deny southerners the right to govern themselves was a subversion of all democratic principles. Congress did not listen. Instead, a supplementary act was passed which ruled that the President could not directly give orders to the officers of the army. To permit him to exercise the functions of a commander-in-chief was to ask for a coup d'etat, said the Radicals. So by law he was limited to giving orders through the General of the Army, Grant. It would be illegal for any soldier to accept a Presidential order which did not come through Grant. The President was also expressly forbidden to order the General of the Army away from Washington without that officer's consent.

The President protested anew against what his friends called the "Force Bills." Such acts, they said, set up military satraps, Caesars; they trampled over the civil rights of the American citizens of eleven states. Stevens replied that if anything, the bills were too mild and that anyone who opposed them was all for "hugging and caressing those whose hands are red and whose garments are dripping with the blood of our and their murdered kindred."

Congress generally agreed with Stevens, or at least to the extent that its members routinely voted to override the Presidential vetoes of the "Force Bills." Those members with full knowledge of who had drawn up the bills smiled.

For Secretary of War Stanton had been their author. When Congress met to convene he had sent a note to the Radical Congressman George Boutwell of Massachusetts asking him to call at the War Department. Stanton took Boutwell into a private room where they could be alone. The Secretary of War told the Congressman that he was more worried over recent developments than he had been at any point during the war. He was fearful that the President would reorganize the government by assembling a new Congress composed of rebels and northern Copperheads. Johnson would then throw out the real Congress with bayonets. He must be limited, the Secretary said. Then Stanton dictated the terms of the military bills which Boutwell introduced under Stevens' direction and which Congress passed.

His military power gone, the President still controlled

the government's civil officers. On the Swing Around the Circle he had told an audience in St. Louis that he was going to get rid of his enemies in the government: "I will kick them out just as fast as I can." The Radicals countered that good men must be given protection. "There, sir, is the duty of the hour," Sumner told the Senate. The Congress must act because there was a President of the United States who had "become the enemy of his country."

"Do not forget," Sumner went on, "that we stand face to face with an enormous and malignant usurper, through whom the Republic is imperiled. You must not forget that the President is a bad man, the author of incalculable woe to his country. . . . Search history and I am sure you will find no elected ruler who, during the same short time, had done so much mischief to his country. He stands alone in bad eminence."

So the Tenure of Office Bill was passed through both houses of Congress. The President vetoed it. Congress passed it over his veto. It became law. It decreed that the President could not discharge any civil officer of the government who had been appointed with the "advice and consent" of the Senate unless the Senate gave its permission. Thus the President would be stymied from making any changes in his official family; thus, said Stevens, Andrew Johnson would be unable to appoint new men who might do his bidding and, by doing so, prove themselves "the most filthy reptiles who ever crawled into office."

But the bill should have been more extensive, Sumner lamented. He had wanted it to cover every federal employee who made as much as twenty dollars a week. He would have extended its protection down to a night watchman, he told the Senate. They must remember with whom they dealt: Jefferson Davis' successor who "exposed himself in a condition of intoxication while taking the oath of office," sold pardons, freed rebels, gave "maudlin speeches" and "degraded the country as it was never degraded before."

Though he said he regretted the battle with Johnson, Sumner did not seem an unhappy man. Perhaps it was that the

Senator's personal life had changed dramatically. The last of his mother's nine children, Sumner had continued to live with her during the twenty-seven years of her widowhood. In June, 1866, his mother died. Four months later Sumner, fifty-six years old and certainly a virgin, his friends said, got married.

The new Mrs. Sumner was Alice Mason Hooper, the widow of a Union army captain. The captain had been the son of Representative Samuel Hooper of Massachusetts, at whose house Johnson had lived during the first weeks of his Presidency. Alice Hooper was twenty-eight, rich, intelligent, strong-willed, beautiful, certainly one of the "catches" of Washington and Boston. She was also outspoken. Those who knew her wondered what would happen the first time she ordered Charles Sumner to keep quiet, using one of her favorite expressions: "God damn you!"

The couple moved into an elaborate home, where they gave elegant dinner parties for such guests as Stevens, Speaker of the House Schuyler Colfax, and the leading members of the diplomatic corps. One visitor was a young Prussian attaché whose frequent attendance upon the new bride became an immediate subject of Washington speculation.

Sumner's numerous enemies jibed at him for his December-May marriage. Strange that he had not "selected a sable daughter of Africa" for his bride, declared Garrett Davis of Kentucky in the Senate. Sumner ignored him. It was just another remark from an opponent who spoke "in the voice of slavery."

That voice was still strong in the South, Sumner warned. So the Congress must decide on the standards the South needed to meet before it could rejoin the American nation. Congress ruled that all who had participated in the rebellion could not vote. Thus were excluded five out of six men. Only those who had not joined the southern cause could elect the new legislators, Governors, Senators and Representatives who could shape the new South. The blacks were given the vote and, of course, the northerners who had gone south—the carpetbaggers.

It was the final end of the old order from the Potomac to

the Rio Grande in a South where lemonade parties had replaced champagne and dress balls, and rude carryalls were substituted for the brilliant equipages of prewar days. ("My cart de visite," one lady said of her mule-drawn conveyance.) Before the war the South had far more colleges than the North; now the graduates were subordinate to the field hand and the groom who went to nightly meetings of the Loyal Legion, the arm of Radicalism in the South. There, in ceremonies lit by torches and attended by clanking chains and keening music, the ex-slaves pledged themselves to stand with the Loyal Legion. The pledge, given under a picture of Lincoln, was inviolable. Legion officers, for the most part northerners, told the Negroes that they would yet be given their forty acres and a mule if they abided . by the pledge. Failure to do so could mean threats, beatings, night visits.

What the Legion was, no white southerner could ever really know; but rumors said it stood for barn-burning, rape, race war. The Legion owned guns and ammunition, and its members could be seen drilling and firing off volleys as they sang the old Union army songs. To the southerners a drunk Loyal Legion member seemed infinitely more dangerous than his white counterpart. For it was said that to call the black man to order might result in a night visit from a dozen of his fellow Legion members. Any white who complained to the federal authorities might be charged with obstructing the civil rights of a freedman.

The Chivalrics and Southrons of antebellum days tried to continue their old ways in this new world the war had brought. All through the South they held what they called tournaments. The young Confederate veterans dressed up in medieval attire and called themselves the Knight of Truth or the Lord of Duty. Riding full tilt, they tried to put a lance through a circle so that they might receive a crown from the Queen of Love and Beauty.

Other organizations suddenly appeared in those late winter and early spring days of 1867 when congressional Reconstruction got under way. One group was formed in Pulaski,

Tennessee, when some young veterans—boys, really—decided to organize a club. Why not call themselves the Kuklos, one young man asked. It meant "band" or "circle" in Greek. But the name was cumbersome. Another boy called out, *"Call it the Ku Klux."*

The first great parade was held on July 4, 1867, at night. Wearing high-peaked hats and long robes, the Klan came riding on horses draped in white. They appeared in cities and villages with funereal slowness and in deathlike silence. They moved in long, disciplined lines, circling the square and traversing the nearby streets to come into the square again. Silently they moved in obedience to unspoken orders from their leaders. They moved too, men said, in response to something that was noble and heroic. They were brother to those secret organizations made up of other victims of despotism: the Confrèries of medieval France, the Carbonari of Italy, Vehmgericht of Germany, the Nihilists of Russia.

In their view they alone stood ready to protect the disenfranchised South from the fanatic Puritan allied to the barbaric African. They alone opposed the carpetbagger who had come to pick the bones of the defeated foe, and the southern scalawag who collaborated with the oppressor for his own profit. They were the opposition to bayonet government.

Soon the new voting regulations would put illiterate field hands into the statehouses of the South. There the blacks would order up gold watches, Westphalian hams, imported mushrooms, champagne, velvet tête-à-têtes, perfumes, ladies' hoods, bonnets, chemises. Everything would be charged to the taxpayers, among whose number the new legislators were not to be found, because they had nothing that could be taxed.

The new congressional Reconstruction state governments, led by Governors born in Maine or New Jersey, quadrupled prewar taxes, floated enormous bond issues, sold railroad concessions. The northern journalist James S. Pike observed that there were southern Governors spending thirty or forty thousand dollars a year while receiving salaries of less than one-tenth that amount. The South Carolina Legislature, largely black under congressional Reconstruction, kept a taxpayer-financed bar open day and night. All drinks, food and cigars were free. The voters who put the legislators into office often appeared at the polls carrying a bucket for the mess of ballots they would take home for supper.

"Manufactured voters," said General Sherman contemptuously, and from the ranks of the blacks came what the journalist Pike thought was "the most ignorant democracy that mankind ever saw . . . the slave rioting in the halls of his master, and putting that master under his feet. And, though it is done without malice and without vengeance, it is nevertheless completely and absolutely done."

In the volunteer schools, the Yankee schoolmarms taught the black children to sing "John Brown's Body." It was rumored the Loyal Legion encouraged former slaves to address their prewar masters by their Christian names. Observing the Legion musket drills, the Vicksburg, Mississippi, correspondent of the New York *Herald* noted a change: the question in the South no longer was, "What shall we do with the nigger?" Now it was, "What will the nigger do with us?" There was always the possibility that the carpetbagger state governments or the Congress would confiscate land and give it to the freedmen.

Yankeedom was putting into practice in another man's home the abstract theories of a speculative humanitarianism, the southerners told each other. And nothing could be done about it. Any protesting white man would be seen as one of the rebels at whose hands three hundred thousand Boys in Blue had perished.

So the Ku Klux rode out. Notes were pinned to the town pump or to the coffins they left in the yards of men's homes: *The Lion Tracks the Jackal, the Bear the Wolf. The Serpent and Scorpion Are Ready. Some Shall Weep and Some Shall Pray. The Death Watch Is Set. The Last Hour Cometh. The Moon Is Full. Burst Your Cerements Asunder. The Guilty Shall Be Punished.*

The hooded men came at night to the Negro cabins,

white shrouds floating as they rushed by, shouting, "We are the Ku Klux, straight from hell!" They told the frightened listeners they had come from a spot between the moon and the seven stars, and were the Confederate dead of Shiloh, Chickamauga, Manassas Gap and Gettysburg. They had returned to warn of the horrible monster who lived in the swamps and ate nothing but nigger meat. Silently they sat in their white robes on the gravestones which members of the Loyal Legions would pass on their way to meetings.

Daggers Glimmer . . . Some Live Today, Tomorrow Die . . . The Dark and Dismal Hour Draws Near . . . When the Black Cat Is Gliding Under the Shadows of Darkness and the Death Watch Ticks at the Lone Hour of Midnight, Then We Pale Riders Are Abroad. Perish the Guilty! When the Finger of the White Skeleton Points to the New-Made Grave, Brothers Strike!

Spare None!

On occasion a lone horseman rode into a Negro settlement, a long, red flannel tongue dangling from his mouth and animal horns suggestive of the devil attached to his conical hat. He was thirsty. A bucket of water would be emptied. Bring more, he would command. Again he would empty a bucket—into a goatskin bag hanging from his throat but concealed under the flowing white robe. Good water, the freedmen would be told, and most welcome, for the rider had not had a drink since he was killed at the Battle of Atlanta three years before. A warning would follow about what happened to darkies who forgot their place, and then the rider would slowly drift away, his horse's hoofs wrapped in muffles making no noise.

"We are in the hands of camp followers, horse holders, cooks, bottle washers and thieves," said the former Confederate General J. H. Clanton of Alabama. "We have passed from the hands of the brave soldiers who overcame us and are turned over to the tender mercies of squaws for torture." In the legislatures of the southern states employees frittered their time away, messengers, porters, pages, doorkeepers, chaplains, sergeants-at-arms, boards and commissions set up to perform useless tasks. Their salaries and their bribes drove up taxes so that soon the rates would be 800 percent higher in Mississippi than before the war, 500 percent in North Carolina. To object was to be called "an enemy of the colored man and the Unionist."

A Member of the British Parliament visited Louisiana and asked if there were any great curiosities he might observe. He was told there was one that could not be seen in any civilized country. Then he was taken to the legislature. (If the new statesmen were "turned loose in the Zoological Gardens," said the Mobile *Tribune,* "the animals would collapse with laughter.")

The South Carolina Legislature vote of one thousand dollars to its Speaker to recompense him for a bet he lost on a horse race typified congressional Reconstruction in the South's view. To Thad Stevens and Charles Sumner in Washington here was justice for those who made the rebellion. And of course, the southerners said, the ex-slaves would always vote the way Stevens and Sumner desired. The Loyal Legion carpetbaggers would tell them that the Bible mentioned only two classes of voters: the Republicans and the Sinners. (At Selma, Alabama, a man arose in front of the polling place and held up the blue ticket denoting the conservative slate. "No land!" he shouted. "No mules! No votes! Slavery again!" Then he held up the red Radical ticket. "Forty acres of land! A mule! Freedom! Votes! Equal of a white man!")

To protect what they had, and what they wanted to do, that mass of idealist, opportunist, missionary, looter, philosopher, free-booter, experimenter and soldier of fortune which formed the Reconstruction gathered itself to fight. The enemy was the Ku Klux and the other lesser organizations who claimed in their membership virtually every able-bodied white man of the South: The Knights of the White Camelia, the Pale Faces, the White Boys. Here were no ghosts or haunts, the Loyal Legion told its people. Men began to defy the hooded figures, and, quickly responding, The Invisible Empire of the Ku Klux Klan with its Grand Cyclops and Genii, its Night Hawks and Ghouls, went from tomfoolery to something else. One of the Alabama founders remembered years later, "Three notably offensive Negro men were dragged from their beds, escorted to the old boneyard (three-quarters of a mile from Tuscaloosa) and thrashed in the regular antebellum style until their unnatural nigger pride had a tumble, and humbleness to the white man reigned supreme."

The members of the Klan told one another they were really peace police, but soon they were leaving signs on doors ordering people to get out of town, and horsewhipping carpetbaggers and scalawags. And then the lynching and raping began.

In the summer of 1867, federal cavalry, dispatched by the Reconstruction state governments, came pounding down the empty roads separating the small and silent towns. But when the soldiers arrived it was always too late. The Ku Klux had melted back into the sullen population. "Education is the ruination of the nigger generation," the Klansmen sang, and they burnt the schools.

They sang, also:

> Oh, I'm a good old Rebel,
> Now that's just what I am
> For this "Fair Land of Freedom"
> I do not care a damn.
> I'm glad I fit against it—
> I only wish we'd won
> And I don't want no pardon
> For anything I've done.
>
> I hate the Yankee Nation
> And everything they do;
> I hate the Declaration
> Of Independence too.
> I hate the glorious Union
> 'Tis dripping with our blood;
> I hate the striped banner—
> I fit it all I could.

I can't take up my musket
And fight 'em now no more.
But I ain't a-goin' to love 'em,
Now that is certain sure.
And I don't want no pardon
For what I was and am;
I won't be reconstructed,
And I don't care a damn.*

From Washington came congressional ukases granting more power to the federal commanders. In Louisiana, Sheridan removed the mayor of New Orleans and the Governor of the state, appointing as replacements men described to the President as "imported Yankees" sent down to "irritate and insult" the citizens. From Washington also came new tax laws aimed at helping the foundry and mill owners and railroad magnates of the industrializing North but ruinous to the cotton and tobacco planters of the agricultural South.

The President, that "cipher" to Sumner, was helpless. Congress was Radical. There remained the third branch of the government, the Supreme Court. Before it was voted out by Negro and carpetbagger ballots, the "Johnson government" of Mississippi appealed to the Court to restrain the President from enforcing the bills passed over his veto. At once Congressmen rose to say it was they who represented the people, not the Supreme Court.

Let the Court "defy a free people's will," said Representative John Bingham of Ohio and the Committee of Fifteen, and the people, "insulted and defied," would demand, and get, a Constitutional amendment abolishing the Court. Representative George Boutwell echoed the threat: perhaps it was time for the legislative branch to put certain matters above the jurisdiction of the high Court. Such bills were then introduced. One passed. The President vetoed it on the grounds that it was subversive of the Constitution in that it upset the three-part checks-and-balances system of the American govern-

* First printed in the Augusta, Georgia, *Weekly Constitutionalist,* July 10, 1867, and "respectfully dedicated to Thad Stevens."

ment. Congress passed the bill over his veto. The Justices then dismissed Mississippi's "Johnson government" case on the grounds that they had no jurisdiction in the matter.

The "Johnson government" of Georgia sought to put the Force Bills aside by appealing to the Court to restrain Secretary of War Stanton from sending troops to the South. The Court ruled that he was an agent of the President and therefore no other branch of government could interfere with him. Other attempts to get the Court to act also failed. Soon the last of the "Johnson governments" would be replaced by the congressional Reconstructionists. There would be no more appeals.

King Andrew the Indecent, though de-fanged, was still dangerous, Congressmen told one another. The Thirty-ninth Congress was about to end, but to adjourn for several months might prove fatal. The despot in the White House—he was believed by many to be the secret Grand Wizard of the Ku Klux Klan—would run amok, bring in troops and raise the Confederacy's Stars and Bars on the Capitol's flagstaff.

Therefore the Fortieth Congress must be convened as soon as the Thirty-ninth ended. So, on March 4, 1867, the Senate doors were opened, and everyone filed out. The Chamber stayed empty for half an hour and then the legislators and spectators returned to see the new Senate president pro tem, Bluff Ben Wade, declare the Fortieth Congress in session. The President's new Attorney General, Henry Stanbery, declared it was absolutely illegal for Congress to convene itself in special session without a Presidential call. Nobody paid any attention.

Perhaps the most outstanding new member of the Congress was Representative Benjamin Butler of Massachusetts. Physically he was grotesque. His left eye was disfigured from birth, and the eyelid drooped over it. According to Colonel Theodore Lyman, Butler had "a set of legs and arms that look as if made for somebody else, and hastily glued to him by mistake." His features habitually wore a wild look, and his manner of expressing himself caused people to believe that the legend his father had been hanged as a pirate was very likely correct. A political opponent charged by Butler with having a venereal disease said nature had put her seal on him by giving him a face like a "Borneo ape" which, "like a wrecker's light, warns all whom it may concern to be on the lookout."

A supporter of Jefferson Davis for the Democratic Presidential nomination in 1860, Butler became a political General in the Union army, commanding the wartime occupation forces holding New Orleans. Rumors of bribery, the shipment of contraband, personal confiscations and illegal sales of cotton dominated his reign.

But it was his "Woman Order" which made him famous, or infamous. One day as Butler walked under a New Orleans balcony, six women upon it sneered, turned, lifted their skirts and walked inside. "Those women evidently know which end of them looks the best," Butler roared out, and declared that any woman who by "word, gesture or movement" showed contempt for a United States officer should be regarded and treated "as a woman of the town plying her avocation."

In effect he was inviting his soldiers to use the women of New Orleans as they wished. The Confederate government in Richmond declared Butler outside the rules of civilized warfare, an outlaw to be shot if captured. Prime Minister Lord Palmerston told the House of Commons that "Englishmen must blush to think such an act has been committed by a man belonging to the Anglo-Saxon race." Butler routinely cursed the Confederate authorities and said Palmerston was a good example of the wife beaters of England.

During the funeral procession of a Union officer Butler heard the laughter of a lady belonging to an illustrious New Orleans family. He confined her to jail for two months, saying she was not "a vulgar woman of the town but an uncommonly vulgar one." She was permitted to speak to no one save her maid and Butler himself. He hanged a New Orleans gambler on the spot where the man had defiantly torn down the United States flag. Behind his back people referred to him as "Beast Butler."

While Butler commanded at New Orleans his brother circulated in Union-held areas, putting pressure on men to sell him cotton and turpentine at cut-rate prices. When the deals were brought to light Butler said his brother did it to save the government the cost of other ballast to be used on ships headed north. To "Beast" was joined the nickname "Spoons," commemorating his stay in a requisitioned southern mansion. The family silver had vanished while he lived there.

Disliked by his own troops—cries of "Lobster-eyed son of a bitch" and "Who stole the spoons?" came from the ranks when he passed by—he went north to command an amphibious landing aimed at reducing the Confederate stronghold of Fort Fisher in Virginia. His conduct would have brought him before a firing squad in a European army. In charge of an overwhelming force, he completely botched the operation. Grant said he must be relieved of any command for the good of the service, and so, attended by the usual uproar which marked his comings and goings, he gave up the military life.

Withal, he was an effective if brutal lawyer. When Lincoln's death put Andrew Johnson into the White House, Butler was immediately sent for by Ben Wade to offer legal advice to the new leader. Johnson conferred with Butler and asked what obligations rested upon the Union because of Grant's liberal terms to Lee. Butler replied that since the war was over, it was no longer a question of dealing with prisoners of war, but rather with war criminals. Therefore Johnson had the legal right to hang the Confederate leaders, including Lee, and in fact should do so.*

Then Johnson ceased his talk of executions and the Radicals revolted, their ranks to be joined by Ben Butler, who ran for Congress when the President made his Swing Around the Circle. During the campaign he termed his detractors fools

* Johnson communicated this opinion to Grant, who replied that the day Lee was arrested would be the day Grant gave up his commission.

and said he had faced their masters in New Orleans. "I have hung your betters," he roared as shouts of "Spoons" and "Fort Fisher" came up to him. "Do you suppose that I will flinch before you? A man who has smelled gunpowder can stand rum and garlic!" Johnson to him by then was a monster usurper, Booth's accomplice, a drunken traitor. The Radical sweep put him into the House of Representatives of the Fortieth Congress as it convened after the half-hour pause between sessions. Within three days he rose to say: *Impeach.*

10

It was not the first time that word had been spoken on the floor of the House. Representative Benjamin Loan of Missouri had earlier declared there was a usurper in the White House who had come to power through an assassin's bullet bought by rebel gold. Representative James M. Ashley of Ohio, a close friend of Secretary of War Stanton, agreed, and asked that the Committee on the Judiciary be authorized to look into the question of whether the President should be impeached. The resolution passed by overwhelming vote. ("Damn your conscience!" snapped Thad Stevens at one man who said his conscience would not permit him to vote in the affirmative.)

The Committee began its hearings. Witnesses alluded to alleged profits on a railroad built during the President's Military Governorship of Tennessee. There were suggestions that the President sold pardons to ex-rebels. Ben Butler searched for evidence to tie him in with the assassination of Lincoln. Nothing solid turned up. The President cooperated throughout, turning over his bank records and everything else that was requested.

Representative Ashley, the sponsor of the impeachment

inquiry, came before the Judiciary Committee in the capacity of expert witness. He left the members with their mouths hanging open. "I have a theory," he declared. It was that President Harrison and President Taylor had definitely been poisoned and that an attempt had been made to poison President Buchanan. The object in each case had been to put their respective Vice Presidents into their places. In line with his theory Ashley had concluded that Johnson arranged Lincoln's death. Perhaps, he added, all of his testimony was not legal evidence.

Ashley's appearance ended any chance that the committee members would vote to impeach. But the threat was at least useful to the Radical leadership as a means of keeping the President in line. "Though for the present," wrote the young French journalist Georges Clemenceau, "the Radicals are limiting themselves . . . to binding Andrew Johnson with good brand-new laws. At each session they add a shackle to his bonds, tighten the bit in a different place, file a claw or draw a tooth, and then when he is well bound up, fastened, and caught in an inextricable net of laws and decrees . . . they tie him to the stake of the Constitution and take a good look at him, feeling quite sure he cannot move this time."

But, the future Premier of France noted, the President was occasionally capable of bursting loose for a moment: "Then Seward, the Delilah of the piece, rises up and shouts: 'Johnson, here come the Radicals with old Stevens at their head; they are proud of having subjected you and are coming to enjoy the sight of you in chains.' And Samson summons all his strength, and bursts all his cords and bonds with a mighty effort, and the Philistines (I mean the Radicals) flee in disorder to the Capitol."

In June, 1867, the President slipped his bonds, sending orders to the military commanders in the South. These new orders were based on Attorney General Stanbery's considered interpretation of the "Force Bills." The "little monarchs," Stanbery said, did not have the power to remove Governors and judges. Nor could they put aside laws passed by the "Johnson government" legislatures or uniformly deny ex-Confederates the vote.

Congress rushed to the rescue of the Generals. Stevens rammed through supplementary Reconstruction regulations that specifically authorized the military to remove civilian officials in the South if a local army commander wished. The new regulations also repeated the ruling that ex-Confederates could not vote. The expected veto came, Johnson reiterating that American citizens were being denied the protections given them by the Constitution, that hundreds of years of American and British tradition were being ignored so that feudal powers could be entrusted to military chieftains wielding the "rod of despotism" and trampling their subjects with the "armed heel of power." Congress passed the supplementary act over the veto.

In the South the Ku Klux rode. The carpetbagger regimes raised up white-officered black militia to combat them, with the ex-Confederates who were both the taxpayers and the Klan paying the bill. In the welter of conflicting interests and motives which was the Reconstruction the idealists suffered, for the scavengers scorned them as fools and the natives ostracized them. Lonely, those men and women who had gone South to uplift God's image in ebony began to drift home. The ambitiously begun schools closed and were forgotten. With the war's end thousands of ex-slaves had poured into The Freedmen's Savings and Trust Company the sum of twenty million dollars, their deposits coming mostly in dimes and quarters and half-dollars. Now infected by corruption, the bank crashed. The blacks who had put pathetic trust into the little bankbooks with a busy bee on the cover were the losers.

Perhaps, just after the surrender, the South's white men might have given the Negro something approaching equality, or at least fairness. "Let us be scrupulously just in our dealings with him," General Wade Hampton of South Carolina had said, setting up a schoolhouse on his plantation. "Let us assist him in his aspirations for knowledge, and aid him in its acquisition." But that opportunity had disappeared in the bitterness brought about by the Reconstruction legislatures and the terror born of the lynchings of the Ku Klux Klan.

And the North did not care. For twenty years the nation had argued and fought on great issues. Now the passion was gone. In the fall of 1867 the voters of Ohio, Pennsylvania, New York and Maine clearly showed they were turning from Radicalism. A Democrat was elected Governor of New York. In the other states, the impressive Republican majorities of the previous year shrank markedly. Kansas and Minnesota defeated proposals to give Negroes the vote. Even the old Abolitionist stronghold of Ohio voted "no" by a margin of 40,000 and then rejected the Radical Ben Wade for reelection. A new type of political leader was rising on the tide of increasing disinterest in the SOUTHERN OUTRAGES columns. He cared nothing for ideology, everything for technique. His interests were power and money, the coming Gilded Age and not the great past. Stevens he understood and feared. Sumner was beyond understanding.

For the Senator from Massachusetts seemed to live in the past. To give his speeches on the Slave Power seemed absurd two and a half years after the war. Sometimes he seemed to realize the old rallying cries had lost their magic and at his clubs would tell people that what he had to say was history itself, and they had better listen. Then he would forget himself and lecture the Senate on the great crusade against the powerful planter aristocracy of the South. He did not seem to understand that to the rising political generation the battle was finished.

The new Senators smiled discreetly. Roscoe Conkling of New York, ruthless and ambitious, mimicked him. Bewildered and caught off guard, Sumner wondered why the others snickered. With his constant denunciations of the rebellion, of John C. Calhoun and Jefferson Davis, he reminded Senator James W. Nye of the man who killed a woodchuck and then kept pounding at the body to show the woodchuck there was punishment after death.

Human Rights, the Secessionists and the Nullifiers filled

Sumner's speeches, along with his sincere feelings about the freedmen. Let the bars come down, he said, and the blacks would give to America their generosity, simplicity, fidelity, which, married to the "more precocious and harder" characteristics of the whites, would result in a civilization where "men will not only know and do, but they will feel also."

Few northerners listened. Let the blacks, now free, make their own way. The Senate voted down Sumner's bill to give the freedmen free schools and free land. He went home and wept.

In the days immediately following Abraham Lincoln's assassination, Secretary of War Edwin M. Stanton, seeking John Wilkes Booth, sent detectives north into Canada and cavalry patrols south into Virginia and beyond. On his recommendation Andrew Johnson signed a proclamation declaring that Jefferson Davis instigated the murder. The War Department offered one hundred thousand dollars' reward for Booth and his accomplices and threatened to hang anyone who aided the fugitives. In the end Stanton's men flushed Booth out of the barn in which he had taken refuge. Almost all of Booth's little circle was soon behind bars, including Lewis Paine, Seward's assailant, and George Atzerodt, the cloddish boatman from Port Tobacco who had been assigned to plunge a knife into Andrew Johnson's heart. Minor conspirators were also arrested. Only John H. Surratt, Booth's most capable accomplice, escaped. In his stead Stanton arrested his mother, Mrs. Mary Surratt.

Swearing he would hang the conspirators before Lincoln's body was interred at Springfield, Stanton and the Judge Advocate General, Joseph Holt, convened a court of army officers. The defendants were put in irons, and head-sacks covered their faces at all times save when they were brought into the courtroom. Throughout the proceedings Mrs. Surratt maintained her innocence. She said she had known the assassin only as her son's friend and therefore had made him welcome in her home. She had known the remaining conspirators as other friends of Johnny Booth. She declared she knew nothing of any illegal plans.

Her words had the ring of truth. Middle-aged, plain, a widow, the proprietor of a boardinghouse, Mrs. Surratt seemed bewildered by what was happening. Many people quailed at the idea of hanging her. But among those who wanted her to swing were Stanton, the Judge Advocate Holt and Congressman John Bingham of Ohio (and the Committee of Fifteen), temporarily appointed assistant prosecutor of the trial.

The panel of officers, including Brigadier General Lew Wallace, the future author of *Ben Hur,* handed down their verdict: the rope for Paine, Atzerodt, David Herold, who had been taken with Booth, and Mrs. Surratt. Long jail terms were given the minor conspirators.

It was widely expected that the new President would grant Mrs. Surratt a last-minute reprieve. Execution morning came. The condemned woman's daughter, Annie, seventeen, went to the White House to plead for her mother's life. The President gave orders that she was not to see him. Senator James Lane of Kansas and the President's friend Preston King were detaining Annie at the base of the stairwell leading to Johnson's office when Secretary of State Seward came down from a conference. The young woman clung to him, begging for mercy, but he told her it was useless. She began to scream. Seward moved away, and Secretary of the Treasury McCulloch, looking on, saw Annie Surratt collapse on the stairs. The President's daughter, Martha Patterson, ministered to the girl.

All through the day the officers in charge of the execution waited for instructions from the White House not to hang Mrs. Surratt. Even as the prisoners came shuffling to the scaffold General Winfield Scott Hancock expected a reprieve. He had posted couriers along the way to the White House who could speed the word on.

On the scaffold Lewis Paine told the soldiers around him that Mrs. Surratt was innocent. General Hancock, still thinking a reprieve might come, slowed the proceedings to allow time for the word to reach him. But no messenger appeared.

Two soldiers removed Mrs. Surratt's bonnet and put a rope around her neck and a hood over her face. Watching from a second-floor window overlooking the scene, Annie Surratt fell to the floor, unconscious. A moment later her mother and the three men were hanging from the ends of the four ropes.

That was in the summer of 1865. In the years that followed the government made little effort to find Mrs. Surratt's escaped son, John. The reward which had been offered for his capture was withdrawn. Surratt was serving with the Papal Guard in Italy when an acquaintance from Maryland recognized him and, not knowing there was no longer any reward, informed the American authorities of his whereabouts. Surratt fled, to be captured in Alexandria, Egypt, and brought back to Washington. In the early summer of 1867 he went on trial on charges of having conspired to kill Abraham Lincoln.

By August his trial neared its end. John Surratt stood an excellent chance of being acquitted. Two years previously Surratt's mother had swung from a rope, but by the summer of 1867 the jury, like the rest of the country, was anxious to have done with the war, even with the now-distant murder of Lincoln.

In his summation defense lawyer Richard Merrick alluded to the hanging of his client's mother and indicated she had certainly not deserved execution. Indeed, Merrick went on, he had heard a rumor that the panel which found Mrs. Surratt guilty had attached to the sentence a recommendation of mercy, but that the recommendation had not been seen by the President, to whom it was addressed. Now, he went on, the government was also attempting to hang the son in the same underhanded fashion as the mother. A second defense lawyer also referred to the rumored recommendation for pardon.

The prosecution lawyers privately questioned Judge Advocate Holt. Then Edwards Pierrepont, the senior counsel of the prosecution, said in court that President Johnson had looked at the entire record of the trial of Mrs. Surratt after the death sentence had been handed down. There had indeed been a recommendation of mercy. The President had seen it but ignored it. "He signed the warrant for her death with the paper right before his eyes."

That was on Saturday, August 3. The Sunday morning papers carried the story. On Monday the President ordered Stanton to let him have the complete record of the conspiracy trial. He looked at the sentence and saw his signature.

Above his name was the recommendation for clemency, signed by five of the nine officers who had made up the trial panel. But the President had never seen the recommendation before. Either it had been torn out two years before when the record was given to him for his signature or Holt had somehow concealed it from his vision.

Johnson had been tricked. He had been responsible for the death of a woman whose guilt was doubted by a majority of the sentencing panel. Ever since then his enemies had said that the President sent Mrs. Surratt to the gallows to silence someone who could implicate him in Lincoln's murder. That was why the conspirators had been forced to wear hoods which made speech difficult. But their heads could not be covered indefinitely. And that was the reason why Johnson killed them.

To those rumors the Radicals added another. The reason the President had not seen the mercy petition and had not received Mrs. Surratt's daughter was obvious. He had been drunk.

All these rumors and deceptions, the President reflected, could be laid at Stanton's door. Holt was Stanton's tool. Unarmed with Stanton's orders, he would never have dared to rip out or conceal the clemency recommendation. Why had Stanton done it? Perhaps to promote the idea that the South was so irremediably evil that it made even the motherly Mrs. Surratt a murderess deserving execution. Now the same Stanton sat in the War Office conniving with the Radicals who in Johnson's eyes were responsible for the military satraps, the hooded horses and riders, the profligate southern legislatures, for all the sorry work of congressional Reconstruction.

"Within my knowledge he is one of us," Charles Sumner

had said of Stanton, his close friend. Alone of all the Cabinet ministers who disagreed with Johnson's policies the War Secretary had stayed on in the Cabinet, thus becoming the Radical spy in the enemy's camp. At Cabinet meetings he rarely offered his views. When asked for an opinion, he usually said the President should do as he wished. But he never attempted to hide the fact that he usually thought that what the President wanted to do was wrong.

Four days prior to looking for the first time at the mercy recommendation for Mrs. Surratt, the President had remarked to Grant that he could no longer tolerate Stanton. Grant had urged him to remember the Tenure of Office Act which held that the President could not dismiss a Cabinet minister without the advice and consent of the Senate. The act, Grant pointed out, "was intended specifically to protect the Secretary of War."

But the President was beyond caring. All his life he had been thought to be an uncompromising fighter who never backed away from a battle. "A. Johnson the Pigheaded," said George Templeton Strong. In fact the President was slow to move. (Gideon Welles thought Johnson's chief fault was that he could not make up his mind.)

Now he acted. If Stanton had given support from the beginning, everything would now be all right, Johnson told his secretary, Colonel William Moore. Instead, Stanton had backed "this damned extreme gang," the Radicals. The Mrs. Surratt matter was the last straw. He handed Moore a note and told him to give it to the Secretary of War.

> Sir: Public considerations of a high character constrain me to say that your resignation as Secretary of War will be accepted.
>> Very respectfully yours,
>> Andrew Johnson,
>> President of the United States.

A reply came back shortly.

> Sir: Your note this day has been received, stating that

public considerations of a high character constrain you to say that my resignation as Secretary of War will be accepted.

In reply, I have the honor to say that public considerations of a high character, which alone have induced me to continue at the head of this department, constrain me not to resign the office of Secretary of War before the next meeting of Congress.

Edwin M. Stanton,
Secretary of War.

The President could not discharge Stanton, but under the Tenure of Office Act he still possessed the right of suspending him. He would leave Mr. Stanton hanging on the "sharp hooks of uncertainty" for a few days, he said, and sent for Grant. Would Grant consent to act as Secretary of War ad interim until Congress convened in November, three months in the future? If at that time the Senate voted to restore Stanton to office, would Grant join in a fight to keep him out? Or, if Grant then preferred not to get involved, would he give the President notice so that someone else could see the case through?

Physically unimpressive, shy, taciturn, Ulysses Grant was a man who but a few short years before the war had burst into tears on a street in Galena, Illinois, because he could not sell the firewood he was forlornly peddling. He was so elemental a man that Henry Adams thought that he should have been extinct "for ages" or at best lived in a cave and "worn skins." But by the summer of 1867 Grant was a potential President of the United States. General of the Army, Savior of the Republic, he had climbed as high as any soldier could. Now the highest office dangled before him. Grant hesitated to accept Johnson's offer. In the end he said he would serve as Secretary ad interim. If it came to a fight with the Senate, he would probably hang on. If he should change his mind, he would resign and let the President appoint someone else.

Stanton bowed before the hero of Appomattox and accepted suspension, saying he was submitting to superior force.

Grant had occupied the War Secretary's office less than a week when the President ordered him to transfer General Philip Sheridan from his post as Military Governor of Louisiana and Texas to the Indian badlands of the West. Grant told Johnson it would be a calamitous mistake to remove the Military Governor most beloved of Radicalism. Sheridan's continuance in power at New Orleans, Grant said, was the "will of the people."

But the will of the people had not been canvassed on this particular subject, Johnson replied. And he was President. Grant ordered Sheridan to quit New Orleans in favor of General Winfield Scott Hancock. The deposed officer went north to the accompaniment of torchlight parades and receptions organized by the Radicals for a great war hero sacrificed by the despot of the White House.

When his replacement, Hancock, let it be known that he felt the civil power should dominate the military, Johnson hailed him for his liberalism. The President then announced that Congress should offer Hancock an official vote of thanks for his statement. In reply the House of Representatives declared, "The House utterly condemns the conduct of Andrew Johnson, President of the United States, in having dismissed from the command of the Fifth Military District the gallant soldier Major General Philip Sheridan."

By then the last faint semblance of good manners had vanished from the exchanges between the Congress and the President. Looking back years later, it seemed to the longtime Washington observer Henry Adams that "at times the whole Senate seemed to catch hysterics of nervous bucking without apparent reason," that "Senators passed belief" and "were more grotesque than ridicule could make them." He did not find greater sweetness and light at the other end of Pennsylvania Avenue. "You can't use tact with a Congressman!" Adams remembered a Cabinet minister expostulating. "A Congressman is a hog! You must take a stick and hit him on the snout!"

During the final months of 1867 constant alarms passed through the country. When General William T. Sherman came to Washington for a rest from his Indian-fighting duties Secretary of the Interior Orville Browning begged him not to return to the West during such a period of political unrest. Congress was planning to arrest and depose the President, Browning said. It would be the President's duty to resist, and Grant's reliability in such an emergency was questionable. Therefore, Browning added, it was vital that the influential Sherman remain in the capital so that he could play a part in the struggle. Sherman replied that Browning overestimated his influence. In any case he did not wish to climb to power over Grant's shoulders. "I still urged that I thought he should remain here," Browning wrote in his diary, "as by so doing he might prevent revolution and civil war."

From the other side of the fence, Radical now when once he had been a Presidential supporter, George Templeton Strong wrote in his diary, "People say that Johnson's more intimate pals talk as if he contemplates a coup d'etat, a purging of Congress after the manner of Cromwell. He is a public calamity, anyhow. One might be pardoned for hoping he would undertake some great crime and outrage, if one were sure he would be hanged for it."

Strong was not the only person thinking of a possible Presidential attack on Congress. The French correspondent Georges Clemenceau took note of the panicky rumors which swept the capital when the Governor of Maryland asked Secretary of War ad interim Grant for some cannon for his militia. There was immediate frenzied speculation that the Marylanders, largely officered by ex-Confederates, wanted the cannon to march on Washington and there militarily back up the despot. "MARYLAND AND THE PRESIDENT PREPARING FOR WAR," headlined the Cincinnati *Commercial*. Grant rejected the request for arms. In turn the Maryland Governor vowed he would get the cannon elsewhere, which prompted Representative Samuel Hooper of Massachusetts to write to Sumner that many Bostonians believed the northern Governors would "have to call for armed Loyalty to sweep down Washington and Maryland."

Sumner took Hooper's words as additional proof that he must continue with his work. Yet at fifty-six he felt tired and ill from a gradually worsening heart condition which he attributed to the Brooks assault. He longed for retirement and an end to strife. His weariness was not entirely a result of his physical condition. Much of it came from his marriage to the widow of Hooper's late son. Shaky almost from the start, the relationship ended after less than a year, when Alice Sumner, nearly three decades his junior, left her husband. The reason, she said, was "that what every matured woman considers a just desire was not fully granted."

Washington society believed that it understood her words and called Sumner behind his back The Great Impotent. He moved into a new home, selling his family's house in Boston to raise the money. From that house, he told Longfellow, he had buried his father and mother, a brother and three sisters, and now he was leaving it "the deadest of them all."

In his new home he began to prepare a revised collection of his speeches. Eventually it came to fifteen volumes: the speeches themselves, authorities he had relied upon for his facts, press comments, letters received. He would sit up nights rewriting the speeches for their publication, putting in additional footnotes to explain once more his positions against the Slaveocracy, the Slave Power, those who warred on human rights. He also worked on his book and picture collections, wandering the shops and negotiating with dealers in Europe and America. Vast clutter surrounded him: volumes piled on the floor, papers, letters which he liked to read to admiring visitors. To save money so that he could extend his collections he kept no horse and carriage.

Despite his fame, he seemed remote from human affairs, a weary titan dwelling on Mount Sinai. "I, long since, ceased to take any interests in individuals," he said to Julia Ward Howe.

"You have made great progress, sir," she replied. "God has not yet got so far—at least according to the last accounts."

If Charles Sumner was low in spirits, Thad Stevens at seventy-five was not. Suffering from dropsy, rheumatism, jaundice, his legs almost too weak to carry him, his heart and liver giving out, the essence of the man remained unchanged. He had spent the summer and fall of 1867 at a resort hotel, sitting muffled in blankets and arranging races for children, with the winner getting a silver quarter. Then he would organize handicap races for the losers, so that eventually each child received a coin. For once the harsh lines of his face relaxed.

But he had not really changed. Considered the Great Commoner * in Europe, and the American Prime Minister, Old Thad remained pitiless in his dealings with others. He did not stoop to pity himself even though he had grown so weak that he was unable to sit upright during the train ride to Washington for the November opening of Congress. He lay on a bed arranged for him on the floor of the coach, his voice sinking to an indistinguishable murmur at the end of each sentence. But the eyes were the same, the intelligence unimpaired. On November 21, 1867, he was stretched out on a sofa in his committee room as the Congressmen assembled. He rose only once: when Sumner came in.

The feud of the still-powerful Radical leadership with the President dominated all other congressional considerations. The Radicals demanded and received from the White House all documents relating to Johnson's suspension of Stanton. Meanwhile the Committee on the Judiciary reopened its hearings on the question of whether it should vote to impeach. Congressman Ashley—"Impeachment Ashley" to his colleagues —visited a convicted perjurer in jail when the man's wife told Ashley that her husband had absolute proof that Johnson had conspired to kill Lincoln. The convict, who called himself Sanford Conover, informed Ashley that he could produce letters from Johnson to Jefferson Davis and John Wilkes Booth. Ashley affected to believe him, adding it would be useful to have proof that Booth told friends that the then-Vice President knew of the assassination plan. Ashley dickered over the price

* "Commoner" in the sense of a House of Commons parliamentarian.

of the alleged letters. But he did not offer enough to satisfy Conover, who wrote the President all about the "diabolical designs" and "nefarious conspiracy" of "Ashley and Co."

Thus betrayed, Ashley turned to the former head of the United States Secret Service, the capable but eccentric LaFayette C. Baker. Baker swore that he had once seen a letter from Johnson to Jefferson Davis. According to Baker the letter had been written by Johnson when he was Military Governor of Tennessee. In it, Baker said, Johnson suggested lines of strategy to Davis and promised that Tennessee would be turned over to the Confederacy. Unfortunately the letter was not in Baker's possesssion, but he would make every effort to find it.

The House Judiciary Committee questioned Annie Surratt, asking her whether Johnson had been a co-conspirator with Booth. She said she knew nothing. An actor friend of the assassin was brought to testify about Booth's friendship with Johnson; the actor said Booth had never discussed it. Why had Booth called upon Johnson—or at least sent up his card—the day of the assassination? No one knew. The Radicals said the explanation could have been found in the missing pages in Booth's captured diary, had Johnson not ripped out the incriminating evidence.

Radical enough in its composition to believe anything of Johnson—its members would have impeached the President for stepping on a dog's tail, wrote Secretary Welles—the Committee on the Judiciary recommended impeachment in December. The committee based its recommendation on the grounds that the President illegally usurped power, violated the law, "retarded the public prosperity, lessened the public revenues, disordered the business and finances of the country, encouraged insubordination in the people of the states lately in rebellion . . . revived and kept alive the spirit of rebellion" and "humiliated the nation."

The House of Representatives considered the impeachment recommendation, while in the Senate the Radical Charles Drake of Missouri called for at least a joint Senate-

House resolution of censure upon the "double-skinned rhinoceros," Johnson, "the nightmare that crouches upon the heaving breast of this nation."

But neither censure nor impeachment vote passed. The public, which had lost interest in politics, appeared to approve the rejections. Johnson would be a fit subject for a book to be titled *Andrew's Adventures in Blunderland*, said George Templeton Strong; he was a "caitiff" and such a fool as was almost unmatched in history, yet to Strong it seemed best not to impeach him. "Far better to let him go on eating dirt" for the remaining fifteen months of his term. After that he could "set up a tailor shop in Tennessee, conducted on strictly Constitutional principles."

That solution also appealed to Senator James W. Grimes of Iowa. "While the President has been guilty of many great follies and wickednesses," he was not guilty enough to set an example which might make the United States like a South American republic where the ruler was ousted the moment the populace turned against him in sentiment. Better to "submit to two years of misrule, which is a very short space in the lifetime of a nation, than subject the country, its institutions and its credits, to the shock of an impeachment."

With Congress in continual session, Washington's social season was brilliant. From the North's great victory had come bonnets decorated with aigrettes of diamonds, flutters of lace and silk, room corners adorned with potted bushes and trees, rising railroad shares, gold stickpins and rings and such a display of wealth and splendor on the part of the "newly enriched" as to make the writer E. F. Ellet think the scene almost like a carnival. The journalist Emily Edson Briggs wrote that never had such costly clothing been seen; studying a handsome blonde in royal purple she was reminded of the Psalmist: "They toil not, neither do they spin, yet Solomon in all his glory was not arrayed like one of these."

In the dispirited and sullen South the forest came back to reclaim the cotton fields. The former Confederate officer Richard Taylor looked at the so different North and contemptuously said that now the jewels of southern ladies were flaunted by northern women. Richard Taylor, the son of President Taylor and the brother-in-law of the imprisoned Jefferson Davis, asked Charles Sumner to aid in obtaining Davis' release. Taylor recalled the experience: "I was delighted to listen to beautiful passages from the classic as well as modern poets, dramatists, philosophers, and orators . . . Burke, or Howard, Wilberforce, Brougham, Macaulay, Harriet Beecher Stowe, etc., but I failed to get down to the particular subject that interested me."

Taylor tried Thad Stevens and found him completely candid. "He wanted no restoration of the Union under the Constitution, which he called a worthless bit of old parchment. The white people of the South ought never again to be trusted with power, for they would inevitably unite with the northern 'Copperheads' and control the government." As for helping Taylor free Davis, Stevens said it was silly to refuse permission at this point but that he would not say so publicly —why should he relieve Johnson of the responsibility? *

On New Year's Day the President received with his daughters. General Sherman's daughter came in light buff grenadine over a green silk gored skirt with a full train; other women wore lavender silk trimmed with folds of black velvet, sky-blue silk trimmed with white satin, black velvet cloaks and black moiré antique with white furs. Mrs. Johnson was upstairs as usual, pale and emaciated and permitting herself to say that she and the President had been happier when he was simply a prosperous tailor back in Greeneville.

When the holidays ended the Senate turned to the question of whether it would give consent to the removal of Stanton as Secretary of War. There was every reason to believe that the Senators, following the dictates of the Tenure of Office Act, would not allow Stanton to be replaced.

But what would Secretary of War ad interim Ulysses Grant do if the Senate ordered him out so that Stanton could

* Davis eventually went free on bail and was never tried. The technicalities involved in selecting a proper site for a trial seemed insurmountable.

return? Everything hinged upon the General's decision. So the President repeated to Grant his request that the General inform him in advance if he did not wish to join in a fight against the Senate. Then Grant could resign and the President would name a new Secretary ad interim who would hold the post while the issue was fought through the Supreme Court. There, the President said, the Act would be declared unconstitutional in "half an hour."

On Saturday, January 11, Grant talked with the President for more than an hour. He said he could not decide how he would respond if the Senate ordered Stanton returned to the War Office. He then asked Johnson about the ten-thousand-dollar fine and the jail sentence waiting for anyone who violated the Tenure of Office Act. Johnson replied that he was so certain the Act would be overthrown by the Supreme Court that he, the President, would pay the fine and take the jail term himself if he were wrong. All he asked was that the office not be surrendered to Stanton until the Court ruled.

The General was not entirely reassured. The two men agreed to talk again on Monday, two days later. Grant left. Perhaps he thought he had made his position clear; more likely he did not have a position.

On Monday the Senate voted thirty-five to six that it did not accept the President's discharge of Stanton.

The news of the vote reached Ulysses Grant. People came in its wake to speak to him. The great soldier of his time was now befuddled. Ambition mixed with his uncertainty. Grant sat down and wrote out his resignation as Secretary of War ad interim. He then went to an evening reception at the White House, where the President asked him why he hadn't come to their agreed-upon morning conference. Grant made some excuse. He did not mention that he carried his resignation in his pocket.

The next morning at nine Grant stepped into the Secretary's office on the second floor of the War Department Building. He locked the door and put the key in his pocket.

"I am to be found over at my office at army headquarters," he said to Assistant Adjutant General E. D. Townsend and walked over to Seventeenth Street south of Pennsylvania Avenue and diagonally opposite the War Department. He then sent a messenger who carried his resignation to the President.

An hour later Edwin Stanton, smiling, entered the War Department and went upstairs to find the Secretary's office locked. Told that Grant had the key, Stanton asked Townsend to go get it and sat down in the anteroom. In a few minutes Townsend was back to do a mock present arms with the key. Stanton unlocked the door.

By then Grant's resignation had reached Andrew Johnson, who had the General's messenger seek Grant and tell him that the President desired his presence at the Cabinet meeting scheduled for noon. Grant appeared, and sat down in the Secretary of War's chair. However, when the President asked if he had any Department business to discuss, Grant replied he was not present in any function other than that of General of the Army. There followed a barrage of questions. Had Grant agreed either to oppose Stanton's return or at least to hand the War Office over to someone who would? Had he by indirection made it clear at the Saturday conference that he would hold the fort? And had it been understood that there would be another meeting with the President before Grant took any action at all?

Grant stammered out what Secretary of the Interior Browning thought was a series of unintelligible excuses. He had not come for the scheduled conference, he said, because he had not thought the Senate would act so quickly. In addition he had had a meeting with General Sherman. Other "various little matters" had also claimed his attention. Johnson kept hammering at him. Though his excitement and indignation were apparent, the President seemed in control of himself. The word *liar* was not used, but the implication of each question was that Grant had broken his word to the President. And perhaps he had also plotted with Stanton and the Radicals. Embarrassed and unhappy, Grant left. (The

General "slunk away," Welles wrote in his diary.)

That night it was said in Washington that the President, enraged, had kicked over chairs and cursed Grant, and that the two men had narrowly escaped coming to blows. There followed halfhearted attempts on Grant's part to convince Stanton to resign.

There were many cogent reasons why Stanton should give up his office. Ill from advanced asthma, he also found himself in such financial distress that he was unable to pay his children's teacher and had to borrow money to pay his wife's medical bills. His wife begged him to give up the Secretaryship and return to his law practice. But he could not, though he longed to do so. His beliefs would not permit it. Political democracy in America rested in his hands, Stanton said. The President would run amok if given control of the War Department and the army. As Military Governor in Tennessee, Johnson had shown himself ruthless and domineering. As President with access to great military power he would become even more ruthless. In the first instance, the absolute power given Johnson had served the good cause. His use of power now would destroy that cause. Too much had been spent in blood and treasure for Stanton to leave. So the Secretary remained in his War Department office one block from the White House. The old gray-colored building could be reached from there by a shaded passageway that ran along a four- or five-foot-high wall. At night the wall was lit by flickering gas jets. Because no telegraph existed in the White House, Abraham Lincoln had been in the habit of walking down that passageway to visit the War Office telegraph operator, whose machine had told of the terrible battles that were being fought.

Now no President came down that walk and no Secretary of War went to Cabinet meetings. Yet Secretary Seward needed military reports on British Columbia, Secretary McCulloch requested troops to guard gold shipments along the Mexican border and Postmaster General Randall asked for cavalry to patrol postal routes in unsettled Texas. So Stanton's salary was paid and money supplied for War Department needs. The Senate through the Tenure of Office Act had ruled that mutual detestation between a President and Secretary did not give the higher official the right to remove the lower.

But Johnson was not quite helpless. He ordered Grant, the head of the army, not to accept any future orders issued by Stanton. Grant left for Richmond on an inspection tour, brooding about the situation in which he found himself. He was trapped in the middle between his Secretary of War and his commander-in-chief. Other factors entered into his thinking: the fact that Johnson's hints that Grant had broken his word were finding their way into newspaper stories; that the Radicals had it in their power to help win a Presidential nomination and an election before the year was out.

Upon his return Grant sent the President a note. In order that there be no confusion about certain matters in future, the General wrote, he would no longer accept verbal orders from the President. Johnson returned the note with an indication that future orders would be written down.

Grant acknowledged receipt of the note. He added another point: he would henceforth accept orders from the Secretary of War.

Johnson had had enough. He cut all ties to the army chief with a letter outlining the General's apostasy as a man who had given his word to do something he had not done. Grant wrote back angrily saying the President offered "many and gross misrepresentations."

"And now, Mr. President," Grant's letter concluded, "when my honor as a soldier and my integrity as a man have been so violently assailed, pardon me for saying that I can but regard this whole matter, from the beginning to the end, as an attempt to involve me in the resistance of law, for which you hesitated to assume the responsibility in orders, and thus to destroy my character before the country."

Tottering around on a cane, weakening moment by moment, Old Thad said Grant was now in the church of the Radicals.

11

His Cabinet ministers advised Johnson to let Stanton stay in the War Department. Nor was there any point in fighting the Senate. After all, Secretary McCulloch pointed out, there was still the possibility of an impeachment proceeding.

"Impeach and be damned," the President replied. He could not go on with Stanton remaining in the Cabinet. He would be President on his own terms or not at all. He said he would bring Sherman to Washington and promote him to the rank of General of the Army so that he might act as counterbalance to the now antagonistic Grant. Let the Radicals plot against him then. "This will set some of them thinking," he said to his secretary, Colonel Moore.

But Sherman was horrified at the proposal. The vision of two opposing armies, one commanded by himself and the other by Grant, arose in his mind. "The President would make use of me to beget violence," he wrote his brother, Senator John Sherman of Ohio. He asked his brother to fight the proposed promotion.

The President dropped the plan, substituting for it a

proposal that Sherman become Secretary of War. The General demurred. Suppose Stanton refused to vacate the office? "Oh, he will make no objection," the President said. "You present the order and he will retire. I know him better than you do. He is cowardly."

But Sherman had seen enough of the bitter and divided city that Washington had become in the early days of 1868. He had known Grant, he said, in the midst of death and slaughter, with men slitting their mules' throats in order to eat; but never had he seen him so troubled as he was now, caught in the fight between Congress and the President. Sherman told the President he did not wish to be Secretary of War.

Johnson turned to General George H. Thomas, the hero of the Battle of Chickamauga. The President had grown to like and respect Thomas during his days as Military Governor of Tennessee. He would appoint him General of the Army and send him to Stanton with orders that the Secretary get out. But the situation was delicate for Thomas. He was a Virginian whose family had considered him as dead from the day in 1861 when he decided to remain with the army of the Union in preference to going with that of the Confederacy. But he was yet a southerner. And like Grant and Sherman, Thomas had a soldier's disdain for a political position. He declined Johnson's offer.

But there was another General Thomas—Lorenzo P., the Adjutant General of the army. His stature could not possibly be compared to that of Sherman or to the hero of Chickamauga, for Lorenzo P. Thomas was generally considered to be a fool and the next thing to a confirmed alcoholic. Tall, thin almost to the point of emaciation, he had seen no action during the war. In actuality, his nominal underling, Assistant Adjutant General Townsend, performed his duties as Adjutant General. Lorenzo P. Thomas, Stanton had been known to say, was only fit for "presiding over a crypt of Egyptian mummies like himself." Of late the Secretary of War had him off inspecting military cemeteries.

On February 21, 1868, at nine in the morning, President Johnson handed General Thomas two written orders. Five weeks had passed since Stanton's return to the War Department.

Thomas took the orders and left the President. A few minutes later Secretary of War Stanton looked up from where he sat on his worn leather couch near the window of his office and beheld a subordinate of whom he had never held a high opinion. Thomas said, "I am directed by the President to hand you this."

Stanton read the papers Thomas gave him. One, addressed to Stanton, ordered him to get out of the War Office. The other contained Thomas' nomination as his replacement.

Stanton was flabbergasted. It seemed impossible that the President intended to rely upon this nonentity. Sherman must be in the wings. Perhaps memories of the Grand Review in 1865 and Sherman's refusal to shake hands came flooding back.

"Do you wish me to vacate at once, or am I to be permitted to stay long enough to remove my property?" Stanton finally asked.

"At your pleasure," Thomas replied. He appeared to believe the matter was closed, and when Stanton asked for copies of the orders, Thomas willingly sought out Assistant Adjutant General Townsend to ask his aid in the work. When Thomas returned with the copies, he found that Stanton had hurriedly sent for Grant and that after talking with the General of the Army his attitude had changed.

"I want some little time for reflection," Stanton announced. "I don't know whether I shall obey your orders or not." Thomas left to see Johnson, optimistically declaring that there would be no trouble. He would go to the War Department in the morning and take up his new duties. That would be the end of Stanton.

The same thought entered Stanton's mind along with the belief that Thomas' appointment was preparatory to the coronation of a despot or monarch. He sent messengers flying to the Senate and House asking for help.

Before those messengers made it to their destinations, a messenger sent by the White House arrived at the Senate with an announcement of the appointment of Lorenzo Thomas as Secretary of War ad interim. The message was placed on the desk of the lame-duck Senator from Ohio, President Pro Tem Bluff Ben Wade, where it was casually picked up by Wade's friend Zachariah Chandler of Michigan.

When Chandler took in the meaning of the nomination —that Johnson had declared a new war on Stanton and the Radicals by refusing to abide by the Tenure of Office Act—he dropped the papers and rushed around the Senate floor to spread the news. A moment later Stanton's messenger arrived. He brought word that the Secretary was under siege. Would the Senators come to his aid?

At once a flood of messages of support was dispatched to the embattled Secretary. Succinct for once, Charles Sumner grabbed a pencil and from his desk wrote a one-word note: "Stick."

Then with several other Senators, Sumner went to see Grant. Rumors of impending violence were spreading through the city and the terrible fears of prewar days were being reborn in new circumstances. The specter of the horror of civil conflict rose again. Where did the General of the Army stand?

As always Grant appeared imperturbable. How, he asked, could Johnson order troops into action? Stanton sat in the chair of the Secretary of War; he, Grant, stood at the head of the army. Militarily there was nothing for the Radicals to worry about. (The White House's impotence was not lost upon the President or his advisers. "A pretty state of things," wrote the worried Presidential secretary William G. Moore in his diary. "Were the White House to be besieged, the President could not send an order to the troops that would be obeyed. The order would have to be given to Grant first.")

Encouraged, the Senators returned to the Capitol building, where the two houses of Congress discussed the crisis. It was, Representatives and Senators said, an open bid for a coup d'etat. Louis Napoleon had once been addressed as "President"; now he sat in the Tuileries as His Imperial Majesty the Emperor of the French. Thad Stevens rasped, "What good did your moderation do? If you don't kill the beast it will kill you!"

At nine o'clock, lights burning, the Senate was still debating what action to take. A letter arrived from Stanton: "If the Senate does not declare its opinion, how am I to hold possession?"

Within an hour the Senate voted a resolution that Johnson could not legally oust Stanton. A group of Senators presented the Secretary with the news. With the Senators was Judge David Cartter of the District of Columbia Supreme Court. He had driven Stanton and Secretary of the Navy Welles through the frightened crowds in the streets to Ford's Theatre on the night Lincoln was shot. Judge Cartter declared that if it was illegal to violate the Tenure of Office Act, then Lorenzo Thomas had apparently committed a crime. Let him be arrested. A warrant was made out and men assigned to serve it on the General. As for himself, Stanton said, he would physically remain in his office night and day until the issue was decided.

By one in the morning most of the crowd in Stanton's office had left. Senator John M. Thayer of Nebraska hung back as the others departed. Five months earlier, speaking, he said, on his responsibility as a United States Senator, he told a gathering that "today Andrew Johnson meditates and designs forcible resistance to the authority of Congress," but that when he made his fight he would find "five hundred thousand armed men from Pennsylvania, New York and Ohio will fly to arms and tramp the soil of Maryland to reach the beleaguered capital and rescue it from the hands of rebels and traitors." Now the moment he had predicted appeared to be at hand. "Mr. Secretary," Thayer said to Stanton, "would you like to have company tonight?"

"Well, Senator, if you feel disposed to stay with me, I shall be very glad to have you."

An armed soldier brought in a light meal which Stanton nibbled at and then abandoned. He moved to the window and gazed at a line of sentries surrounding the building. The General of the Army had ordered them to stand guard. When a full battalion was in place Stanton asked its commander what he would do if General Thomas ordered him to withdraw his men. The commander replied that the battalion took orders only from Grant. Stanton and Thayer lay down on the two couches, but Stanton could not sleep. Thayer dozed fitfully.

A block away the President also remained awake. At two in the morning Colonel Moore, his secretary, received a message from Johnson. The President had learned that an intoxicated General Thomas was talking too much about what he would do with Stanton. The President wished that Moore would take him in hand. Moore sent word that when daylight came he would go to Thomas.

A short time later Stanton shook Thayer awake. "Senator," Stanton said, "I believe the troops are coming to put me out." Thayer could hear the tramp of marching soldiers coming from the direction of the White House. He looked at his watch. Just 4:00 A.M. They waited. The sound of marching grew louder, then stopped. It began again and receded, and they realized it was the changing of the guards.

Two hours later Colonel Moore went to General Thomas' residence to discover the General had left with "two gentlemen." Moore eventually found Thomas at his lawyer's office, where he was free on five thousand dollars' bail. The "two gentlemen" were a District of Columbia deputy and marshal. Judge Cartter had sent them to arrest Thomas on charges of violating the Tenure of Office Act. They took him into custody when he returned from a ball. There he had let it be known that he was the man to throw Stanton into the street if necessary. "Suppose Stanton resists?" a man at the ball had asked him.

"I expect to meet force with force," Thomas said.

"Suppose he bars the doors?"

"I will break them down."

Moore steered his charge to the President. The arrest need not worry them, Johnson said. General Thomas was

Secretary of War ad interim. "Go and take charge," Johnson ordered. Thomas saluted and marched toward the War Department, his approach noted by a group of Radicals clustered around Stanton. "There he comes!"

Thomas came up the stairs and into Stanton's room, where the Secretary and the others sat in a semicircle with Stanton at the center.

"Good morning," Thomas said.

"Good morning, sir," Stanton said.

"I do not wish to disturb these gentlemen, and will wait."

"Nothing private here," Stanton said. "What do you want, sir?"

"I claim the office of Secretary of War, and demand it by order of the President."

"I deny your authority to act and order you back to your own office."

"I will stand here," Thomas replied. "I want no unpleasantness in the presence of these gentlemen."

"You can stand there, if you please, but you cannot act as Secretary of War. I am Secretary of War. I order you out of this office and to your own."

"I refuse to go, and will stand here."

"How are you to get possession?" Stanton asked. "Do you mean to use force?"

"I do not care to use force, but my mind is made up as to what I shall do. I want no unpleasantness, though. I shall stay here and act as Secretary of War."

"You shall not," Stanton said. "And I order you, as your superior, back to your own office."

"I will not obey you, but will stand here and remain here."

"I order you out of this office and to your own. I am Secretary of War and your superior."

Thomas took a new tack. He crossed to the room on the opposite side of the hall and began issuing orders to the officers there. Stanton followed him and told the men not to obey. "I am Secretary of War, and I now order you, General Thomas, out of this office and to your own quarters."

"I will not go," Thomas said. "I shall discharge the functions of Secretary of War."

"You will not."

"I shall require the mails of the War Department delivered to me and shall transact the business of the Office."

"You shall not have them, and I order you to your own office," Stanton said once more.

They were getting nowhere. But it was obvious there would be no violence, no apocalyptic clash of troops. The matter would be decided elsewhere. So the Radicals in attendance departed. Thomas and Stanton stood facing each other.

"The next time you have me arrested," Thomas said, "please do not do it before I get something to eat."

Stanton laughed. "Well, old fellow, have you had any breakfast this morning?"

"No."

"Nor anything to drink?"

"No."

"Then you are as badly off as I am, for I have had neither." Stanton put his hand around Thomas' neck and then ran it through his hair. "Schriver," Stanton said to Major General Edmund Schriver, "you have got a bottle here. Bring it out."

Schriver offered Stanton a small vial from which, he said, he occasionally sought relief from dyspepsia. Stanton divided the whiskey equally for himself and Thomas. Thomas knew it was an equal division because Stanton held the two glasses to the light to see that each man had the same amount. Presently a messenger brought in a full bottle. Stanton uncorked it and poured more generous portions. "Now," he said, "this at least is neutral ground."

They chatted, Stanton asking how the report on the national cemeteries was progressing. Thomas replied that he would soon finish and submit the report. Looking on, Assistant Adjutant General Townsend asked himself if this was a ruse by Stanton to make Thomas acknowledge him as Secretary of War. When, later, Townsend asked Stanton if this were the case, he was rewarded with a mock expression of surprise.

Thomas left, and went about saying to anyone who asked that indeed he was master of the situation. He ran into a man from his home town, Newcastle, Delaware. When the man portentously said that Delaware had her eyes on the native son and expected him to stand firm, Thomas straightened up and asked, "Am I not standing firm?"

"But are you not going to kick that man out?" asked his fellow townsman.

"Oh, some of these days."

From such encounters came predictions of the approach of appalling violence. In New York City, George Templeton Strong heard that Copperheads, roughs, bummers, bounty jumpers and "varied canaille" were organizing a volunteer army to defend the President and "make a muss" at Washington. From Galveston, Texas, a man wrote the President: *"Arrest Congress!* Which will stop further legislation. Court-martial Grant and Stanton as army officers insubordinate to their chief!" From Canton, Ohio, another correspondent wrote that the only question before Johnson was whether he could marshal enough military force to back him: "If you can, in God's name and the name of the people put that contemptible spy out of the War Office and then defend yourself as President of the United States. If revolution must come, let it come now."

The President sent for General W. H. Emory, the officer commanding the Department of Washington, to ask whether, as rumored, large-scale movements of troops were underway. Emory said no actions were being taken. Word of the officer's visit to the White House spread through Washington and immediately Congressmen were telling one another that Johnson was going to make this General Emory his military chieftain. Here was new proof that Johnson intended to play the part of a Cromwell, a Napoleon I, an emperor or despot. Blood and terror were in the air, rumors of revolution, coup d'etat, civil war.

The Senate-House Committee of Fifteen met briefly and then Thaddeus Stevens announced that the group voted overwhelmingly to recommend impeachment of the President. No specifics, the equivalent of charges, were offered. They would come later, it was indicated. Few noticed that the matter was illegally taken out of the hands of the House Committee on the Judiciary. The need of the moment was to slay the dragon, wrote the journalist Emily Edson Briggs. Grant had crushed the head of the reptile in Virginia and Sherman had cut the monster in half in the west, but "it is left for a loyal Congress to deal with that part of the serpent which it is said never dies till the sun goes down."

Stevens sought an immediate decision on the Committee resolution, but too many House members wanted to speak on it and so the vote was put forward. But the clock was stopped so that, officially, February 22 would not end until the vote was recorded. Thus the first step of impeachment would be taken on the birthday of George Washington.

The Representatives opened fire. James "Impeachment" Ashley declared that Stanton's dismissal was "the smallest of the many offenses of which this man has been guilty." Johnson, said Ben Butler, a man who was drunk on the day he became Vice President, "humiliated the nation and all the people," and "dishonored us in the presence of the civilized world." He was the product of John Wilkes Booth, who made Lincoln a martyr and put in his place a scoundrel who brought the Confederacy back from the dead and tried to make the General of the Army his co-conspirator and the War Department his tool.

"Ungrateful, despicable, besotted, traitorous man," said John Farnsworth of Illinois, "this accidental President made so by the assassin's pistol." Representative John Logan of Illinois called Johnson The Great Patricide, who had "dragged, as a demagogue, the robes of his high official position in the purlieus and filth of treason. . . . He has done every act a man can conceive not only calculated to degrade himself, but to destroy the rights of the American people."

"I am in favor of the official death of Andrew Johnson without debate," said John Shanks of Indiana. "I am not surprised that one who began his Presidential career in drunkenness should end it in crime." The House concluded its denunciations on the afternoon of February 24.

Stevens spoke the final words before the Representatives voted to impeach and send the case to the Senate for trial. They were not discussing whether the President was guilty of technicalities, Old Thad said. (They were not out to discover if the President had stolen a chicken, Ben Butler put it.) It was instead the very meaning of the war that concerned them: the future relations between North and South, the course of the Republic, and the question of whether one man, even if he be President, could dominate a great nation.

What they did, Stevens said, would "endure in its consequences until this whole continent shall be filled with a free and untrammeled people or shall be a nest of shrinking, cowardly slaves." The vote for impeachment was 126 to 47.

The following day, February 25, 1868, Stevens went before the Senate to say that he, "in the name of the House of Representatives and of all the people in the United States," impeached Andrew Johnson, President of the United States, for high crimes and misdemeanors.

12

The Constitution defines the grounds for impeachment as treason, bribery, or other "high crimes and misdemeanors." Some Senators, the House impeachers knew, would vote Andrew Johnson guilty on any charge preferred. Declared Senator Sumner: "Never in history was there a great case more free from all just doubt." Here was a man who "patronized massacre and bloodshed and gave a license to the Ku Klux Klan." To be against his immediate conviction and banishment from public office was to "quibble." Let the President be tried on narrow grounds, Sumner said, let him be found guilty and gotten rid of. That was all that mattered. As there was no Vice President, his replacement would be the president pro tem of the Senate, Bluff Ben Wade of Ohio. That would suit Sumner.

But not every Senator was ready to act as unhesitatingly as Sumner. Therefore a catchall collection of articles of impeachment—the equivalent of an indictment—must be devised by the board of managers who would represent the House and then take the case to the Senate.

The first article dealt with Johnson's unquestioned violation of the Tenure of Office Act. But did this transgression provide sufficient reason to remove an American President? It was certain that Senator John Sherman, the General's brother, would not think so. At the time of the Act's passage he had spoken against it, saying that no decent man would wish to stay in office after his chief, the President, asked him to leave. Anyone who refused to resign his office would thus "show he was unfit to be there." A second article was created to satisfy Sherman. It said that even if the President had the right to remove Stanton, he had no right to appoint Lorenzo Thomas to replace him.

Seven more articles followed, essentially rephrasing the first but adding also the charge of conspiracy between Johnson and Thomas. Johnson's questioning of the Washington garrison commander General Emory about rumored troop movements was cited as a violation of the law that he must go through Grant in all army matters. The tenth article was the production of Ben Butler. It charged the President with delivering before and during his Swing Around the Circle "certain intemperate, inflammatory, and scandalous harangues" aimed at exciting feelings against Congress. These statements, the article said, were made "with a loud voice" and were unmindful of the dignities and proprieties of the Presidency.

It was left to Stevens to summarize all the charges in the eleventh and final article. Never was so great a malefactor treated with such gentleness, he declared, adding he would therefore produce not a single article, but "one and a half." Old Thad included an allusion to Johnson's statements that the Congress was not legally constituted because it prohibited southern members. That might catch a vote or two, he said. The Senator did not live who wished to hear that he held his seat illegally.

Stevens told his friends in his whispering, weak voice that it would not be difficult to get the Senate to convict. No jury could fail to find the Great Criminal guilty beyond doubt. He added Johnson behaved the way he did because he was still on his "Inauguration drunk."

A similar thought suggested itself to former Assistant

Secretary of War Charles A. Dana's New York *Sun*. Either the President was demented or an opium addict, the paper said. In any event, he should plead not guilty by reason of insanity.

George Templeton Strong wrote in his diary that the President would object to being tried before a Senate that did not contain supporters of the rebellion and then would resign of his own volition. Good riddance, Strong thought. "The sooner we are rid of him, the better."

Moorfield Storey, Sumner's young secretary, also thought a trial would not be held. The President would wait until the last minute, Storey wrote his father, and then, like a "thoroughly ill-bred dog," would send in his resignation.

But Johnson had no such intention. At Cabinet meetings he never mentioned the impending trial. Even in casual conversations he did not bring up the subject. It was different for his wife. An invalid closeted upstairs, Eliza Johnson said she wished she was home. "But for the humiliation and Mr. Johnson's feelings," she told one of her rare visitors, "I wish they would send us back to Tennessee—if it were possible, give us our poverty and peace again, so that we might learn how to live for our children and ourselves. I have not seen a happy moment since I came to this house."

The President's silence worried Secretary of the Interior Browning. At the end of the Cabinet meeting on February 28, while the House was preparing articles of impeachment, Browning remarked that he felt the Cabinet members should give the President the benefit of their opinions. Secretary of State Seward demurred. The President had not asked for opinions. Browning persevered. The Secretary of the Interior said he did not wish to thrust his views on his chief, but he felt it was his duty to speak out. In any case the members of the Cabinet ought to understand each other. Save, of course, for the Cabinet member entrenched in the War Department Building.

Supported and encouraged by those who saw Edwin Stanton as a sentinel at the post defending liberty, the Secretary of War was yet at odds with his wife. She said his conduct was silly and told his clerk-bodyguard, Sergeant Louis Koerth, that she would not send him anything to eat. Stanton ordered Koerth to obtain food at Koerth's own home and then slipped out himself to a predawn farmers' market to buy more. With Koerth in attendance, Stanton prepared a stew and put it on the fire in his office. Watching the flames, he and the sergeant fell asleep. The sergeant awoke to hear, "Koerth! Koerth! Wake up, man, the stew is burning!" Senator Sumner and Stanton's son by his first marriage went to Mrs. Stanton. She relented and sent her husband food, clothing, blankets, pillows.

Urged on by Browning, the President's advisers talked strategy. Noah L. Jeffries, the Registrar of the Treasury, said the President should announce that he was submitting the Tenure of Office Act and the military "Force Bills" to the Supreme Court for a decision on their constitutionality. Johnson should also make a public statement beforehand that if the laws were declared legal he would immediately resign the Presidency. If the Congress would not agree to this test, then the President should arrest his principal foes. Only fifty armed men would be needed. Secretary Welles told Jeffries the idea was madness. The General of the Army was a member of the conspiracy. "Fifty military men," Welles said. "What could they do?" No soldier could stand against Grant. Certainly not General Emory, the Washington garrison commander. Jeffries and Welles argued the matter as Johnson listened in silence.

Upon one question the President's advisers were united: Johnson must not dignify the Senate proceedings by appearing in person. Johnson, however, wanted to appear so that he could put his tormentors to flight. His appearance was also sought by Ben Butler, who pictured the Great Criminal literally standing before the bar of justice, forbidden to take a seat until it should be the Senate's pleasure that he do so. To Butler's sorrow his colleagues did not go along with this plan. "Too weak in the knees or back," he said.

Butler's free-and-easy manner worried some of the other Radicals. A fellow manager told Butler, "This is the greatest case of the times, and it is to be conducted in the highest possible manner." Butler replied the matter would be tried according to the law—just like a horse-stealing case.

Had he been younger and in better health, the dominant man among the group of managers would of course have been Thaddeus Stevens. He was appointed chairman of the managers, but struck everyone as a dying man. Thin and pale, his eyes swallowed up in cavernous sockets, his skull showing through the skin, he sat swathed in blankets during the meetings of the board of managers. Butler and some of the others livened the sessions by gorging themselves on great slices of cheese they cut with their penknives. Stevens could eat nothing save an occasional cracker. But for the first time in decades he took liquor. As a young man he had been a social drinker, but the death of a drinking friend had turned him into a teetotaler. (In his own fashion Stevens announced his abstinence by dragging the contents of his wine cellar to the street, where he emptied the bottles in the gutter.) Now to keep up his strength he sipped brandy.

According to the journalist Emily Edson Briggs, Stevens was like the setting sun surrounded by the glory of the departing day; he was like the taper which, burning low in the socket, sends up a brilliant flame for a moment before it expires. This last great achievement of his life—the banishment of the Great Criminal—was, Mrs. Briggs wrote, the act of a man whose body was broken but whose spirit lived. Hardly able to walk, he was carried about in a chair by two young Negroes. For them he got out a weak joke: who, he asked, would take care of him when the two of them died?

Into the void left by Stevens stepped Ben Butler. He realized that the man primarily responsible for dislodging a President might eventually replace him. And the task itself appealed to Butler. He set to work on an opening address to the assembled Senators.

Still people wondered if the trial would actually take place. Samuel Pomeroy of Kansas, a Radical Senator, told Colonel Moore, the President's secretary, that if Johnson would replace his entire Cabinet with Radicals, including Butler, the trial could be called off. Moore relayed the message to his chief. "I will have to insult some of those men yet," Johnson sighed. Radicals had also told Secretary Seward that if he did nothing to hinder the trial he would be continued in office under Johnson's successor, President Wade. Seward's customary urbanity deserted him when he heard the offer. "I will see you damned first!" he replied. "The impeachment of the President is the impeachment of his Cabinet."

And so the work went forward. On March 4, 1868, at one in the afternoon, the Senate's main doors were thrown open and the committee of managers entered, two by two and arm in arm, Stevens in the lead leaning heavily on Representative Bingham.

"The managers of the impeachment on the part of the House of Representatives," called out a sergeant-at-arms. As president pro tem of the Senate, Benjamin Wade occupied the seat of the presiding officer. Studying his harsh face, Representative Shelby Cullom of Illinois asked himself what would happen if Johnson was convicted and then refused to give up his office to his former friend. Suppose, like Stanton, he decided to fight his removal. Would the result be civil war, the guillotine?

Others also began to view in a different way the man who was now the potential eighteenth President of the United States. "Johnson in the White House is bad enough, but we know what we have," Representative James G. Blaine of Maine said to Cullom. "Lord knows what we would get with old Ben Wade there."

The managers took their seats at a long table. Sumner got up from his desk and went to sit by Stevens. Together they and the others listened as Representative Bingham read the eleven articles, the counts of the indictment offered by the House in its own name and the names "of all the people of the United States, against Andrew Johnson, President of the United States, in maintenance and support of their impeachment against him for high crimes and misdemeanors in office." The reading took twenty minutes. At the end Wade said the

Senate would take notice and form itself into a high court to hear the case.

The following day, March 5, the Senate met again. The galleries were jammed. As provided in the Constitution, Chief Justice Salmon Chase took his seat as presiding officer of the trial. He swore in the Senators as jurors:

"I do solemnly swear that in all things pertaining to the trial of the impeachment of Andrew Johnson, President of the United States, I will do impartial justice, according to the Constitution and the laws: So help me God."

Standing with his hand raised, Sumner swore to be impartial. There was a dispute when Wade's name was called. Should he vote on a matter which could transform him from a lame-duck Senator into the President in the White House? The question was put to a vote, Chase's right to make the decision himself being challenged by the Radicals. The Senators voted that Wade could serve as a juror like the rest of his colleagues.

The high court then adjourned until March 13. At the White House the President was told that Wade had already selected his Cabinet. "Old Wade is counting his chickens before they are hatched," Johnson said with a chuckle. Rumors spread that the President had turned superstitious. As a result, spiritualists sent in messages from Lincoln offering advice. In fact the President remained as calm as though nothing out of the ordinary were occurring. The whole thing was in God's hands, he said. He showed no emotion when someone told him there was a rumor that Stevens had just died. He did not believe it. Stevens was like Vesuvius, he said, "which at times withdrew into itself all its heat and vapor, only to burst forth again in flames and lava." So it was with Old Thad. "A sort of temporary paralysis, which would be succeeded by a flow of living passion."

To plead his case the President had engaged five lawyers, each to be paid two thousand dollars out of the President's pocket. (In order that it might not be said that a government employee was serving him in a personal capacity, one of his lawyers, Attorney General Stanbery, resigned his post.) Perhaps the most eminent defender was William M. Evarts of New York, as prominent an attorney as any in the country. To Evarts the Republican, Andrew Johnson the President was anathema. Only four months earlier the lawyer had denounced him while speaking under a banner inscribed ANDREW JOHNSON: TRAITOR, RENEGADE, OUTCAST. Now Johnson was a client, and personal feelings were entirely submerged as Evarts and the others filed into the Senate Chamber on March 13 to begin the proceedings.

Young-looking despite his Olympian posture and visage, dressed in the robes of the Chief Justice, Salmon Chase told the sergeant-at-arms to summon the accused to judgment. "Andrew Johnson," cried the sergeant-at-arms, "President of the United States, appear and answer to the articles of impeachment exhibited against you by the House of Representatives of the United States."

Although everyone knew the President was not coming, all eyes turned to the main door. It opened. In walked Ben Butler. The Senate collapsed in laughter. As for Butler, it seemed to one observer that a hurt look came over his features. Why was the awful name of the Great Criminal flung at him?

When order was restored, former Attorney General Stanbery told the Senators that he and his colleagues had not had sufficient time to go over the case. Therefore, they asked a recess. Forty days was the period of time they had in mind.

"Forty days!" roared Ben Butler. "As long as it took God to destroy the world by a flood!" Representative Bingham demanded instant action. Perhaps Bingham had in mind the rumor that tens of thousands of ex-Confederates were massing for an attack on Washington. Perhaps it was the rumor that rebel sympathizers had secreted nitroglycerin in buildings all over the city.* But this was not a police-court matter to be

* The Houston *Telegraph* gave full voice to the rumors, accepting all as fact and reporting in its February 25, 1868, edition that the War Department had been burned, Lorenzo Thomas murdered and Stanton wounded in the fighting which erupted when Grant declared himself dictator and put Johnson under arrest. "General war inevitable," the paper told its readers. Meanwhile the Louisville *Democrat* reported that Congress was to be driven away at "bayonet point." The newspaper asked its readers: "Are you ready once more to take the musket, still warm from the last shot that struck down the rebellion, for a new battle?"

put through with railroad speed, Stanbery replied. They compromised by voting a ten-day delay.

But it would be ridiculous, Charles Sumner said, for Congress to continue in the same relation to the Great Criminal as before. Were Senators expected to send bills to and receive messages from one who shortly would be banished from office and into outer darkness? All business should be suspended until the trial ended, Sumner said. He was so certain that Johnson would be found guilty that he was already writing up legislation that would forbid the ex-President to hold public office again. Ben Butler, also convinced that Johnson was finished, sent telegrams to friends predicting that "Wade and prosperity are sure to come in with the apple blossoms." Speaker of the House Schuyler Colfax said: "He will be convicted without doubt."

More cautious, Thad Stevens studied the names of the Senator-jurors. Conviction required a guilty vote by two-thirds of the Senators—thirty-six out of fifty-four. If only a simple majority was needed to convict, there would be no doubt of the outcome. A two-thirds vote was different. But what if a few Senators from safe carpetbagger regimes could be added to the high court? Whispering instructions to subordinates straining to hear his words, Stevens moved for quick readmission of Arkansas to the Union.

With the Presidential conventions only months away, with an election scheduled for the fall, Ulysses Grant possessed more influence than any other man in the country. And he had decided that acquittal would encourage Johnson to run amok. According to Grant, only the President's lack of courage had prevented total "riotousness" in the White House. A not guilty verdict would give Johnson courage. Seemingly without a temper—he had lost his composure only once during the war, when at Shiloh he saw a teamster abuse a horse—Grant had arrived at a state of mind where he was almost irrational in his detestation of the President. After years of adulation, Grant found his word questioned because of his broken promise to hold the War Office against Stanton. He blamed Johnson for putting him into such a situation and hated the President more than he had ever hated any Confederate. On a Washington horsecar he saw Senator John B. Henderson of Missouri, who was known to lean toward a not guilty verdict. The General sat down and asked if Henderson had changed his opinion about the impeachment.

"No, General, I am of the same mind about it."

"Do you think you can defeat it?"

"Well, I can't warrant that," Senator Henderson replied. "We have friends enough against it to defeat it, but I cannot give a pledge that we shall actually defeat it."

"Well, I hope you won't," Grant said.

"Why, General, you wouldn't impeach Johnson?"

"Yes, I would impeach him if for nothing else than because he is such an infernal liar!"

"I very much regret to hear you say it. I regret it because on such terms it would be nearly impossible to find the right sort of man to serve as President!"

Even before the trial began, letters demanding a guilty verdict poured into Senators' offices. Fessenden of Maine resented the proffered advice. The writers had not taken an oath as the Senators had. Nor would they hear all the evidence. "I cannot and will not violate my oath," Fessenden said. "I would rather be confined to planting cabbages for the rest of my days."

But there was too much at stake to be fussy, the Radicals said. Opponents of impeachment might fear that conviction would "Mexicanize" the American government—since obtaining its independence from Spain half a century earlier the Mexicans had had innumerable presidents, dictators, generalissimos, caudillos and jefes, not to mention an Emperor—but the Radicals did not care. The American system of government would be endangered and all future Presidents emasculated and made into figureheads; *if you don't kill the beast it will kill you,* Stevens had said.

On March 23 the defense lawyers came to the White House before going to the Senate Chamber. The previous night Johnson had suddenly declared that he was planning to accompany them, and it was only with difficulty that they dissuaded him from doing so. But now in the last moments before the great trial he was calm as he said good-bye to them. (His Cabinet was less hopeful than the President. Welles wrote in his diary, "Every member, I think, considers conviction a foregone conclusion." In the name of the Constitution, Welles wrote, the Senate was going to shoot down the faithful sentinel who stood guard over the Constitution. People were already paying farewell calls to Cabinet members. Perhaps they felt it would be unpleasant and embarrassing to do so after conviction.)

Appearing almost unconcerned in the eyes of the body-guard William Crook, the President shook hands with the lawyers on the White House portico.

"Gentlemen," he said, "my case is in your hands. I feel sure you will protect my interests." They left, Crook escorting them at the President's request. They drove to a Senate Chamber which, with its red carpet, rose chairs and sofas, seemed to the journalist Emily Edson Briggs suggestive of molten heat. She observed Chief Justice Chase's daughter, Kate Chase Sprague. Mrs. Sprague was the wife of the Senator from Rhode Island and the all-too-obvious good friend of Roscoe Conkling of New York. Dressed in silk tinted the shade of a dead forest leaf, she also wore matching gold ornaments. Chase himself had a cold, haughty, handsome face. Kate had far more charm. As clever as she was stunning, she stood out among the other beautiful women in the galleries, many of whom had brought opera glasses. They seated themselves in such fashion that their flowing crinolines blocked anyone else from sitting nearby. Somehow, though, they always found space when a friend arrived bearing one of the yellow entrance tickets of which each Senator was issued four and each Representative two.

The situation did not appear hopeful, thought the bodyguard Crook, up in the galleries. Crook worshiped the memory of Abraham Lincoln, whom he regarded as almost a supernatural being capable of foreseeing his own death, a foresight demonstrated when he said "Good-bye, Crook" in place of the usual "Good night, Crook" on the night Lincoln attended Ford's Theatre. In Crook's eyes Johnson was no Lincoln. But the bodyguard esteemed the silent man. To-gether they took long walks, exchanging not a word. Once at a cemetery they silently looked at the long rows of soldiers' graves until Johnson breathed that they were in the center of a city, a city of the dead. The President was considerate of the people who served him, Crook thought. Johnson had established a White House mess where employees could eat instead of going out for lunch. Even though the President never seemed to notice what was going on around him, he arranged for his driver to be given a hot toddy when the man was soaked in a cold rain.

He did not deserve this fate, Crook thought to him-self as the lawyers took their places in front of the raised desk at which Chief Justice Chase sat. It was one in the afternoon. The managers were already seated, Stevens im-mobile, his eyes closed. For a moment Crook felt something akin to terror. Mrs. Briggs noted the absolute silence, no pages scurrying about with messages, no coughing.

Evarts, dignified, reasonable, arose to present the Presi-dent's case. The Tenure of Office Act was unconstitutional. The Congress had assigned to itself rights that it did not have under the Constitution. The President's sworn duty by the oath he took three hours after Lincoln's death forbade him to accept the Tenure of Office Act. As for the charge that he had defamed Congress in his Swing Around the Circle, he stood on his rights of free speech, guaranteed by the Constitution. The Senate adjourned. That night Andrew Johnson held a long-scheduled social reception. Perhaps he had been engaged in working on the bill of fare as his counsel spoke, Mrs. Briggs reflected. In like manner Louis XV concerned himself with powders and paintbox, with Madames DuBarry and Pompadour, while France's great storm was brewing. Mrs. Briggs noticed that many of the guests were foreigners. They are the last to

247

leave a sinking dynasty, she thought to herself. It also seemed to her that men outnumbered women at the affair by a ratio of ten to one. "There is no surer sign of deterioration in entertainments than the absence of women," she wrote.

Crook was surprised to see so many people at the reception. He had anticipated an empty White House. He was further shocked to discover some fifteen Radicals gathered together in the East Room. They were laughing and teasing one another. "What are you here for?" one asked.

"And you," the other replied. "What are you doing here yourself?"

"Why," said the first, "I wanted to see how Andy takes it."

But neither Crook nor the guests could know what thoughts were going through the President's mind. For Johnson greeted all callers in such unconcerned fashion as to make it appear the whole gathering had "come to congratulate him on his statesmanship." Mrs. Briggs agreed with Crook. Smiles lit up the President's "unreadable face," she wrote. But she added that the party was a farce, a beehive swarming with black-coated honey bees and few queens. Secretary of the Treasury McCulloch was there, in her view sleek and oily, with a mouth that snapped shut like a tobacco box closed up and put away for future use. Also present was Secretary Welles— The Old Man of the Sea to Mrs. Briggs. They must be present for the purpose of dividing up and sharing the honor they feel slipping away, she decided. At eleven o'clock the Marine Band packed up its shining horns and left, and the guests vanished. Mrs. Briggs departed too, leaving the Executive Mansion to what she thought must be uneasy dreams.

The next day the trial resumed at one in the afternoon. Ben Butler took the floor. He had worked on his speech with great industry, thinking to himself that the opening argument would be the most important of the trial and that whatever followed would not be of much consequence. He wore a black evening suit with white tie.

For the first time in the history of the world, Butler began, a nation was bringing before its highest tribunal its highest official for a trial and a possible ouster from office. It was well that the Constitution provided for a Presidential impeachment, for otherwise, short of assassination, how could the country be rid of "a tyrannical, imbecile, or faithless ruler"?

And what a ruler it was that Congress impeached! "By murder most foul he succeeded to the Presidency, and is the elect of an assassin to that high office!" Butler's voice rose in such fashion as to make Crook think the occasion was being made too theatrical, almost unreal.

Butler cried out that there were no precedents for a ruler who had returned rebeldom to power over the bodies of three hundred thousand Union dead. Strict interpretation of any law by the Senator-judges was not called for. "Bound by no law . . . you are a law unto yourselves, bound only by the natural principle of equity and justice." Yet even on narrow lines the President was plainly culpable. He had overridden the Tenure of Office Act at his pleasure. He had not accepted that Act, which was a law of the United States. He had played fast and loose with it; he had ignored it; he had attempted in underhanded manner, just as the "criminal brought to bay makes to escape the consequences of his act," to bypass the law. And he was not ashamed of what he had done. Here was a brother to Cromwell and Napoleon.

Butler discussed the Swing Around the Circle. The President of the United States, resting, is in a hotel. Outside, in the darkness, "a noisy crowd of men and boys, washed and unwashed, drunk and sober, black and white." They make the "night hideous by their bawling." The President rushes to a balcony from where he proceeds to express his opinions on the wisdom, expediency, justice, worthiness, objects, purposes and political motives and tendencies of the Congress. These observations are received with hisses, cheers, laughs, groans. He yells into the darkness. Voices reply, "Mind your dignity,

Andy." He does not obey this considered injunction. He yells some more. Someone shouts out, "Traitor!" On this "fitting, Constitutional occasion," the President sees fit to answer.

Previously bored with the trial, Sumner laughed at Butler's gibes. Butler went on, "Never again, if Andrew Johnson go quit and free this day, can the people of this or any other country by Constitutional checks or guards stay the usurpation of executive power."

Butler talked for three hours, concluding: "I speak, therefore, not the language of exaggeration, but the words of truth and soberness, that the future political welfare and liberties of all men hang trembling on the decision of the hour."

That night the defense lawyers reported to their client. "What are the signs of the zodiac today?" he asked. The President seemed calm, as did his entire family. Martha Patterson told a friend, "I do not know how it will end. All we can do is to wait." *

But the odds against the President seemed very great. Newspaper opinion was overwhelmingly in favor of conviction. He should be removed, said Horace Greeley's New York *Tribune,* not only for breaking the Tenure of Office Act but because he was also guilty of treason, drunkenness, adultery, murder. The general conference of the Methodist Episcopal Church met in Chicago and entertained a motion asking an hour's prayer for the President's conviction. When a member of the conference inquired whether, by requesting the Senators to vote in such fashion, they were urging them to violate their oaths of impartiality, the motion was withdrawn and replaced with another that stated Senators were being bribed and corrupted and that the Almighty should be besought "to save our Senators from error." The motion passed and the conferees prayed for the allotted hour.

From the Republican Campaign Club in Chicago came a message for Trumbull of Illinois: it would be unwise for the

---

* Not always so restrained, she had nicknamed the Secretary of War "Brute Stanton." His aide, Assistant Adjutant General Townsend, was "Aunt Nancy."

Senator to show himself on the streets of Chicago if he failed to vote for conviction. He would be strung up on the nearest lamppost.

Johnson was "the lost cause," Mrs. Briggs wrote, and sometimes in private it came to the President that perhaps conviction and disgrace were waiting. The Senate was corrupt, he told his secretary, Colonel William Moore. You could not depend upon it to do what the interests of the people required. Therefore it was certainly possible that he would be convicted. But he did not care, so long as the nation itself felt he was innocent. Yet it was depressing for a man to labor for the people and not be understood. "It is enough to sour his very soul," the President told his aide, adding that perhaps Moore ought to look around for a new job.

Those close to Johnson tried to keep up his spirits. "I am now in regular training, like a prizefighter," Stanbery told him. "I have a man to come and rub me down, to keep in good condition. I feel that we will win, and that you, Mr. President, will come out all right. As the boys say, I feel it in my bones." Secretary of State Seward said he would bet anyone a basket of champagne that the verdict would be acquittal.

After Butler's opening address the board of managers put into the record all the documentation needed to make a considered case against Andrew Johnson: a copy of the oath whereby the President swore to execute his office; a certification from Chief Justice Chase that the Justice had administered the oath in the Kirkwood House; Abraham Lincoln's nomination of Edwin M. Stanton as Secretary of War and Johnson's note discharging him from that post. The managers also submitted Johnson's messages to Congress, which were read aloud. Senators drifted into the cloakroom in order not to hear the readings, which droned on and on. They listened to the testimony Stanton gave before the House committee which originally took up the question of impeachment.

The secretary of the Senate then swore in the man who had served the arrest papers on Lorenzo Thomas. The man told of finding General Thomas at a masquerade ball. How did he know it was the General if masks were worn? "I saw his shoulder straps and I asked him to unmask." The certificate of service was put into evidence.

Witnesses to Thomas' attempted takeover from Stanton said that everyone had been amused by Thomas' reiteration that he wished no *on*pleasantness. Had the General, Butler asked one witness, emphasized his desire that things be pleasant, or was he emphasizing the *on* in "*on*pleasantness"?

"Well, sir, I can only state what General Thomas said."

"The emphasis is something."

"*On*pleasantness was the expression used."

As the trial progressed, Chief Justice Chase's attitude increasingly alarmed the Radicals, particularly Charles Sumner. When Chase and Sumner had served as fellow Senators they had strolled about arm in arm and Sumner had said of Chase that he was his dearest friend. The two men had talked of buying a house together. Between them they constituted a majority of the then-tiny group of Senators who could be called Abolitionists. Chase had moved from the Senate to be Treasury Secretary for most of the war's duration (he put his own face on the new greenbacks) and from there to the Chief Justiceship. Summer had raced from the Senate to inform him of his confirmation to that post.

Salmon P. Chase's feelings for the downtrodden were sincere and self-sacrificing, yet he was at the same time a man who could stoop to unsavory financial dealings. Intensely ambitious, noble and yet avaricious, Salmon P. Chase had a great deal to win or lose by his conduct during this trial. He was a potential candidate for the Presidency, which he had sought with half-mad intensity for so long. As opposed to Chase, Ulysses Grant was small-bore. Certainly there was at least a possibility that the Republicans would turn to one of their long-time stalwarts in place of a politically ignorant soldier. Chase also appeared giantlike as compared with Johnson's successor should there be a conviction. "The idea of that horrid Ben Wade being put over my father!" cried the beautiful Kate Chase Sprague when a Philadelphia *Evening Star* reporter interviewed her.

Yet with so much at stake for himself, the ambitious

man had put aside ambition and submerged all personal feelings. Looking only to the law and to the right as he saw it, the Chief Justice sometimes made rulings which favored the defense. There were those who believed that his display of independence was the most admirable thing he had ever done. Always a corner cutter where his career was concerned, he was rigidly impartial now.

Charles Sumner was not among those who found Chase's actions inspiring. His old friend's rulings bewildered, then angered him. "Alas, poor Chase," he said, and moved to limit Chase's role in the trial: "Resolved, that the Chief Justice of the United States, presiding in the Senate on the trial of the President of the United States, is not a member of the Senate, and has no authority, under the Constitution, to vote on any question during the trial, and he can pronounce decision only as the organ of the Senate, with its assent."

But the language was too brutal for most members of the Senate. If the Senators outraged Chase's dignity he might in his majestic fashion decline to participate further in the proceedings. That would end the trial. A more tactfully worded resolution was passed: Chase would rule on all questions of evidence and his rulings would stand unless a member of the Senate requested a vote on a particular one. The result of the vote would then govern.*

The presentation of evidence went on, the managers addressing Chase as "Mr. President," which implied he was acting chief of the Senate with limited powers, and the defense calling him "Mr. Chief Justice," which implied a higher position. Lorenzo Thomas' possible resort to violence was analyzed by the managers: he had axes, crowbars, armed men in mind when he spoke of supplanting Stanton. A clownish fellow townsman of Thomas was produced, one George Washington Karsner. Karsner apparently viewed the entire controversy as a challenge to Delaware's position in the world. "Said I to him, 'General, the eyes of Delaware are upon you.'"

Everyone laughed.

* In effect, some observers said, the Senate was now both judge and jury.

"Order!" cried Chase.

" 'Stand firm, General,' said I . . . 'I think Delaware will expect something from you.' . . . Just before I left I renewed the desires of Delaware."

"Order! Order!" shouted Chase.

They went on to examine General Emory, the officer commanding the military forces in Washington. Had not Johnson asked him about troop disposition in the District? Why? The lawyers wrangled.

Horace Greeley's New York *Tribune* published an interview with General Grant. He had found it "not inconsistent with his duty as a soldier to announce it as his opinion that the only hope for the peace of the country is the success of the pending impeachment trial." Grant felt the country was in a grave emergency, reported the *Tribune*. "He feels national security demands the removal of the President. . . . When the General of our armies entertains this conviction, there is no room for doubt as to the duty of the Senate."

Johnson read the interview and said to his secretary, Moore, "What an idea!"

Other, wilder, newspaper articles appeared. Two Senators had suffered upset stomachs. It must have been poison. People should be careful about drinking water without making certain it came straight from the well. Money was being shipped from banks in New York to Washington, to be used for bribes.

By then Chase's duplicity was accepted as a proven fact by all Radicals. When it was reported that an undecided Senator was seen leaving a dinner party at the Chief Justice's home, Ben Butler roared, "We are sold out!" Detectives were hired to keep watch over Chase's house to see just which Senators called upon him.

One Senator often seen in the Chief Justice's home was his son-in-law, the husband of the beautiful Kate. William Sprague was one of the richest young men in the country, perhaps the richest, with interests in mills, railroads, banks. Handsome, the commander of his Rhode Island regiment when Kate met him, he seemed to be a brilliant catch. But he was a wastrel.

His behavior when intoxicated was revolting. At a White House dinner he drank too much and attracted the attention of the President's younger daughter, Mary Stover. "I would not take more if I were you," she said. "There are a pair of bright blue eyes looking at you."

"Damn them," he replied. "They can't see me."

"Yes, they *can,*" Kate said, "and they are thoroughly ashamed of you!" Sprague drained another glass and then slammed it down on the table.

His business ethics were such that during the war he had involved himself in running Confederate cotton through the blockade to his mills. These transactions could have easily resulted in treason charges. They had come to light in the last days of the war and had been the subject of a report by General John Dix which was en route to President Lincoln's desk when Lincoln died. The report did not reach his successor. But Secretary of War Stanton knew about the transactions and could be assumed to have transmitted the information to his Radical allies. Even if Stanton unaccountably kept quiet, Sprague could be destroyed by Ben Butler. When Butler was in command at New Orleans, Sprague wrote a safe-pass letter for one of his cotton smugglers. The smuggler was to show Butler the letter if the ship should be stopped. Sprague did not know if the letter ever came to Butler's attention, but he could be sure that if it had, Butler would not have forgotten it or failed to realize its implications. Sitting in his seat watching Butler's efforts to force Andrew Johnson out of the White House, Sprague could not doubt that if necessary Butler would use the letter to get his vote for conviction.

Meanwhile Kate Chase Sprague railed at her husband to vote for acquittal. She did not know that he was at the mercy of the Radicals. She thought only of her father. If the Senate acquitted the President, Ben Wade would return to Ohio, no longer a contender for the 1868 Republican nomination. Kate had barely left girlhood behind her when she held the second place in social Washington behind Mrs. Lincoln (for Secretary of State Seward's wife was ill and Kate's father, then Secretary of the Treasury, was a widower). She could become the first hostess in the land if her father were elected to the White House. So while her worried husband wondered how he should vote, Kate Sprague ceaselessly lobbied for acquittal.

The board of managers went on to present Johnson's feud with Grant after Grant gave up the office of Secretary of War ad interim. They then examined the newspaper stenographers who had taken down Presidential speeches in short-hand—this in connection with Butler's article accusing the President of defamation of Congress. (When one of the stenographers said he had cleaned up the President's speech before giving it to his editor, making "You and I saw" from "You and myself has seen," Butler professed horror that the man had thus tampered with the President's great constitutional right of freedom of speech.)

Butler made great sport with the Cleveland speech of the Swing Around the Circle, putting on the witness stand the stenographer who had taken it down along with comments shouted by the audience.

"Was anything said about not getting mad?" Butler asked.

"The words used were, 'Don't get mad, Andy.' "

"Did he appear considerably excited at that moment when they told him not to get mad?"

People could not help smiling then, or when Butler questioned a witness who made reference to a friend who was— a tailor. But Sumner's young secretary, Moorfield Storey, wrote his family that he wondered if Butler's tomfoolery would go down so well when read fifty years in the future. As with his employer, Storey felt that the only important matter was to remove Johnson from office. Concerned about the persistent rumors that the President kept shifting troops around the city, Storey hesitantly wrote his family that he could not believe Johnson would order them to fight when conviction was announced. "The suicidal folly of such a course is evident. Still Johnson is an exception to all rules. It only shows the folly of leaving a man, impeached for high crimes, in full possession of all the powers of the government, and the command of the army and navy." Rumors spread that the President intended to send marines under the command of Secretary of the Navy Welles to force Stanton out of the War Office.

On April 9 the managers concluded the presentation of their evidence. It had taken them three weeks to do so. By then Moorfield Storey was so filled with the trial that it invaded his sleep. He dreamed that the family cat, Rose, was possessed of a vote of immense importance and that to his horror she ran away from him. He also dreamed that Sumner told him he really wanted to vote for acquittal. He wrote a young lady friend that he told Sumner all about it and "worked him up to quite a pitch of excitement, and had hard work to make him understand it was only a dream."

Even when awake and away from the Senate Chamber the secretary was not free of the trial, for it brought forth a flow of threatening letters to Sumner. Storey's duties included reading the correspondence. He wrote a friend, "The Ku Klux send letters every day, filled with gallows, coffins, skulls, daggers and corpses, announcing to Charles * that the avenger is on his track, and that he will be awakened at midnight only to find his room filled with masked figures, and to meet his doom at their hands. . . . The drawings which accompany these epistles remind me of my own efforts. They seem to be the work of schoolboys."

Former Attorney General Stanbery and William Evarts were the most prominent figures of the defense effort to counter the points which the managers made. But Stanbery was not a well man and his strength was failing. So most of the work was left to Evarts. The responsibility did not depress him. One Sunday evening he ran into Manager George Boutwell of Massachusetts at a dinner party given by Sumner. (The usual prohibition against lawyers mixing socially with jurors did not apply when the jury consisted of the United States Senate.)

---

* Storey was young and a bachelor, and no doubt his young lady was impressed to learn that he offhandedly referred to Senator Sumner by his Christian name, at least in letters to young ladies.

Evarts remarked that he had not been out of his hotel room all day, but had spent it going over the case. Boutwell indicated that Sunday was supposed to be a day of rest. Evarts replied, "Yes, but you know what the Bible says we may do in case an ox or an ass falleth into a pit, particularly the latter, and especially when he has been in it so long." He did not know, and perhaps would never know, that Ben Butler had paid spies to search the wastepaper basket of his hotel room seeking clues to the lines of defense. Years later Butler still boasted of it.

The defense presentation of evidence opened with a speech by defense lawyer Benjamin Robbins Curtis. This case was a trial, Curtis said. Nothing more. "Here party spirit, political schemes, foregone conclusions, outrageous biases can have no fit operation. The Constitution requires that there should be a 'trial' and in that trial an oath, which each of you has taken, to administer 'impartial justice according to the Constitution and the laws.' "

Curtis questioned whether Edwin Stanton was even covered by the Tenure of Office Act. He had been appointed by Lincoln, not by Johnson. Now President in his own right, Johnson was not serving Lincoln's term. Could he be entirely bound by Lincoln's acts? It would be similar to claiming that after a monarch died, the crown prince become king was merely serving out his father's reign.

But even if the law did cover Stanton, Curtis went on, it had not been violated. For Stanton was still in his office at the War Department. There had only been an attempt to remove him. The whole issue of his discharge was moot.

Finally, whether Stanton was covered or not or removed from office or not, the Act itself was unconstitutional and therefore not valid legislation. The President had no choice but to resist it. Directed solely against the President, it could be contested only by the President. If he did not question this law, no one else could, and it would never be tested by the Supreme Court for its validity. That was why he had violated the Act. There had been no conspiracy on his part. He had obeyed all other laws.

Curtis turned to the speeches of the Swing Around the Circle. The Constitution, he said, spoke of treason, bribery and other high crimes and misdemeanors as impeachable offenses. No mention was made of offensive speeches. To judge exactly what was proper talk could lead to guillotines and scaffolds and to the kind of order which prevailed in the Czar's empire.

Curtis ended, Ben Butler thinking to himself that everything possible had been said for the President. The defense presentation of witnesses began. Lorenzo Thomas took the stand.

The Senators and spectators saw a fussy man, no longer young, with a slender waist and tapering fingers. According to Emily Edson Briggs, if the poet who wrote "Frailty, thy name is woman" had seen Thomas, he would have added a qualifying phrase indicating that nature sometimes makes mistakes. That Stanton had put his arm around Thomas' neck and run his fingers through the man's hair suddenly seemed a natural act to her. The General through his testimony did not emerge as a strong figure. He described his military career as that of a messenger boy who always obeyed orders: "I was sent . . . The first duty he placed me on . . . He sent me . . ." No violence was ever contemplated during his attempted takeover. He had said he would "kick out" Stanton because his fellow Delawarian, George Washington Karsner, had used the phrase. He simply repeated Karsner's phrase.

"Are you certain the 'kicking out' came from him?" Stanbery asked.

"Yes, sir—oh, yes. I want to say one thing. I did not intend any disrespect to Mr. Stanton at all. On the contrary, he has always treated me with kindness, and I would do nothing to treat him with disrespect."

Butler cross-examined. Had not General Grant recommended Thomas' retirement?

Yes, but "The President did not put me aside."

And his relations with Stanton? "You would not harm a hair of his head, certainly not kick him?" Certainly not. But

259

had not Stanton repeatedly sent Thomas away from Washington, preferring to have Assistant Adjutant General Townsend perform Thomas' duties? And if so, why?

"I did not suppose he wanted me in the office, though there was no unkind feeling," Thomas replied.

"Only he did not want you there?"

"I do not suppose he did."

"It was perfectly kindly, except that he did not want you about?" Butler asked. "Now, if you will pay attention to my question, General Thomas, and answer it, you will oblige me."

Looking on, Moorfield Storey said to himself that Butler was making Thomas pitiable, and that Butler's effrontery took the breath away. Thomas became confused about when he was selected to replace Stanton. First he named one day, then another.

"I want you again to pay attention to my question. How early did you swear that you received an intimation that you would be made Secretary of War?"

"I should like to divide those two things," Thomas replied to Butler's question. "I told you that I corrected my evidence."

"I am dividing them. Now I am getting to what you swore to first. By and by I will come to the correction, perhaps. Now answer my question. What did you swear to first before you took advice?"

Stanbery jumped up to object. " 'Took advice'! Monstrous!"

Butler kept going. Thomas became more and more confused. "The honorable manager is trying to mix things up," he complained.

"Now listen to the question and answer it!" Butler replied. "That will be better."

Evarts and Stanbery tried to protect their witness, and their exchanges with Butler grew very sharp. "We object to your arguing with the witness," Stanbery said. "Ask your question."

"Do not interrupt me," Butler snapped. He went to

Thomas' statements that he would use force if necessary. Had he meant that?

"I suppose I did not mean it, for it never entered my head to use force."

"You did not mean it?" Butler pressed.

"No, sir."

"It was mere boast, brag?"

"Oh, yes."

"How was that? Speak as loud as you did when you began!"

Butler got on the subject of whether the President had told Thomas to "take charge" of the War Department. Had that been the phrase, or was it "take possession"? Originally Thomas had said the words were *take possession;* now it was *take charge.* Why?

"I think the words were put into my mouth. I do not recollect distinctly."

"The same as Karsner put in about the 'kicking out'?"

"Yes."

"And you are rather in the habit, are you, when words are put in your mouth, of using them?"

Finally Butler let him go. That Thomas was a weakling and a nincompoop was made abundantly clear. But could he be viewed as the fearsome tool of a power-mad Nero?

General Sherman was put on the stand. He had been summoned from his Far West post. When he called at the War Department to visit Assistant Adjutant Townsend, he found the place barricaded. Stanton took more precautions than were considered necessary for officers traveling through dangerous Indian territory, Sherman told people. "Maybe, however," Sherman said, "he deems himself in greater danger here than I would be among the Indians, and damn me if I feel as safe here as I did on the Plains. I feel as if I were liable to be entrapped by politicians and correspondents." He laughed heartily.

On the stand Sherman testified that the President asked him to take over as Secretary of War, but he had refused.

Stanbery fell ill. It was almost completely Evarts versus Butler now. Yet from time to time Thad Stevens, eyes closed, motionless, with his elbows on the arms of his chair and his fingers interlaced under the swaddling blanket, raised his head as a signal to Butler to hear a few whispered words. So frail that people thought he was literally dying before them, he missed nothing. Wrote Georges Clemenceau: "If it were not for the fire smouldering in the depths of his piercing eyes, one might imagine life had already fled from that inert body, but it still nurses all the wrath of Robespierre."

An old preacher friend wrote Stevens urging that he repent his sins: "At present, in every part of the United States, people believe that your personal life has been one prolonged sin; that your lips are defiled with blasphemy! Your hands with gambling! And your body with women!" But the last thing on Stevens' mind was to make peace with the Almighty. He was too worried that the vote would go the wrong way. Working through subordinates, he drove forward his motion to admit the two Senators-elect from Arkansas. Elected by what was called an "Africanized" constituency, they would be automatic votes for conviction. Could such men, who had not been sworn as jurors for the opening of the trial, and who in that capacity had not heard the early evidence, vote at the end of the trial? "Of course," Sumner said.

It seemed to Mrs. Briggs that the "impeachmentites" would succeed. She wrote, "A new day already dawns in the East, and the coming man stands before the people, whom destiny has called to be the leader and to guide the ship of state into a peaceful sea. All hail! Benjamin F. Wade."

Wade had not said a word during the trial. Whenever a point was put before the Senate for a vote, he abstained. No one knew if he planned to participate in the final vote which would determine if he vaulted from lame-duck Senator to President of the United States. It did not seem decorous for a man to vote for himself on such a matter, but decorum was not Bluff Ben's strong suit. (One day Chief Justice Chase could not find his robe. It had fallen on the floor of Wade's office, where Chase dressed each day. Wade picked it up. "There's your damned old robe, Chase," he said, and flung it through the air.)

The lawyers wrangled over admission of testimony the defense wanted to introduce to show the President's purpose in dismissing or attempting to dismiss Stanton. The defense contended Johnson was not acting as a revolutionary but that he simply wanted to test the Tenure of Office Act. Butler maintained that what Johnson had or had not said to people did not constitute evidence. "I have had a great many things said to me that I should be very unwilling to have regarded as evidence," he declared. "For instance, here is a written declaration sent to me today: 'Butler, prepare to meet your God. The avenger is abroad on your track. Hell is your portion.' "

But the view of the defense prevailed. Secretary of the Navy Welles took the stand. Butler greeted the Secretary by suggesting that Johnson, like a king who could do no wrong, was attempting to hide behind his Cabinet ministers. Evarts countered that Welles would simply indicate his chief's frame of mind. The Secretary would speak of the counsel offered the President by his advisers. The lawyers argued the point. Finally Chase ruled that Welles' testimony could be included. But Senator Howard of Michigan called for a Senate vote on Chase's ruling. The "nays" dominated, and Welles stepped down. "Judges!" he wrote in his diary. "O, what judges!"

Chase was shocked by the vote. Surely, he said to intimates, the defense had a right to call Cabinet ministers to testify. But nothing more could be done. Muzzled by the Senate vote, the defense was forced to conclude its case.

13

On the night of April 21 defense attorney William Evarts asked the eminent Union General John M. Schofield to visit him at the Willard Hotel. He told Schofield the President wished to nominate him for the post of Secretary of War, replacing Thomas, the ad interim minister. Evarts was frank to say the President's advisers wanted the nomination sent to the Senate before the close of the impeachment trial.

Schofield discussed the proposal with Grant. The General of the Army was not happy to see Johnson relieved of the embarrassment of having Thomas hung around his neck. But, as he said to Schofield, there was "no reasonable doubt of the President's removal." Therefore he had no objections to Schofield's acceptance of the proffered post. Schofield would make President Wade a good Secretary of War.

The President sent the nomination to the Senate. Schofield was regarded as an upright soldier. He would not likely become an instrument for revenge in the hands of an acquitted Johnson. Grant suddenly saw that the appointment reassured still-undecided Senators. He told Schofield not to accept the nomination. By then it was too late. Schofield's appointment might well cost the Radicals a precious vote or two, which they could not afford to lose. So a group of Radicals began meeting each day at the home of Senator Pomeroy of Kansas. The question on their agenda was always the same: what pressures could still be applied to Senators who had not already made up their minds?

Willey of West Virginia was a reverent Methodist; the Radical caucus sent Bishop Matthew Simpson to speak and pray with him. Trumbull of Illinois showed the same concern as Sumner for Negro rights; stories of new Ku Klux outrages were detailed to him. The Radicals believed Henderson of Missouri might succumb to pressures from home; letters poured in on him, and Missouri papers wrote editorials warning him to vote for conviction. Grant also had him in for breakfast. The General told Henderson that conviction was certain. President Wade's Cabinet had already been picked. (Ben Butler would be Secretary of State.) And Grant was to be Wade's successor. The Radicals promised to back the General, provided he agreed to retain Wade's Cabinet. "Good God, General," Henderson said. The trial was a bad situation, Henderson told his fiancée. "If I vote for Johnson, it is sure to cost me reelection to the Senate, and I know you will not like that."

"You go ahead, John," his fiancée replied. "Don't consider me. I don't care at all. Do what you think is right. That is the way I will be happy." He remained undecided.

Edmund Ross of Kansas remained a question mark. He had no political experience. Two years earlier the Governor of Kansas had appointed Ross to the post vacated by Senator Jim Lane, who had shot himself. It was believed the suicide resulted from the vituperation poured upon Lane for his support of Johnson's policies. There had been no intimation from the state Governor, Ross' regimental commander during the war, that he might be appointed to the Senate. Ross himself had not solicited the post.

In Washington, Ross boarded with an old acquaintance from Kansas, Robert L. Ream. His landlord had a slim and attractive daughter, Vinnie, a young sculptress hardly out of school and barely past twenty-one. Despite her youth she had received a commission to do a statue of Lincoln for the Capitol, and was provided with a studio in the building. Word of Ross' frequent visits to the studio reached the Radical caucus along with information that Vinnie Ream was urging Ross to vote against conviction.

The Radicals convinced themselves that Vinnie Ream was conducting a highly improper relationship with the Kansas Senator. Congressman George Washington Julian of Indiana was assigned to have a talk with the young woman. Less vituperative in his language than certain other Radicals—Wade's profanity revolted him—Julian nevertheless spoke harshly to Miss Ream. She had better understand, he told her, that if she had any influence with Ross it should be used in favor of conviction. If she lobbied for acquittal, she would live to regret it.

The Radical caucus soon found one meeting a day was not enough to track down rumors and plan strategy. Government had almost come to a standstill, and the country's business interests delayed important commitments until the outcome of the trial.* In such an atmosphere rumors flew about, then died with lightning speed. The caucus met twice daily.

The Radicals continually discussed the case of Chase's son-in-law, Senator Sprague of Rhode Island. Chase's impartiality during the trial would seem to have ended his hopes for Radical support for the Presidency. However, all might be forgiven if the Senate voted for conviction. Sprague could be appealed to on the grounds that a guilty verdict would result in Radical support for his father-in-law. And there were the cotton deals of wartime hanging over his head. The caucus had good reason to think that Sprague would be incapable of voting not guilty.

The Ministership to Great Britain was held out to

---

* Dressmakers, however, did very well. Every woman wanted a garment done in new "Impeachment Blue."

Fessenden of Maine. Perhaps he was not as immovable as he appeared. On the chance that he was not, the Radicals organized a letters-from-home campaign to help him see things the Radical way. "Is it possible that you have turned traitor, and that your name will be handed down with that of Benedict Arnold?" "If for nothing else, to satisfy those who elected you, you are bound to vote for conviction." The Senator was besought "not to crush the people of Maine with shame and misery."

The defense lawyers arranged a counterattack through Senator James W. Grimes of Iowa, who was strongly against conviction and believed the nation would never recover from the shock attendant to driving a President from office. Grimes thought of Sumner and Stevens as ruinous, dangerous anarchists and said so. (The Radicals spread the rumor that Grimes' position was not due to principle, but to jealousy of Wade. They also said Grimes was the father-in-law of the editor of the Chicago *Tribune* and had joined the paper in an anticonviction conspiracy.)* Grimes had been asked by a group of moderate Senators to produce some proof that if Johnson were acquitted he would not, as the Radicals had it, "do rash things, go on in his excesses, encourage the ex-rebels." Grimes felt it would be useful for Johnson to offer suitable assurances. But if the President made such a public declaration, it would constitute an admission of guilt. Furthermore, since he was on trial, he must speak through his counsel. Perhaps something could be done unofficially, the President's lawyers indicated to the Iowan. Grimes discussed the problem with Senator Reverdy Johnson of Maryland, another Presidential supporter, and Senator Johnson got word to the President that he would be pleased to see him at the Senator's house on a particular night.

The President arrived to find that Grimes was a fellow guest. The three men had some rambling talk about old times in the Senate. Then Reverdy Johnson introduced the subject

* No daughter of Grimes was married to the editor.

which had brought them together. The President excitedly and indignantly said the Radicals had no warrant to declare that he would run amok if he were acquitted. He would never do anything against the Constitution. Grimes, listening, thought him eloquent. If he had ever doubted Andrew Johnson's intentions, he did so no more. The President was a patriotic and law-abiding man, Grimes told himself.

The next day Grimes met with three undecided Senators. "You may rely implicitly upon this," he said. "I know Johnson's purposes in the event of acquittal. You need not fear his behavior will cause you to regret your vote, whichever way you may cast it. . . . He has no thought of wrong or rash doings."

The President must have welcomed the chance to speak in his own defense to Grimes and Reverdy Johnson. For his lawyers were not fierce enough for him. During the managers' presentation of evidence Ben Butler had once denounced him as the soul of corruption, assassination, cowardice, murder. In reply Evarts had simply remarked that never before had he listened to such a harangue in a court of justice. " 'Harangue,' " said the President to his secretary, Colonel Moore. "And I believe he thinks he did a most smart and dreadful thing." Evarts, Johnson said, had missed a chance to administer a rebuke to Butler and ringingly defend the President before the Senate and the entire country. For a time he considered telling Evarts what he thought, but managed to hold his tongue.

Yet it was hard for him to remain calm. "Impeachment of me for violating the Constitution!" Johnson said to Colonel Moore. "Damn them! Have I not been struggling ever since I have been in this chair to uphold the Constitution which they trample underfoot?"

It was one of the few times he lost his composure while what he called "the show" went on. In later years his daughter Martha Patterson would remember a particular brass chafing dish as her symbol of those days. At night her father and his lawyers would gather around the chafing dish while she stirred its contents—Welsh rarebit, often. He did not rant and condemn his enemies at those moments but instead read aloud from Chapter Twelve of First Samuel: *Behold, here I am: witness against me before the Lord. . . . whose ox have I taken? or whose ass have I taken? or whom have I defrauded? whom have I oppressed? or of whose hand have I received any bribe to blind mine eyes therewith?*

His enemies kept repeating he must be convicted or he would ruin the country. "Set up anarchy in general, and preside over it with a sceptre," he said scoffingly. But that was nonsense. He would never turn against anything in the Constitution. He would leave that to the Jacobins, Stevens and Sumner, who in their misguided idealism would remake the world in a day. If they convicted him, there would be no fight, no barricaded White House. And those who had convicted him would one day suffer the fates of the men who signed the death warrant of Charles the First. Like Cromwell, their bodies would be exhumed and hanged from a scaffold.

But would two-thirds of the Senate vote for conviction? Increasingly it appeared that the race was going to be very close. Stevens' attempt to get the "Africanized" states accepted into the Union in time for the vote was going to fail, so there was no danger to the President from new Senators. But the Radical caucus' work on the fence-sitters seemed to be bearing fruit. Henderson of Missouri became so distraught as a result of the pressure applied by Radical Congressmen from his home state that he considered resigning his seat in the Senate. Almost buried under the telegrams from constituents urging him to bring in a guilty verdict, he finally lost his temper. YOU HAVE NO RIGHT TO INSTRUCT ME IN SUCH AFFAIRS, he wired. I AM AN HONEST MAN. I WILL OBEY MY CONSCIENCE AND NOT YOUR WILL.

Fessenden of Maine, also under telegraphic bombardment, controlled his usual fiery temper when replying to demands that he find Johnson guilty. IF HE WAS IMPEACHED FOR GENERAL CUSSEDNESS THERE WOULD BE NO DIFFICULTY IN THE CASE. THAT HOWEVER IS NOT THE QUESTION TO BE SETTLED.

On April 22, one month into the trial, the final arguments began. The President was not fit for his post, said Manager John A. Logan of Illinois. He had willfully, maliciously, deliberately, criminally, violated the law. He had stood in the way of peace and the healing of wounds, and had produced discord and strife. "Incendiary . . . false . . . malignant . . . revolutionary . . . indecent. Who will cherish as a household word his dishonored name? None, none, no, not one. No, sir. The virtues that should adorn a Chief Magistrate fled on the induction of this criminal into that high office.

"Almost from the time when the blood of Lincoln was warm on the floor of Ford's Theatre, Andrew Johnson was contemplating treason. . . . His great aim and purpose has been to subvert law, usurp authority, insult and outrage Congress, reconstruct the rebel states in the interests of treason, insult the memories and resting places of our heroic dead."

Manager George Boutwell followed. He spoke through the session of April twenty-second and into the session of the twenty-third. "Base . . . gross . . . unjustifiable . . . evil."

What punishment could possibly be great enough to expiate the sins of the Great Criminal? Boutwell had the answer. "Travellers and astronomers inform us that in the southern heavens, near the Southern Cross, there is a vast space which the uneducated call the hole in the sky, where the eye of man, with the aid of the powers of the telescope, has been unable to discover nebulae, or asteroid, or comet, or planet, or star or sun.

"In that dreary, cold, dark region of space, the Great Author of celestial mechanism has left the chaos which was in the beginning. If this earth were capable of the sentiments and emotions of justice and virtue, which in human beings are the evidences and the pledge of our Divine origin and immortal destiny, it would heave and throw, with the energy of the elemental forces of nature, and project this enemy of two races of men into that vast region, there forever to exist in a solitude eternal as life."

Reflecting upon this tremendous toss, Moorfield Storey decided that such a throw would imply a certain amount of sharpshooting skill on the part of Mother Earth. It would certainly not be easy to aim Johnson exactly into the untenanted chaos of the hole in the sky. But that had apparently not entered into Boutwell's calculations. The expression on the manager's face clearly showed pride in his selection of the appropriate spot for Johnson. That self-satisfaction was noted by William Evarts. He leaned over to his fellow defense attorney, Curtis, and whispered, "I'll put Boutwell into that hole so that he never will get out again."

Boutwell finished. The friends of liberty throughout the world would rejoice when the Senate gave its verdict on the criminal at the bar. Peace and prosperity would return with his banishment—whether to the hole in the sky or simply to Greeneville, Tennessee. "I do not contemplate his acquittal—it is impossible."

Defense attorney Thomas A. R. Nelson spoke. He practiced law in Johnson's home town and had spent his career in less exalted places than the one in which he now found himself. Nor was he physically impressive, for he was crippled in one leg and limped as he walked. Perhaps he had been included in the defense staff so that he could appear as character witness for a man he had known forty years.

Nelson declared that if all the things said about his fellow townsman were true, then whips should be issued the populace to lash him about the world. He could be exhibited as a monster. The sight of him would make people's hair stand on end like a porcupine, and his name could be used to frighten naughty children.

But were all the things true? "Who is Andrew Johnson?" asked Nelson, and spoke about the days when war was on the horizon and rebel armies gathered across the Potomac. Johnson then stood "within ten feet of the place in which I stand now." He spoke for the Union. From there he had gone to make his fight at Nashville. Now he would be judged in that Senate Chamber where he had spoken and which he had left.

Let the jurors cleanse their minds of preconceptions, Nelson said. Let them forget the press, "the mightiest power known to the land," that power greater than President and Senators and Representatives. Forget the calculations of who would vote guilty and who innocent. Forget, above all, the contention of the managers that the Senators were a law unto themselves. For that view would permit the overthrow of all the values that went by the name of American justice and principle. "I know that now-a-days it excites almost ridicule with some to hear anything said in behalf of the American Constitution." But it was upon that Constitution that the President was making his fight. "We talk about our social equality. We talk about all being free and equal. It is an idle song, it is a worthless talk, it is a vain and empty expression unless that liberty and that equality are enforced." And it was the Constitution which decreed enforcement.

Nelson halted, to resume the next day. He took up an issue raised by Manager Boutwell in his hole in the sky speech. Boutwell had remarked that Judge Jeremiah Black had originally been one of the lawyers of the defense, but had withdrawn. As Nelson put it, Boutwell had implied Johnson was such a leper that Judge Black could not stomach being a part of his defense. According to Nelson the facts were different: Black's law firm represented an investment group that was pressing for United States military action against Santo Domingo. The group hoped to recover a tiny island, Alta Vela, whose valuable guano deposits the investors had exploited before being expelled by Santo Domingo. One warship would do the job. In support of their claim they had obtained the signed backing of Managers Butler, Logan, Bingham and Stevens. The support of these managers had been acquired by Black's firm after the impeachment proceedings began.

The managers' backing had created a delicate situation for the President. If Johnson complied with the request for action against Santo Domingo, it would appear that he was trying to appease the managers who might receive unspecified rewards. For all he knew, Johnson said, each manager might

272

have been offered half a million dollars for his signature. If he dispatched a vessel, it would look as if he was sending American sailors into action in order to save his own skin. And his counsel was involved in all this! "Judge Black won't do!" he said.

When Black withdrew from the case, he wrote the President: "Unless you can do something for your friends, it is useless for me longer to apply my personal and professional powers when defeat stares us in the face." Black then told newspaper reporters that the President's case against conviction seemed hopeless.

Many of the President's intimates agreed with Black. They begged the President to reconsider. If he sent the ship, Black would come back. And, it was implied, the managers would be appeased. "I would rather be put to death than suffer such humiliation," Johnson said.

There would be no ship and no Judge Black. "Many seem to have supposed that, as I was now in trouble, I might be forced to do things that I would not do under other circumstances," he said to his secretary, Moore. "They will find out their mistake."

Such were the facts in the Alta Vela matter, defense attorney Nelson told the Senate. The President did his duty as he saw it, knowing that the managers would be made even more intense in their desire to get rid of him; he also realized that Black would resign from the case and that his resignation would be taken to mean that he thought the President's case was hopeless. Why had he taken the decision? It would have been a simple matter to bludgeon the Santo Domingo government into submission. But to do so would not have been honorable. It would have been "pollution."

But the Alta Vela matter was not finished. Ben Butler arose to say that he and the other managers must deny the insulting implications of Nelson's remarks. He, Butler, had been the first of the managers to endorse the claim of the group Black represented, and he swore he had done so months before the impeachment procedure began. "Every element of falsehood" was in Nelson's insinuation. The man was a liar.

Nelson responded angrily. Butler's words were "foully and falsely" wrong. "So far as any question that the gentleman desires to make of a personal character with me is concerned, this is not the place to make it. Let him make it elsewhere if he desires to do it."

"Does the gentleman know what he is saying?" Butler demanded.

Nelson did. He had asked Butler to challenge him to a duel. He went on to say that he would produce the signed statements of the managers endorsing the claim of Black's clients. They would show the dates those endorsements were made.

"I trust not until they are shown not to have been mutilated," Butler shot out.

"Sir!"

Edmunds of Vermont asked that the matter be put aside. A personal dispute between the two men had nothing to do with the trial. Chase ordered the question dropped. But the next day Sumner asked that the Senate officially reprove Nelson for language which, "besides being discreditable to these proceedings, is apparently intended to provoke a duel or to signify a willingness to fight a duel, contrary to law and good morals."

Nelson tried to speak, but Sumner cut him off several times. Finally Butler suggested the whole matter be dropped. Nelson indicated he had spoken in anger and meant no disrespect to the Senators. Sumner's resolution was tabled.

William S. Groesbeck of Cincinnati, Black's replacement, spoke. This case was based on Stanton. Where was the willful force and violence which the President's foes attributed to him? Was it seen in the moment when the President's tool, old Thomas, permitted Stanton to run his fingers through his hair? What were the President's thoughts on the whole matter? "We offered to bring in here the Cabinet. You would not hear them. You shut their mouths, and remitted to us the man from Delaware and the empty utterances and boastings of Lorenzo Thomas. What great truth searchers are these managers in this case!"

As for Johnson's alleged slandering of Congress, let Senators remember the Sedition Act of 1798, which forbade citizens to speak ill of the government. It was the most offensive law ever passed in America, Groesbeck said. Now the tenth impeachment article concentrating on the President's words about Congress duplicated it. Let the tenth article be passed into law, Groesbeck said. Here was how it might read: "*Be it enacted,* That, if the President . . . shall say anything displeasing to Congress . . . or if he shall misquote or carelessly quote the sacred Scriptures, or . . . use bad grammar, then, and in either of such cases, he shall be guilty of a high misdemeanor, and upon trial and conviction thereof shall be fined in any sum not exceeding $10,000, or imprisonment not exceeding ten years."

Most of his listeners gave him the laugh he expected. Then he became serious. "Andrew Johnson tried to pluck a thorn out of his very heart. . . . You fastened it there, and you are now asked to punish him for attempting to extract it.

"He is not learned and scholarly, like many of you. He is not a man of many ideas, or of much speculation. But by a law of the mind he is only the truer to that he does know. He is a patriot, second to no one of you in the measure of his patriotism. He may be full of error. I will not canvass now his views. But he loves his country. He has the courage to defend it, and I believe to die for it if need be. His courage and his patriotism are not without illustration. . . .

"How can you single out this man, in this condition of things, and brand him before the world, put your brand of infamy upon him because he made an ad interim appointment for a day, and possibly may have made a mistake in attempting to remove Stanton? . . .

"I do hope you will not drive the President out and take possession of his office. I hope this not merely as counsel for Andrew Johnson, for Andrew Johnson's Administration is to me but as a moment, and himself as nothing in comparison with the possible consequences of such an act.

"No good can come of it, Senators."

On Monday, April 27, 1868, Old Thad, wraithlike, was

carried in by his two Negro servants. He was so weak that he could hardly stand. They had to raise him to his feet so that he might speak. Here, Stevens said, was the trial of the chief servant of a trusting community arraigned before the bar of justice. That was interesting. Here was the Chief Executive Magistrate charged with betrayal, high crimes, misdemeanors. That was most interesting. Here was a man accused of seeking to usurp the power of a nation of millions that he might better misrule them. That was intensely interesting.

"Wretched man!" Andrew Johnson had committed perjury when he took the Presidential oath in the Kirkwood House. Were he honest, he would have said he would obey only the laws of the land which he approved; and of course those did not include the Tenure of Office Act. "Pettifogging political trickster!" How extended would be that "track of infamy which must mark his name, and that of his posterity!"

Stevens' legs gave out. He asked permission to speak while seated. He was on his last reserves, the voice steadily growing weaker. What a fatal day it was that inflicted Andrew Johnson upon the people! "Wretched man, standing at bay, surrounded by a cordon of living men, each with the axe of an executioner uplifted for his just punishment!"

It was Congress, Stevens said, upon whom the task of reconstructing the South should have fallen. Johnson had usurped the legislative power to set up new state governments, resurrecting the late Confederacy into an empire of his own. Now let Congress send him away and end his despotism, his unholy ambitions, his lust for turmoil and bloodshed. Let the Senate call him guilty.

For the first time in the trial a voice had spoken out and said what the trial was really about. Then the voice faltered. The physical Stevens was finished. Ben Butler picked up the speech and read from where Stevens had broken off. Andrew Johnson was unwilling to obey the laws, Butler cried out. Let him go back to his village obscurity.

Huddled in his blankets, immobile, the exhausted Stevens and all the others listened as Stevens through Butler declared that Johnson's claim that he merely wished to test the Tenure of Office Act had come as an afterthought. He really wanted to see Stanton's head rolling at the foot of a guillotine. After that the subjugation of the country to his will. *Put him in the stocks!*

It was time for William Evarts. Slender, with his left hand stuck in the back pocket of his frock coat, he gestured with his right, waving his gold-rimmed eyeglasses. His speech was exhaustive—it took three days for him to deliver it. (He sought to become immortal by being eternal, said Manager John Bingham.)

Once upon a time, Evarts said, Andrew Johnson had taken an oath. It was a promise, not only to fulfill the duties of his office as President, but also an oath to preserve, protect and defend the Constitution of the United States.

Abraham Lincoln had taken that oath and had said that it was a solemn vow registered in heaven. So it was with Lincoln's successor. Now he was on trial for obeying that oath. It was his adherence to the Constitution that was on trial.

And to speak of "congressional omnipotence" and to put aside the President was to put aside the Constitution. That was not something to be done lightly. And what exactly had the President done? What, precisely, was his crime? He had removed a member of the Cabinet. That was hardly an unprecedented occurrence, still less an act of terror. It could hardly be termed total depravity. It was not the same thing, for example, as snatching away a newborn child from its mother and destroying it before her eyes.

Yet, Evarts went on, consider the punishment selected for the President by Manager Boutwell, he of the hole in the sky! Effusion of blood or sequestration of property would not do for the honorable manager, still less banishment from office. Nothing would satisfy save instant transportation to the region of outermost planets.

But to accomplish that, Evarts said, would likely create so great a shock of nature as might unsettle even the footing of the members of Congress. That would be perilous. How, then, was the President to be removed to the hole in the sky? "Why, in the first place, nobody knows where that space is but the learned manager himself, and he is the necessary deputy to execute the judgment of the court. . . . The honorable and astronomical manager shall take into his own hands the execution of the sentence. With the President made fast to his broad and strong shoulders, and, having already essayed the flight by imagination, better prepared to execute it in form, taking the advantage of ladders as far as ladders will go to the top of this great Capitol, and spurning then with his foot the crest of Liberty, let him set out on his flight, while the two houses of Congress and all the people of the United States shall shout, 'Sic itur ad astra.' " *

Everyone looked at Boutwell. He had a weak smile on his lips and seemed to be suffocating. When the laughter died down Evarts continued. "But here a distressing doubt strikes me," he said, beaming. "How will the manager get back? He will have got far beyond the reach of gravitation to restore him, and so ambitious a wing as his could never stoop to a downward flight." Therefore Boutwell and his passenger, beyond even the awesome power of a congressional subpoena, would become a new constellation. They would whirl through the heavens together for all time to come.

The lawyer spoke of the three powers of the American system: judicial, legislative and executive. Would Congress undertake to weaken forever one of these branches? Would the Senator-jurors make their own branch a tyranny, in contradiction to the founders of the nation who held that inordinate power must not accrue to any single arm of the government? And all this for the proposed removal of Edwin Stanton?

But perhaps he had spoken too soon, Evarts said. There was the tenth article, which charged the President with improper language directed toward Congress. A grave matter. Yet reflect on certain statements made by various gentlemen pres-

* "Thus onward to the stars."

ent. Consider a remark Mr. Senator Sumner once offered upon the floor of this self-same body: the President was the "enemy of his country." When the Senator had been called to order, Sumner's ally, Senator Anthony, had offered a guide to the proper courtesies which should prevail between the legislative and executive branches. Senator Anthony had said that Mr. Sumner's words did not exceed the usual latitude of senatorial debate. Senator Sherman agreed with that view, declaring the words were perfectly in order. Did not the rule about proper phraseology, Evarts asked, work both ways?

Then there was the question of propriety among members of the House of Representatives. Consider some words exchanged by two members of that great body who now sat together as managers. Here, said Evarts, was Mr. Bingham of Ohio discussing Mr. Butler of Massachusetts:

" 'It does not become a gentleman who recorded his vote fifty times for Jefferson Davis, the arch traitor in this rebellion, as his candidate for President of the United States * to . . . cast an imputation either upon my integrity or my honor. I repel with scorn and contempt any utterance of that sort from any man, whether he be the hero of Fort Fisher not taken or of Fort Fisher taken.' " †

To which Butler had replied, making reference to Bingham's role as assistant prosecutor at the trial of Booth's coconspirators:

" 'If during the war the gentleman from Ohio did as much as I did in that direction I shall be glad to recognize that much done. But the only victim of the gentleman's prowess that I know of was an innocent woman hung on the scaffold, one Mrs. Surratt.' "

To which Bingham had offered: " 'Such a charge, without one tittle of evidence, is only fit to come from a man who lives in a bottle and is fed with a spoon.' "

* In the 1860 Democratic Presidential Convention.
† As previously noted, the disaster at Fort Fisher was the final display of military incompetence which caused Grant to demand Butler's dismissal from the army.

All roared. "Now," Evarts said, "what under heaven that means I am sure I do not know." More laughter. (Everyone knew that "Spoons" was one of Butler's nicknames in honor of the silver he supposedly stole from a New Orleans home; and all knew that Grant had said that Butler had gotten his troops miserably bottled up in a wretched pre-Fort Fisher campaign.) "But it is within the common law of courtesy in the judgment of the House of Representatives. Now, to be serious, in a free republic who will tolerate this fanfaronade about speech-making? Who will tolerate public orators prating about propriety of speech?

"Without apologizing, for no man is bound to apologize before the law or before the court for the exercise of freedom of speech, it may be freely admitted that it would be very well if all men were accomplished rhetoricians, finished logicians and had a bridle on their tongues."

He was approaching the end of two days of speaking. Cardinal Wolsey, he said, had once remarked that in political times it would be possible to impanel a jury which would rule that Abel killed Cain. By the same token, it might be possible that an American Senate would rule that Andrew Johnson meant to breed commotion and civil war. Evarts hoped not. He indicated his regret that his argument was taking so long, and gracefully thanked the Senate for its indulgence by quoting the English judge who replied to a lawyer who said he would proceed if it were the court's pleasure, "The court will hear you, sir, tomorrow. But as to pleasure, that has long been out of the question."

The following day, May 1, Evarts considered the history of ad interim appointments and concluded the President had a right to make one. He alluded to the way President John Adams removed a Cabinet minister who said he needed his post because he had no other means to support his family: Adams simply told him to leave. He referred to the Delaware man's statement that Thomas would "kick out" Stanton and derided the opposition's claim this purported evidence showed Johnson planned a coup d'etat. The honorable managers, he said, had found a needle in a haystack. "There is no bristling of bayonets under the haymow, you may be sure."

Evarts went on: even if the congressional view of Reconstruction was correct and that of the President wrong, Johnson had committed no crime within the strictures of the Constitution. "He has always learned to believe that the Constitution must and should be preserved. He loved the country and the Constitution more than he loved his section. I ask you whether he was not as firm in his devotion to the Constitution when he said, in December, 1860, 'Then let us stand by the Constitution and, in saving the Union, we save this, the greatest government on earth.'

"He is no rhetorician and no theorist, no sophist and no philosopher. The Constitution is to him the only political book that he reads. To the Constitution he adheres. For it and under it he has served the State from boyhood up—labored for it, loved it. For it he has stood in arms against the frowns of a Senate; for it he has stood in arms against the rebellious forces of the enemy; and to it he has bowed three times a day with a more than Eastern devotion."

Now, Evarts said, the weak point of the Constitution was on trial: the maintenance of a proper relationship between the departments of the government. If one branch could not be kept from devouring another, then the great experiment of American government would fail.

"If that fails, what can endure?"

The final speakers would be ex-Attorney General Stanbery and Manager Bingham. Ill and feeble, Stanbery remained in bed during the three days that Evarts spoke. Secretary of the Interior Browning thought he looked more dead than alive. The first words of his speech alluded to his debilitated condition. But, he said, although his flesh was weak, his spirit was not. "Unseen and friendly hands seem to support me. Voices inaudible to all others I hear, or seem to hear. They whisper words of consolation, of hope, of confidence. They say, or seem to say to me: 'Feeble champion of the right, hold not back.' "

He had not known Johnson personally when he was asked to become Attorney General, Stanbery said. His only acquaintance in the Cabinet had been Edwin Stanton. Two years had passed since his appointment. Now he wished to tell the Senators something of what he had learned in that time. "Listen for a moment to one who, perhaps, understands Andrew Johnson better than most of you; for his opportunities have been greater.

"From the moment that I was honored with a seat in the Cabinet of Mr. Johnson not a step was taken that did not come under my observation, not a word was said that escaped my attention. Never, in word, in deed, in thought, in action, did I discover in that man anything but loyalty to the Constitution and the laws.

"Yes, Senators, with all his faults, the President has been more sinned against than sinning. Fear not, then, to acquit him. The Constitution of the country is as safe in his hands from violence as it was in the hands of Washington. But if, Senators, you condemn him, if you strip him of the robes of office, if you degrade him to the utmost stretch of your power, mark the prophecy: the strong arms of the people will be about him. They will find a way to raise him from any depths to which you may consign him, and we shall live to see him redeemed and to hear the majestic voice of the people, 'Well done, faithful servant; you shall have your reward!' "

He sat down. The last word in the President's defense had been said.

The next day, as Manager Bingham prepared to sum up, Senator Grimes' seat was empty. From the start, Grimes had been against conviction and defended the President by saying he would not run amok if acquitted. A rumor spread that Grimes had died, and in the galleries jubilant Radicals sang, "Old Grimes is dead, that bad old man, we ne'er shall see him more." Chase gaveled them into silence and Bingham invoked the spirit of Patrick Henry, who said that Caesar had his Brutus, Charles I his Cromwell and George III their examples. And Andrew Johnson? Let his executioner be the laws, which the Constitution made supreme and not playthings "because it suits the pleasure of his highness, Andrew Johnson, first king of the people of the United States."

If the members should find innocent a man who ignored the Tenure of Office Act, Bingham said, a land of light and knowledge would be converted to a nation of darkness, anarchy, eternal war. To contend otherwise meant the use of cheap lawyer's tricks, as Evarts had done, "so wittily that he held his own sides lest he should explode with laughter at his own wit." To praise the President's good intentions, as other defense counsel had done, was to insult the intelligence of the Senator-jurors. Men of good intentions had deliberately slain innocent children in medieval days, Bingham said, so that the dead souls might go to heaven. No doubt John Wilkes Booth himself had good intentions.

"Guilty and corrupt and oath-breaking . . . hollow and hypocritical," the President thought himself inviolate. In fact he was "violator of oaths, and violator of Constitutions and violator of laws."

Bingham had reached the end of his speech, the end of the trial. "I ask you to consider that we stand this day pleading for the violated majesty of the law, by the graves of half a million of martyred hero-patriots who made death beautiful by the sacrifice of themselves for their country, the Constitution, and the laws, and who, by their sublime example, have taught us that all must obey the law; that none are above the law."

He thanked the Senators for their kind attention. He spoke the last words of the trial: "Before man and God, he is guilty!"

A storm of applause swept the galleries. "Order! Order!" the Chief Justice shouted. "If this be repeated the sergeant-at-arms will clear the galleries." Hisses and derisive laughter sounded.

Senator Grimes—in dire physical straits and late in taking his seat—asked that the galleries be cleared at once. The Senate approved Grimes' motion and Chase ordered all spectators to leave the Senate Chamber. The hissing increased, several Radical Senators joining in. Chase shouted that if the disturbance did not cease, arrests would be made. Trumbull of Illinois moved that the noisemakers should immediately be taken into custody. The Radical Senator Cameron of Pennsylvania moved that the galleries not be cleared. The people, he said, had a right to make their views known.

"Order! Order!" Senators yelled. Guards pushed the scuffling and cursing crowd through the door. Eventually the guards evicted all the spectators, including diplomats and reporters. The Senate voted to meet again so that any Senator who wished to speak might do so. The time limit for each man would be fifteen minutes.

On Monday, May 11, Senator after Senator spoke. Some said they could vote for a particular article but not for another. Others declared they would vote acquittal on every article. Sumner said he would vote "Guilty on all, and infinitely more." Some Senators did not indicate how they would vote. At the end of the day it was clear that if the Senate convicted Johnson, it would do so on the basis of Stevens' sweeping article eleven.

Williams of Oregon proposed that the Senate begin with the eleventh article. The motion was put to a vote. For the first time since the trial began Benjamin Wade responded to his name on a roll call. He voted "yea." The motion carried. They adjourned, to meet again on Saturday, May 16, for the vote.

14

Chase began, "By direction of the Senate the Chief Justice admonishes the citizens and strangers in the galleries that absolute silence and perfect order are required. It will be a matter of unfeigned regret if any violation of the order of the Senate should necessitate the execution of its further order, that the persons guilty of the disturbance be immediately arrested.

"Senators, in conformity with the order of the Senate, the chair will now proceed to take the vote on the eleventh article, as directed by the rule. The Secretary will read the eleventh article."

"That said Andrew Johnson, President of the United States, unmindful of the high duties of his office, and of his oath of office, and in disregard of the Constitution and laws of the United States, did heretofore, to wit, on the eighteenth day of August, A.D. 1866, at the city of Washington and the District of Columbia, by public speech, declare and affirm, in substance, that the 39th Congress of the United States was not a Congress of the United States . . . but, on the contrary, was a Congress of only a part of the states, thereby denying, and intending to deny, that the legislation of said Congress was valid or obligatory upon him, the said Andrew Johnson. . . . and in pursuit of said declaration, the said Andrew Johnson, President of the United States, afterwards, to wit, on the twenty-first day of February, A.D. 1868, at the city of Washington, in the District of Columbia, did, unlawfully, and in disregard of the requirements of the Constitution that he should take care that the laws be faithfully executed, attempt to prevent the execution of an act entitled 'An act regulating the tenure of certain civil offices,' passed March 2, 1867, by unlawfully devising and contriving, and attempting to devise and contrive, means by which he should remove Edwin M. Stanton from forthwith resuming the functions of the office of Secretary for the Department of War . . . whereby the said Andrew Johnson . . . did then . . . commit and was guilty of a high crime and misdemeanor in office."

"Call the roll."

The chief clerk called the name of Senator Anthony of Rhode Island. He stood up.

Chase said, "Mr. Senator Anthony, how say you? Is the respondent, Andrew Johnson, President of the United States, guilty or not guilty of a high misdemeanor, as charged in this article?"

"Guilty."

So many people had been holding their breath as they waited for Anthony to speak that a sound like a great sigh swept through the Senate Chamber.

"Mr. Senator Bayard, how say you? Is the respondent, Andrew Johnson, President of the United States, guilty or not guilty of a high misdemeanor, as charged in this article?"

"Not guilty."

Cameron interrupted the reading of the question to call out his guilty verdict. Everybody laughed nervously. Cattell, Chandler, Cole, Conkling, Conness, Corbett, Cragin, all voted guilty. One quarter of the thirty-six votes needed for conviction had been cast. Telegraph wires sent a running account all over the country, where even in remote small towns men who had placed wagers on the outcome of the trial gathered at newspaper offices.

There was not a hotel room to be had in Washington because of the rush of office seekers and contractors hoping shortly to attract the attention of President Wade or a member of his new Cabinet. All government business was suspended.

At the White House, the President sat silently opening a series of telegrams which reported the votes one by one. Alone, Stanton remained in his War Department office with the window opened to catch the warm spring breeze. Seward was in his office at the State Department. He now expected conviction. He had written out his resignation, to take effect the minute the President was declared guilty.

The voting went on, the silence in the chamber so deep that the smallest sound could be heard. Congressman James A. Garfield said to himself that even in the most trying moments of war there had never been such intensity.

Yet the early voting was actually not important. The verdicts of the Senators whose names came early in the alphabet were predictable. The first undecided Senator would be Fessenden of Maine. The illegitimate son of a college student, he had grown into a cold, haughty man, perhaps, people said, as a result of the stigma. Nevertheless he was an extremely capable, highly regarded Senator. He had been mentioned for the post of president pro tem of the Senate. Had he run for it and won over Bluff Ben Wade, the situation would be very different for a number of Senators who hesitated to put Wade in the White House.

At the start of his career Fessenden had been very friendly with Charles Sumner. Often they would be seen walking arm in arm to the Senate Chamber. Over the years their friendship cooled, and Fessenden had reached the point where he said that if he could be permitted to cut the throats of half a dozen men, Sumner would be his first victim because of his insolent egotism and sanctimonious attitude. Sumner returned his hatred. In 1864 Sumner supported Military Governor Andrew Johnson of Tennessee for the Vice Presidency over the incumbent, Hannibal Hamlin of Maine. It was Sumner's hope that Hamlin would return to Maine, where he would successfully campaign for Fessenden's seat in the Senate. The first half of Sumner's plan had succeeded; Johnson was put on the ticket with Lincoln. The second half failed. So Fessenden rose to stand by his desk as Chase read out the rote question. Fessenden's answer was vitally important. For he was a leader. And there were men to be called upon who had not yet made up their minds.

At the time of Stanton's removal Fessenden wrote Secretary of the Treasury McCulloch, "I meet no man who is not in favor of impeachment if any decent pretense for it can be found." Then he had rethought the matter: "We have many most troublesome and important problems to solve while the folly and madness of such men as Stevens and Sumner keep us in constant peril."

Yet there was still a chance he had not made up his mind. Fessenden had been in his seat early on voting day—he prided himself on never having been avoidably late more than two or three times in his twenty years of public service. The air seemed filled with calculated heaviness, he thought as he waited for his name to be called.

He said, "Not guilty."

The next undecided Senator was Joseph S. Fowler of Tennessee. He was thought to lean toward the Radicals. Fowler had served under Military Governor Johnson and then accompanied him to Washington when he took the oath as Vice President. Thereafter their paths diverged. When Congress submitted the Fourteenth Amendment to all the state legislatures for ratification, Fowler had been an ally of the fervidly Radical Governor of Tennessee, "Parson" William G. Brownlow. Several members of the Tennessee Legislature tried to prevent a vote on the Fourteenth by removing themselves from the chamber and thereby avoiding a quorum. The "Parson" responded by dispatching armed men who dragged the recalcitrant legislators into the chamber where they remained under arrest while the legislature approved the Fourteenth Amendment. Governor Brownlow happily telegraphed the news to Washington, along with the request that his regards be given to "the dead dog of the White House."

As a result of the Tennessee Legislature's action the state was permitted back into the Union, with its two Senators allowed to take their seats. One Senator was David T. Patterson, the husband of Martha Johnson, the President's daughter. (Sumner opposed seating him, raising the specter that Patterson was a friend of the Slaveocracy despite his unquestioned sacrifices for the cause of the Union.) The other Senator was Fowler.

As Fowler hurried to his place in the Senate several Radicals intercepted him, telling him that they had not forgotten that he had said Johnson deserved conviction. He went past them and sat down, to rise when Chase asked that he declare himself.

When Chase finished reading the question, Fowler muttered something. *Guilty,* thought Moorfield Storey. "Did the court hear his answer?" Sumner called out.

Chase asked Fowler to repeat his response.

"Not guilty!" Fowler shouted, so loudly that people blinked and pulled back. To the end of his life Storey believed that Fowler had in an instant changed his mind, that he had said guilty the first time.

They came to Grimes. Two days earlier he had suffered a paralytic stroke and became so ill that this was to be his last week in the Senate. Blisters covered his body. Unable to walk, he had to be carried. Until the last moment it had been doubtful that he would be able to summon the strength to appear. Chase told him he need not rise to deliver his vote, but he insisted on being helped to his feet to deliver the expected "Not guilty."

Henderson of Missouri's turn came. The Radicals had subjected Henderson and Ross of Kansas to the most pressure. Radical members of Missouri's congressional delegation worked on Henderson with such persistence that he offered to resign his seat and let the Governor appoint a new Senator. (His fellow Missourians said it was not his resignation they wanted, but simply his vote for conviction.) Spies followed him everywhere. But when he complained to Sumner he was told, "It is only the wounded bird that flutters." He was bombarded with telegrams demanding conviction, and when a rumor spread that he was going to vote for acquittal he was burned in effigy at home.

He said: "Not guilty."

There followed a dozen or more Senators whose votes were predictable. The chief clerk called the name of Mr. Senator Edmund G. Ross of Kansas. Twenty-four "guilties" had been recorded. Ten more were certain and one, Willey of West Virginia, was near-certain. That meant thirty-five votes for conviction.

But a two-thirds margin was needed—thirty-six. That left the outcome to Ross. All the other undecided Senators had supported the President. Everything that followed Ross' vote would be anticlimactic.

He stood up. Forty years old, bearded, a former printer. The period of the trial had been a murderous time for him. At first his vote had seemed safe for conviction. But he did not consistently join with the Radicals on the various questions regarding admissibility of evidence. Suddenly he became a question mark. Radicals demanded that he tell them his intention, but they were rebuffed.

His fellow Kansan, the Radical Senator Pomeroy, showed him a list which contained the purported opinions of each Senator regarding each of the eleven articles of impeachment. The list claimed that Ross was in favor of five of the articles, including the eleventh. Ross said his colleague presumed too much. He was still undecided. Pomeroy came back two days before the vote to say conviction was certain on the eleventh article and the Radicals assumed that Ross would vote guilty on that article. Ross repeated that he had not made up his mind. He answered telegrams demanding he vote guilty by saying that he would make his decision as his judgment dictated. "Tell the damned scoundrel that if he wants money, there is a bushel of it here to be had," Ben Butler said. Word reached Ross that the Radicals planned to kidnap an undecided Senator and offer terms that he vote Johnson guilty or be killed on the spot.

The night before the vote Senator Pomeroy dined with Ross, urging him to vote for conviction. After Ross returned home General Daniel Sickles, dispatched by Stanton, came to his lodgings. General Sickles stayed until four in the morning in an attempt to get to Ross but was fended off by Vinnie Ream, the sculptress daughter of Ross' landlord, who denied him access to the Senator. A few hours later, as Ross took breakfast with Henderson of Missouri, Radical emissaries approached them. Ross, one man remembered later, was hunted like a fox. Ten minutes before the voting would begin Pomeroy collared him in the Senate lobby. With Thad Stevens looking on, Pomeroy said that a vote for acquittal would spell political death for Ross and an investigation to unearth evidence that his vote had been bought by bribery.

As the men whose names came before his recorded their verdicts Ross sat tearing sheets of paper into strips. They fell into his lap and from there to the floor, and when he stood to give his vote they surrounded him. A piece stuck to his fingers.

He wrote later that he was thinking that to vote Johnson out could bring congressional autocracy. It might create partisan rule whereby a majority would brutally stifle all opposition as a matter of course. Degraded, the office of the Presidency would be subjected forever to the will of the Congress. That was not what the Fathers had intended. The political fabric they had so carefully woven would be ripped open. Through that tear there might come times and conditions which would make it possible for the worst demagogues to destroy the great experiment of political democracy.

Yet Ross did not care for Andrew Johnson as a man, nor for the views he represented. Ross had enlisted in the Union army as a private to fight the South. Discharged as a major, he had returned to Kansas and from there had been active in the statewide protest movement directed against Senator James

Lane's backing of Johnson. Perhaps because of the violent criticism, Lane had committed suicide, and Ross was given his seat. With such a background, was Ross to cast the vote which would save the man who so many believed had betrayed the cause for which the war had been fought?

Ross looked around him and it seemed to him that suddenly his powers of sight and hearing had become enormously developed. Each face in the Senate Chamber appeared clear to him, even those who were farthest away, some with lips apart and bent forward waiting for him to speak. People strained toward him with hand to ear to catch what he would say, and he saw that every fan was folded, that not a foot moved. There was no rustle of clothing, no whispering of any kind.

Sumner looked over at Ross. Surely a Kansas man would do the right thing. The speech that had brought Bully Brooks' cane down on Sumner's head twelve years ago had been about Bloody Kansas. A Kansas man would not turn against all—emancipation, victory in the war, the Fourteenth Amendment, Reconstruction.

Ulysses Grant was going to be President. Even now the delegates to the convention which would unanimously nominate him were assembling in Chicago. Above all things Grant was a man of few ideas and little imagination or passion. That had been the Union's salvation during the war. Just such a man was needed to bludgeon down Robert E. Lee. Ideals, crusades and abstractions would not concern him as President. Money and industrial growth might capture his attention, but never the deeper meaning of the war he had done so much to win. The rights of the blacks would be the last thing he would consider. So the Radicals knew that this was Radicalism's last chance. Its ideological mainstays were already passing off the stage, to be replaced by technicians seeking to exploit the Union's victory and make of it the Gilded Age. Abolitionism had been almost a religion for its believers. For abolitionism to conquer in fact as well as in name, Johnson must be drawn and quartered and the great nation made whole and right.

There remained ten months until Grant took office.

That would be long enough to accomplish abolitionism's and Radicalism's aims. It would have to be long enough, for that was all the time the old prewar group would have.

That was what the whole trial had really been about, Sumner thought. Narrow legalisms such as the Tenure of Office Act were not the issue. Even Stanton, at the time of the submission of the Act, had said it was patently unconstitutional. He had quoted from a pamphlet Charles Francis Adams had written and mentioned something President Buchanan had said, both points showing there was ample precedent against the Act. Johnson at the time had even asked Stanton to draft a veto message. Although he begged off because of rheumatism in his arm, Stanton had given Seward, the eventual drafter of the message, the benefit of his views.

Ross thought: friendships, position, fortune, everything that makes life desirable to an ambitious man, were now at stake here. The necessity to speak was so heavy a responsibility that he found himself driving it away as one fights off a nightmare.

It came to him as he opened his mouth that this was what it must be like to look down into one's own grave.

"Not guilty."

They would adjourn after the last Senator voted, with an agreement to meet again and vote on a different article. But the trial was over, for everyone knew that when the Senate clerk recorded thirty-five out of fifty-four Senators voting for conviction on the eleventh article—one less than a two-thirds majority—the matter was settled. The President's bodyguard, William Crook, jumped up and raced for a door. Behind him came the defense attorneys Nelson and Stanbery.

Moorfield Storey looked at Benjamin Wade. No expression showed in his face. Soon Storey would leave the Senate Chamber just behind Wade and his wife and think, Instead of being the President of the United States with his lady, here were merely Mr. and Mrs. Wade walking home.

All the Senators filed out. *"Fessenden!* You villainous

traitor!" came a voice from the crowd. White-faced, Fessenden kept going.

Nelson and Stanbery piled into a carriage. The driver whipped up the horses and rushed down Pennsylvania Avenue toward the White House. Crook ran along the wooden sidewalks.

At the War Department, Stanton was told the news. An almost feverish feeling overtook him for a moment. He turned his head away. Soon his son would hand a note to Assistant Adjutant General Townsend: *"General: You will take charge of the War Department, and the books and papers, archives and public property belonging to the same, subject to the disposal and directions of the President. Edwin M. Stanton, Secretary of War."*

"Only by one vote," Charles Sumner said. "There is a familiar saying that a man is saved by the skin of his teeth."

"Only one vote."

Nelson and Stanbery raced each other into the White House Library where the President was waiting with Secretary Welles. Though lame, Nelson was the faster runner. He was covered with perspiration. A moment later Stanbery pounded in. It was past lunchtime; uneaten sandwiches rested on the table. Crook came panting up. He had run the entire distance from the Capitol. Crook saw the two lawyers, and it came into his mind that perhaps Mrs. Johnson had not yet been told the outcome. He raced to her room. "He is acquitted!" Crook cried. "The President is acquitted."

She got up from her chair. "I knew he'd be acquitted. I knew it," she whispered.

Crook returned to the library and took the President's hand. Johnson seemed calm, but then tears rolled down his cheeks. He ordered whiskey from the White House cellars and poured some for the lawyers, Welles, and Crook. They all stood up and drank a silent toast. Then they went to work on the sandwiches.

All over the country Radicals surged into telegraph offices. For Ross: KANSAS REPUDIATES YOU AS SHE DOES ALL PER-

JURERS AND SKUNKS. And, from a justice of the Kansas Supreme Court: THE ROPE WITH WHICH JUDAS ISCARIOT HANGED HIMSELF IS LOST BUT JIM LANE'S PISTOL IS AT YOUR SERVICE.

Telegrams flew back from Washington. Fowler wired: I ACTED FOR MY COUNTRY AND POSTERITY IN OBEDIENCE TO THE WILL OF GOD.

Shortly, newspaper extras were on the street, including one which reported, "SUICIDE OF BEN BUTLER." The report was wrong. Butler was already at work on an investigation to discover if any of the Senators who voted not guilty had accepted bribes.

At the White House a message came from Seward: *"My dear friend."*

People began arriving. The President was surrounded by well-wishers. An avalanche of cards was brought in by the ushers, and one man was reminded of the atmosphere which prevails in a royal palace after a coronation. No emotion beyond a slight smile showed on the President's face.

William Crook thought back to the moment when he rushed from the Senate Chamber. The corridor had been jammed with people unable to get in. They were yelling, "What was the verdict?" Out came two young men carrying an old man high on their shoulders. He was waving his arms with an unsuppressible anger. He heard the shouted question and, his face black with rage, gave the answer.

"The country is going to the devil!" Stevens screamed.

15

None of the seven Republicans who voted for acquittal were ever again elected to the United States Senate. They were compared to Benedict Arnold and Judas. One day when Representative James G. Blaine saw Ross enter the White House he felt free to say loudly, "There goes the rascal to get his pay."

Old acquaintances turned away when they saw Ross in the street. When he returned home to Kansas at the end of his term he was physically attacked and beaten. Ross remained convinced that he had done the right thing: "Millions of men cursing me today will bless me tomorrow for having saved the country from the greatest peril through which it has ever passed, though none but God can ever know the struggle it has cost me." The six other Republicans felt much the same way. They too lived out their lives in obscurity.

The decision of the high court of the Senate only intensified the opinions of Thaddeus Stevens about the desirability of evicting Andrew Johnson from the White House. "The block must be brought out and the axe sharpened," he said. "The only recourse from intolerable tyranny is Brutus's dagger."

But Old Thad at long last was a dying man. Two and a half months after the trial he took to his bed for the last time and lay there helpless in Washington's August heat. Mrs. Smith, his housekeeper-mistress, put pieces of ice on his tongue. Seventy-six years of age, he retained his senses to the last. A friend who wished to be kind complimented him upon his appearance. "Ah, John," Old Thad replied, "it is not my appearance but my disappearance which worries me."

On August 11 Mrs. Smith asked him if two black clergymen might be admitted to the sickroom. "Certainly, certainly." When they came in he reached out his hand. Two black Sisters of Charity came in to pray. He died, and South Carolina with its Reconstruction government draped the statehouse in mourning.

The body of Thaddeus Stevens lay in state. Children from the capital's Negro orphanage walked in and one by one were lifted so that they could view his face. In accordance with his desires, they buried him in the one cemetery in Lancaster which did not draw the color line. Upon his gravestone is written:

> I repose in this quiet and secluded spot
> Not from any natural preference for solitude,
> But, finding other Cemeteries limited as to Race by Charter
>   Rules,
> I have chosen this that I might illustrate
> In my death
> The Principles which I advocated
> Through a long life:
> EQUALITY OF MAN BEFORE HIS CREATOR.

Sumner gave the eulogy in the Senate. Stevens ascended now to glory, Sumner said. The light of eventual triumph was upon his path. "Politician, calculator, time server, stand aside: a Hero Statesman passes to his reward."

By then Sumner hoped that, soon, the same would be said for himself. His health was not good, and he suffered from heart disease which he said was brought on by the Brooks attack of twelve years before. The approaching election of Grant aroused no hopes in him, and correctly so. Within a short while his views of the new President were such that when he expressed them to guests at his home he was told that he had better lower his voice or Mrs. Grant, at the White House, hearing the disturbance, would call the police. Grant himself said that no man ever insulted him so ferociously as Sumner did and that if he were not President, he would challenge him to a duel.

People watching Sumner walk through the Boston Public Gardens to look at the statues there speculated that he was envisioning how he would appear one day sculpted in metal. Very likely the people were right, for his thoughts were much on the position he would hold when he was gone. He worked endlessly on the compilation of his speeches he would leave behind.

A diminished figure in a Senate dominated by young technicians devoid of ideological underpinnings, he nevertheless maintained the principles and lived up to the standards which he had held for so many years. But the times were out of joint. Declared *The New York Times:* "In his eagerness to reconstruct the Union in the interest of the Negro, he is prepared to disregard the Constitution, deprive the states of powers expressly vested in them, and remodel everything according to his philanthropic inclinations." Why, people asked, did he simply not petition the Congress to change the blacks into whites?

Sumner did not care. He escorted Senator-elect Hiram Revels of Mississippi, Jefferson Davis' successor, to the ceremony where he took the oath as the first black Senator in history. He continued his attempts to attach an equal-rights provision to all kinds of measures, saying that such was its intrinsic justice that he could not imagine any bill where it would be out of place.

Even after the Republican party all but disowned him and displaced him from his position as head of the Foreign Relations Committee, he fought for his Supplementary Civil Rights Bill. It prohibited discrimination on account of color in railroad cars, hotels and theaters, schools, churches, in the selection of jurors. To Sumner the developing theory of "separate but equal" was an abomination, the old Black Codes in new form. His proposed bill would annul every state law that espoused the doctrine.*

In the last days of 1873 he made his final great speech. It was on his Supplementary Civil Rights Bill. "My desire," he told the Senate, "the darling desire, if I may say so, of my soul, at this moment, is to close forever this great question, so that it shall never again intrude into these chambers—so that hereafter in all our legislation there shall be no such words as 'black' or 'white,' but that we shall speak only of citizens."

Three months later the servants heard him fall heavily in his study. Open on his desk was a volume of Shakespeare with two lines marked:

> Would I were dead! if God's good will were so;
> For what is in this world, but care and woe?

He was lifted up and put into bed. "I am so tired," he murmured. His mind wandered, but kept returning to two subjects. One was the compilation of his speeches. "My book," he kept muttering. "My book is not finished."

The other subject was his Supplementary Civil Rights Bill. His secretary heard him murmur about a bill, and, thinking he spoke of some household obligation, assured him that all bills would be paid. "You do not understand me," Sumner said. "I mean the Civil Rights Bill."

His friend E. Rockwood Hoar came in, and Sumner whispered, "You must take care of the Civil Rights Bill—my bill, the Civil Rights Bill, don't let it fail." By midafternoon, March 11, 1874, aged sixty-three, he was dead.

He lay in state on the catafalque where nine years earlier Lincoln had rested. He was the first Senator ever to lie in the Capitol. The mourning for him, the expression of personal sorrow by multitudes, was greater, James G. Blaine thought, than it had been for any man of his generation, Abraham Lincoln excepted.

* * *

* He also turned his attention to the question of women's rights, saying to the feminist leader Susan B. Anthony as he handed her copies of his speeches, "Miss Anthony, put 'sex' where I have 'race' or 'color' and you have the best and strongest arguments I can make for women."

During the ten months of Johnson's term which remained after his acquittal, the Senate did its best to make him as uncomfortable as possible. Almost anyone he nominated for a government office was certain to be turned down, including former Attorney General Stanbery, whom the President sought to return to his old position. Nominees for minor diplomatic posts were so regularly rejected that finally the President announced he would nominate no one who could not prove in advance that he was acceptable to the Senate.

Presidential messages were put into the record without actually being read out to a Senate which refused to sit through them. So were Presidential vetoes and the State of the Union message. Johnson took it philosophically. Perhaps he was even a little quieter than usual, thought William Crook. When he spoke of his political enemies it was without rancor. Stevens was a most capable man, Sumner a stranger to sordid motives, Grant a great soldier.

The summer of 1868 passed. Election Day came, and Grant's victory. In December, Johnson would turn sixty, and to celebrate the occasion he sent out masses of invitations for a birthday party on the twenty-ninth. They went to the children of official Washington. Hundreds came to dance the quadrilles, polkas, lancers, the schottische and galop. Mrs. Johnson came downstairs and sat in an ebony-and-satin easy chair. She explained why she did not rise when the children were presented: "My dears, I am an invalid."

At the end all the boys and girls did the Virginia reel. President-elect Grant did not permit his children to attend.

The new year of 1869 came in. By then Johnson had issued blanket pardons to all who had served the Confederacy, including Jefferson Davis. He pardoned the minor conspirators jailed for helping Booth and permitted the assassin's family to claim the body.

It came time for his term to end. Up to the last minute he did not indicate whether he would attend the inauguration ceremonies for his successor, who had let it be known he would not ride in the same carriage with the outgoing President or even speak to him. It seemed to some of Johnson's Cabinet ministers that it would appear petty if he failed to attend, and various expedients were suggested. Perhaps he could ride in a carriage going parallel to that of President-elect Grant. That way they would not have any contact.

On Inauguration Day Johnson remained in his White House office as the members of the Cabinet entered one by one. He gave no indication of his plans until Secretary of State Seward suggested that they ought to be leaving for the ceremonies.

"I am inclined to think we will finish our work here," Johnson said. At noon, ex-President, he got up, shook hands with everybody and walked out of a White House left immaculately clean for the Grants by Martha Johnson Patterson. He went home to Tennessee. In the streets of that Greeneville of the runaway apprentice boy, the Mechanic Governor and the tailor-President, where once there hung a banner inscribed ANDREW JOHNSON, TRAITOR, a banner now waved: WELCOME HOME, ANDREW JOHNSON, PATRIOT.

Six years later, on March 5, 1875, he came back to Washington, United States Senator from Tennessee. He seemed to William Crook to be grayer, his face more bleached, more delicate. There were no new lines in his face, just the old ones more deeply graven. He wore the same expression of mingled earnestness and sadness he had shown ever since 1865.

He was wearing a broadcloth suit, standing collar and cravat. He entered the Senate Chamber to be sworn in. Edmunds of Vermont (guilty) was addressing the chair. Edmunds looked over, faltered. Some books on Edmunds' desk tumbled to the floor. Edmunds sat down.

Conkling of New York (guilty) pretended to read a letter, all the while peering at the newcomer from the corner of his eye; Frelinghuysen of New Jersey (guilty) knelt by his desk, apparently searching for something. Boutwell of Massachusetts, he of the hole in the sky, a Senator now, stared straight ahead. Logan of Illinois, another impeachment manager now a Senator, looked into space. Anthony of Rhode

Island, Cameron of Pennsylvania—he had interrupted the Chief Justice's question to shout his verdict—Morrill of Maine (all guilty) looked into space. Morton of Indiana (guilty) wondered what to do as Johnson came by his aisle desk. Johnson stopped, smiled, put out his hand. "There are not many men who could have done that," Morton said later.

Henry Wilson, the Vice President, was in the chair. As a Senator he had voted guilty. He swore in the new Senator from Tennessee, coming down to stand below the podium instead of sitting at it in the usual fashion. There was a roar of applause from the galleries when the ceremony was finished. Johnson turned away. Here in this room he had spoken for the Union, here he had made his Vice Presidential inauguration speech. Here he had been judged.

He headed for his desk. A page handed him a bouquet of flowers. More were heaped upon his desk. Tears came into his eyes. He went into a cloakroom. "I miss my old friends," he said. Ross, Fowler, Trumbull, Henderson—all were gone from the Senate. Fessenden and Grimes were dead. Sumner, Seward and Chase had all died within a year of each other. Stanton was dead.

He gave one speech. Two days later the Senate adjourned. He returned to Tennessee and was at the home of his daughter Mary Stover, talking to his granddaughter Lillie about her approaching wedding when he fell on the carpet, paralyzed.

It was a stroke. His relatives said they would send for a doctor. Johnson forbade it. Then for twenty-four hours he lay in bed and talked of old times, of the tailor shop, his struggles. He died the next day, July 31, 1875.

He was buried on a hill in Greeneville. He had once said in his bombastic way: "Pillow my head on the Constitution of my country, let the flag of the nation be my winding sheet." So they wrapped him in the flag, his fingers gripping its folds, and put under his head the copy of the Constitution he had marked up and written upon ever since he bought it forty years before.

Afterword

Neither in conversations nor in letters did Charles Sumner ever make the slightest personal allusion to Preston Brooks. He had no feeling for the man whose cane had beaten him to the Senate floor. "What have I to do with him?" Sumner asked. "It was slavery, not he, that struck the blow."

It was remarkable that he possessed such an insight, for Charles Sumner had difficulty in understanding the motives of others. That failing made it all the more wondrous that he saw that in the great issues single men become lost, sometimes. Such was the case in the great struggles which drove all those men one hundred years ago. They could be the voices of what they believed, but not the forces behind these things. For the forces they represented and the matters with which they dealt were so great that they encompassed and overwhelmed individuals. Perhaps that is why Stevens is largely forgotten and Sumner himself is often confused with the Fort Sumter whose received gunfire inaugurated the Civil War. Even Lincoln was only a figure in the great drama.

In a world more religious-minded than today's it was thought that Old Thad, Sumner and Andrew Johnson would one day sit as brethren in the Elysian Fields, the rifts between them unimportant when seen next to the great positions whose voices they were. Perhaps they are there now.

Their personal antipathies were, indeed, unimportant. The viewpoints they represented lived on well beyond them, into this century. Likely their debate will remain unresolved in the coming century. There will not be an end in our grandchildren's time.

It took one hundred years for the word *impeachment* to be used in reference to another American President. Never since the instant Senator Ross said "Not guilty" had the concept been introduced in the houses of Congress of the United States. Even Sumner decided at the end that a President should not be driven from office because a majority has come, for the moment, to disagree with his beliefs. "I didn't want to die without making this confession, that in the matter of impeachment you were right and I was wrong," Sumner told ex-Senator Henderson of Missouri, who had voted against conviction.

So it was that when the word was used again it was not used in a political context. Those who were about to impeach one of Andrew Johnson's successors were not so much against that successor's policies as they were against the man himself. His ideologies were far less involved than his troubles or his sins. Johnson stood for far more. So did those who tried to convict him.

The forces that drive men, preordained, perhaps—that is what this book has been about. Not so much the individual men. They were just the symbols. Once, two years before his death, Sumner walked with the magazine editor George William Curtis in the Congressional Cemetery. They passed a cenotaph of the type put up in honor of all Congressmen who die in office. This one had upon it the name of Preston Brooks of South Carolina.

"How did you feel about Brooks?" asked Curtis.

"Only as to a brick that should fall upon my head from a chimney," was the reply. "He was the unconscious agent of a malign power."

Sumner turned away from the cenotaph. "Poor fellow, poor fellow," he said.

Note on Sources

||||||||||||||||||||||||||||||||||||||||||||||||||||||||||||||||||||||||||||||||||||||||||||||||||||||||||||||||||||||||||||||||||||||||||||||||||||||||||||||||||||||||||||||||||||||||||||

The historian Eric McKitrick has remarked that the man Andrew Johnson is not a fascinating figure when taken by himself. His personality, traits and achievements, says McKitrick, are all secondary to the issues with which he was involved. I do not entirely agree, for I find Johnson's rise from humble origins to be of substantial interest, and I think his stand for the Union to be worthy of study. It was an unusual man indeed who would remain in Washington after every other southern Senator had gone home to join the Confederacy.

However, it is true that he does not dominate his era. As I have indicated in the Afterword of this book, the issues did. This fact presents many problems for the student of Johnson's impeachment and trial. For to attempt to understand that impeachment and trial, one must involve oneself with the attitudes of the North and South for the period before the war, with the war itself, with the assassination of Lincoln, with the assumption of power by the new President and his estrangement from his erstwhile supporters. Reconstruction, the carpetbaggers, the Klan—all of which are much the subjects of legend and myth—must be given due consideration. At the end, standing on this pyramid of knowledge, one ought to be able to assess the lasting meaning the events concluded when Senator Ross said, "Not guilty."

This task, which has consumed more than three years of my time, was not rendered more simple by certain concurrent activities in Washington. Many times Sam Ervin's face on the television screen hovered just above the desk where books on Ben Butler lay piled; and sometimes Thad Stevens looked up and gave his fellow Congressman Peter Rodino a baleful stare. (I hasten to say I draw no parallels here at all. I make no guess at what Charles Sumner might have said when the television set revealed that Andrew Johnson's successor had "bugged" his office.)

But to continue. Sufficient research on Johnson's impeachment cannot be done. A lifetime would be too short. That is why I have confined my work to the study of secondary sources. Even there I have had to be selective, otherwise I would still be at my task. The bibliography that follows will indicate the most important of the books I have consulted, but there were others that were looked into at some length. Also consulted were a great number of magazines, including the *American Historical Review, Lippincott's,* the *Atlantic Monthly, Galaxy,* the *Century Magazine,* the *South Carolina Historical and Genealogical Magazine, Pennsylvania Magazine of History, McClure's, South Atlantic Quarterly, Mississippi Valley Historical Review,* the *East Tennessee Historical Society Publications, New York History,* the *Independent, Tennessee Historical Quarterly, Harper's Weekly, Leslie's Illustrated Weekly* and others. The Government Printing Office transcript of the trial itself was of course the main basis for my reportage of the climactic event of this book. House of Representatives Report 182, Thirty-fourth Congress, First Session, gave most of the details of the Brooks attack upon Sumner.

Now that I have finished with these masses of material and have had the honor of getting to know the cast of characters whose actions I have attempted to chronicle, I permit myself to give a thought to that future historian, probably now unborn, who will attempt one day to do what I have done: write an unbiased book about another President and Congress between whom the word *impeachment* was thrown back and forth. I think he or she will be confronted by the same task in some respects that I faced. For very few books on Johnson fail to take a stand. Either Johnson is likened to the Antichrist, or Sumner and Stevens are compared to Satan. There seems little middle ground. The historian who will, half a century or more hence, attempt an unbiased book on the matter of Richard Nixon's proposed impeachment will sympathize with me, should he ever read these words, when I sigh over the wild passion displayed by my predecessors in chronicling Johnson. For by the time that historian begins his work he will properly wish to be as impartial as possible. He will wish to examine his subject from all sides. And while it is true that, at present, few books comparing Richard Nixon's enemies to Lucifer have appeared, we must bear in mind that history and the future may do things that would seem inexplicable today. Not being a seer, I am unable to guarantee what Tomorrow will say. History will put all things right, Andrew Johnson used to say. I will stand on that thought and leave to that future historian the task of giving, if not the final word on Nixon, then at least something approaching the final word. I do not claim for myself that I have accomplished for Johnson what he will attempt to accomplish for Nixon. But I have, I think, at least impartially synthesized that great mass of material, extracts from which are mentioned in the following bibliography.

Bibliography

Adams, Charles Francis, *Autobiography*. Boston, Mass., Houghton Mifflin, 1916.

Adams, Henry, *The Education of Henry Adams*. Boston, Mass., Houghton Mifflin, 1918.

Avary, Myrta Lockett, *Dixie After the War*. New York, Doubleday, Page and Co., 1906.

Barrows, Chester L., *William M. Evarts*. Chapel Hill, University of North Carolina Press, 1941.

Belden, Thomas Graham and Belden, Marva Robins, *So Fell the Angels*. Boston, Mass., Little, Brown and Co., 1956.

Boutwell, George S., *Reminiscences of Sixty Years in Public Affairs*. New York, McClure, Phillips and Co., 1902.

Bowers, Claude, *The Tragic Era*. Boston, Mass., Houghton Mifflin, 1929.

Briggs, Emily Edson, *The Olivia Letters*. New York and Washington. Neale Publishing Co., 1906.

Brock, W. R., *An American Crisis*. New York, St. Martin's Press, 1963.

Brodie, Fawn, *Thaddeus Stevens*. New York, W. W. Norton and Co., 1959.

Brooks, Noah, *Washington in Lincoln's Time*. New York, Century Co., 1896.

Browning, Orville Hickman, *Diary*. Springfield, Ill., Illinois State Historical Library, 1933.

Bumgardner, Edward, *The Life of Edmund G. Ross*. Kansas City, Mo., the Fielding-Turner Press, 1949.

Butler, Benjamin F., *Butler's Book.* Boston, Mass., A. M. Thayer and Co., 1892.

Carter, Hodding, *The Angry Scar.* Garden City, N. Y., Doubleday and Co., 1959.

Chambrun, the Marquis Adolphe de, *Impressions of Lincoln and the Civil War.* New York, Random House, 1952.

Clay, Mrs. Clement, *A Belle of the Fifties.* New York, Doubleday, Page and Co., 1904.

Clemenceau, Georges, *American Reconstruction.* New York, Dial Press, 1928.

Cottrell, John, *Anatomy of an Assassination.* London, Frederick Muller, 1966.

Cowan, Frank, *Andrew Johnson.* Greenesburgh, Penn., Oliver Publishing House, 1894.

Cox, Samuel S., *Three Decades of Federal Legislation.* Providence, R. I., J. A. and R. A. Reid, 1886.

Crook, William H., *Through Five Administrations.* New York, Harper Brothers, 1907.

—— *Memories of the White House.* Boston, Mass., Little, Brown and Co., 1911.

Cullom, Shelby, *Fifty Years of Public Service.* Chicago, A. C. McClurg and Co., 1911.

Current, Richard Nelson, *Old Thad Stevens.* Madison, University of Wisconsin Press, 1942.

DeForest, John William, *A Union Officer in the Reconstruction.* New Haven, Conn., Yale University Press, 1948.

Depew, Chauncey, *My Memories of Eighty Years.* New York, Charles Scribner's Sons, 1922.

Detroit Post and Tribune, The, *Zachariah Chandler.* Detroit, The Post and Tribune Co., 1880.

DeWitt, David Miller, *The Impeachment and Trial of Andrew Johnson.* New York, Macmillan Co., 1903.

Donald, David, *Charles Sumner and the Coming of the Civil War.* New York, Alfred A. Knopf, 1960.

—— *Charles Sumner and the Rights of Man.* New York, Alfred A. Knopf, 1970.

Dorris, Jonathan Truman, *Pardon and Amnesty Under Lincoln and Johnson.* Chapel Hill, the University of North Carolina Press, 1953.

Doster, William E., *Lincoln and Episodes of the Civil War.* New York, G. P. Putnam's Sons, 1915.

Eckloff, Christian F., *Memoirs of a Senate Page,* New York, Broadway Publishing Co., 1909.

Ellet, Mrs. E. F., *Court Circles of the Republic.* Philadelphia Publishing Co., n.d.

Ellis, John B., *The Sights and Secrets of the National Capital.* New York, U.S. Publishing Co., 1871.

Fleming, Walter Lynwood, *The Sequel of Appomattox*. New Haven, Conn., Yale University Press, 1921.

—— *Civil War and Reconstruction in Alabama*. New York, Peter Smith, 1949.

—— *Documentary History of Reconstruction*. New York, McGraw-Hill, 1966.

Gobright, L. A., *Recollections of Men and Things at Washington*. Philadelphia, Claxton, Remsen and Haffelfinger, 1869.

Godkin, Edwin Lawrence, *Life and Letters*. New York, Macmillan Co., 1903.

Grinnell, Josiah, *Men and Events of Forty Years*. Boston, Mass., D. Lothrop Co., 1891.

Hall, Clifton R., *Andrew Johnson, Military Governor of Tennessee*. Princeton, N.J., Princeton University Press, 1916.

Hamlin, Charles Eugene, *The Life and Times of Hannibal Hamlin*. Cambridge, Mass., The Riverside Press, 1899.

Haynes, George H., *Charles Sumner*. Philadelphia, George W. Jacobs and Co., 1909.

Henry, Robert S., *The Story of Reconstruction*. Indianapolis and New York, the Bobbs-Merrill Co., 1938.

Hesseltine, William, *Ulysses S. Grant, Politician*. New York, Dodd, Mead and Co., 1935.

Hoar, George F., *Autobiography of Seventy Years*. New York, Charles Scribner's Sons, 1903.

Howe, M. A. deWolfe, *Portrait of an Independent: Moorfield Storey*. New York and Boston, Mass., Houghton Mifflin Co., 1932.

Jellison, Charles A., *Fessenden of Maine*. Binghamton, N. Y., Syracuse University Press, 1962.

Keckley, Elizabeth, *Behind the Scenes*. New York, G. W. Carleton and Co., 1868.

Korngold, Ralph, *Thaddeus Stevens*. New York, Harcourt, Brace and Co., 1955.

Leech, Margaret, *Reveille in Washington*. New York, Harper and Brothers, 1941.

Lester, J. C. and Wilson, D. L., *Ku Klux Klan*. New York and Washington, Neale Publishing Co., 1905.

Lodge, Henry Cabot, *Early Memories*. New York, Charles Scribner's Sons, 1913.

McClure, Alexander K., *Abraham Lincoln and Men of War-Times*. Philadelphia, The Times Publishing Co., 1892.

McCulloch, Hugh, *Men and Measures of Half a Century*. New York, Charles Scribner's Sons, 1888.

McKitrick, Eric L., ed., *Andrew Johnson: A Profile*. New York, Hill and Wang, 1969.

Merrill, James M., *William T. Sherman*. Chicago, New York and San Francisco, Rand McNally and Co., 1971.

Miller, Alphonse, *Thaddeus Stevens*. New York, Harper and Bros., 1939.

Milton, George Fort, *The Age of Hate*. New York, Coward-McCann, 1930.

Nason, Elias and Russell, Thomas, *The Life and Public Services of Henry Wilson*. Boston, Mass., B. B. Russell, 1876.

Oberholtzer, Ellis P., *History of the U.S. Since the Civil War*. New York, Macmillan Co., 1922.

Paine, Albert Bigelow, *Th. Nast, His Period and His Pictures*. New York, Macmillan Co., 1904.

Pendel, Thomas F., *Thirty-Six Years in the White House*. Washington, Neale Publishing Co., 1902.

Perry, Benjamin Franklin, *Reminiscences of Public Men*. Greenville, S. C., Shannon and Co., 1889.

Piatt, Donn, *Memories of the Men Who Saved the Union*. New York and Chicago, Belford, Clarke and Co., 1887.

Pike, James, *The Prostrate State*. New York, D. Appleton and Co., 1874.

Poore, Ben Perley, *Reminiscences*. Philadelphia, Hubbard Bros., 1886.

Randall, Ruth Painter, *Mary Lincoln*. Boston, Mass., Little, Brown and Co., 1953.

Reid, Whitelaw, *After the War*. Cincinnati, O., Moore, Wilstach and Baldwin, 1866.

Riddle, A. G., *The Life of Benjamin F. Wade*. Cleveland, O., Williams, 1886.

Rosebault, Charles J., *When Dana Was the Sun*. New York, Robert M. McBride, 1931.

Ross, Edmund G., *History of the Impeachment of Andrew Johnson*. Santa Fe, N. M., New Mexican Printing Co., 1896.

Ross, Ishbel, *Proud Kate*. New York, Harper and Bros., 1953.

Salter, William, *The Life of James W. Grimes*. New York, D. Appleton and Co., 1876.

Schouler, James, *History of the Reconstruction Period*. New York, Dodd, Mead and Co., 1913.

Schurz, Carl, *Reminiscences*. New York, McClure Co., 1908.

Shotwell, Walter G., *The Life of Charles Sumner*. New York, Thomas Y. Crowell and Co., 1910.

Smith, William Ernest, *The Francis Preston Blair Family in Politics*. New York, Macmillan Co., 1933.

Stampp, Kenneth M., *The Era of Reconstruction*. New York, Alfred A. Knopf, 1965.

Stewart, William M., *Reminiscences*. New York and Washington, Neale Publishing Co., 1908.

Stoddard, William O., *Abraham Lincoln and Andrew Johnson*. New York, Frederick A. Stokes and Brother, 1888.

Storey, Moorfield, *Charles Sumner*. Boston, Mass., and New York, Houghton Mifflin and Co., 1900.

Strode, Hudson, *Jefferson Davis*. New York, Harcourt, Brace and World, 1964.

Strong, George Templeton, *Diary*. New York, Macmillan Co., 1952.

Stryker, Lloyd Paul, *Andrew Johnson*. New York, Macmillan Co., 1929.

Swisshelm, Jane Grey, *Crusader and Feminist*. St. Paul, Minn., Minnesota Historical Society, 1934.

Taylor, Richard, *Destruction and Reconstruction*. New York, D. Appleton and Co., 1879.

Temple, Oliver P., *Notable Men of Tennessee*. New York, Cosmopolitan Press, 1912.

Thomas, Benjamin P. and Hyman, Harold M., *Stanton*. New York, Alfred A. Knopf, 1962.

Thomas, Lately, *The First President Johnson*. New York, William Morrow and Co., 1968.

Townsend, E. D., *Anecdotes of the Civil War in the United States*. New York, D. Appleton and Co., 1884.

Trefousse, Hans Louis, *Ben Butler*. New York, Twayne Publishers, 1957.

——— *Benjamin Franklin Wade*. New York, Twayne Publishers, 1963.

Trowbridge, John T., *A Picture of the Desolated States*. Hartford, Conn., L. Stebbins, 1868.

Welles, Gideon, *Diary*. Boston, Mass., and New York, Houghton Mifflin and Co., 1911.

White, Horace, *The Life of Lyman Trumbull*. Boston, Mass., and New York, Houghton Mifflin and Co., 1913.

Whitridge, Arnold, *No Compromise!* New York, Farrar, Straus and Cudahy, 1960.

Williams, T. Harry, *Lincoln and the Radicals*. Madison, the University of Wisconsin Press, 1941.

Wilson, James Harrison, *The Life of John A. Rawlins*. New York, Neale Publishing Co., 1916.

Winston, Robert W., *Andrew Johnson*. New York, Henry Holt and Co., 1928.

Index

||||||||||||||||||||||||||||||||||||||||||||||||||||||||||||||||||||||||||||||||||||||||||||||||||||||||||||||||||||||||||||||||||||||||||||||||

316

Swisshelm, Jane Grey, 66-67, 89-90

Talleyrand, Count Charles de, 128
Taylor, Richard, 119, 219-220
Taylor, Zachary, 39, 205
Temple, Oliver, 36, 37, 46
Tenure of Office Act, 191, 212, 220-224,
    236-237, 258, 263
Thayer, John M., 229, 230
Thomas, George H., 226
Thomas, Lorenzo P., 226-228, 230, 237,
    243n., 253, 259-261
  Johnson and, 226-227
  Stanton and, 231-233, 251-252, 259
Tooms, Senator, 22
Townsend, General E. D., 222, 226, 227,
    232, 233, 260, 261
Truman, Major Benjamin C., 55, 56,
    60
Trumbull, Lyman, 163-164, 250-251,
    265, 284
Tucker, Beverly, 102-103
Tyler, John, 82

U.S. Congress
  Civil Rights Bill (1866), 164
  Johnson and, 174, 176, 181-182, 188,
      190, 200, 206, 214-224, 237, 300
    impeachment attempts, 204-205,
        217-219
    impeachment recommended, 234-
        235
    impeachment trial, 241-293
  Joint Committee of Reconstruction,
      136, 142-143, 170
  Tenure of Office Act, 191, 224, 229,
      258
  U.S. Supreme Court and, 199-200
U.S. Constitution
  Johnson's love for, 44-45, 110-112,
      121, 160, 165, 180, 181, 206, 268-
      269, 272, 277, 281, 302
  Thirteenth Amendment, 170
  Fourteenth Amendment, 170-171
U.S. Secret Service, 218

U.S. Supreme Court, 199-200, 221, 239
  U.S. Congress and, 199-200

Vinton, Reverend Francis, 89

Wade, Benjamin Franklin, 85-88, 102,
    133-134, 178, 179, 183, 200, 207,
    228, 241, 255
  Butler and, 202
  Grant and, 87
  at impeachment trial, 262, 284, 293
  Johnson and, 86-87, 91, 144, 242
  Lincoln and, 87-88
  Radical Republicans and, 88, 91, 93
  Sumner and, 110, 118-119, 236
  Welles and, 119
Wade, Mrs. Benjamin Franklin, 86, 87
Wallace, General Lew, 209
Washington, George, 97
Washington, D.C., 12-13, 25, 28
Washington and Lee University, 118n.
Webster, Daniel, 129
Weekly Constitutionalist, 199n.
Welles, Gideon, 117-118, 141, 144, 189,
    239, 248
  on Grant, 223
  at impeachment trial, 263
  Johnson and, 63, 85, 94, 122, 173,
      176-186, 212, 246, 257, 294
  Lincoln's assassination and, 78-82,
      229
  on Radical Republicans, 218
  Seward and, 60
  Sumner and, 137, 169
  Wade and, 119
Welles, Mrs. Gideon, 101
White House, 114, 140-141, 156-158, 301
Whitman, Walt, 81
Willey, Senator, 265, 290
Williams, Dr. Alex, 35, 36, 37
Williams, Senator, 284
Wilson, Henry, 17, 301
Wordsworth, William, 8
Wright, William, 162-163

Yulee, David, 27

320